Description & Setting

WRITE GREAT FICTION

Description & Setting

[TECHNIQUES AND EXERCISES FOR
CRAFTING A BELIEVABLE WORLD OF
PEOPLE, PLACES, AND EVENTS]

BY RON ROZELLE

WD
WRITER'S DIGEST
BOOKS

WRITER'S DIGEST
BOOKS

An imprint of Penguin Random House LLC
penguinrandomhouse.com

ISBN 978-1-58297-327-2

Edited by Michelle Ruberg
Designed by Stanard Design Partners
Interior and cover illustrations by Getty Images
Cover by Nick Gliebe/Design Matters

146122990

[ABOUT THE AUTHOR]

Ron Rozelle teaches Creative Writing on the Texas gulf coast. He is the author of three books: *Into That Good Night*, a memoir, *The Windows of Heaven*, a novel of the 1900 Galveston storm, and *A Place Apart*, a novel set in modern day Ohio. He is the recipient of the Stephen F. Austin Father of Texas Award and the *Image* Magazine Creative Prize. His memoir, *Into That Good Night*, was a national finalist for the P.E.N. Prize and the Texas Institute of Letters Carr P. Collins Award and was selected as the second best work of nonfiction in the nation for the year 1998 by the *San Antonio Express-News*. He has taught writing workshops at numerous conferences and universities, and was twice the memoir teacher at the Newman National Conference at Mississippi College. His articles have appeared in a wide variety of publications, and he was the Barnes and Noble Author of the Month in both the Houston and Dallas markets. He has been a featured author at the Texas Book Festival in Austin and the Texas Folklife Festival in San Antonio. He has a new novel, *Touching Winter*, coming out soon from TCU Press.

[DEDICATION]

for
Victor Platt
and
David Westheimer,
wordsmiths, both

table of

contents

chapter 1

[THE IMPORTANCE OF DESCRIPTION AND SETTING]

One of the first things I learned about the difference between good and bad writing is that good writing is not entirely dependent upon the setting. And bad writing sometimes is.

I was in a college class called The American Novel on the third or fourth floor of the English building, watching the branches of a huge oak tree sway gently outside the open windows in the lazy breeze of a spring afternoon. We were nearly halfway through that odd duck of a decade called the seventies, and the professor used the adjective *transcendental*, which was almost always, in those times, paired with the noun *meditation*.

"Good writing is transcendental," the professor said. "It rises above time and place."

That little pearl has stuck with me ever since. And being for a long time now in the business of writing—good rather than bad, I hope—and teaching it, I can attest that it is true. If it weren't, then only people who grew up in rural Alabama in the early years of the Great Depression would be able to make much of *To Kill a Mockingbird*. But the fact is that any thoughtful reader can make a great deal of it, because *To Kill a Mockingbird* is not about Alabama or the Great Depression. Writing that is only about a time is not literature, it is history. If it is only about a place, it is geography. Literature is about neither; it is about people and all of the wide range of joys and troubles that people tumble into.

Now, having said that, I'd better quickly say this: Even though good writing is not entirely dependent upon the setting, a writer of fiction would be paving the way to miserable failure if he did not first create, using every tool at his disposal, the most clearly depicted time and place he could come up with. Because a story will not get very far—more specifically, your reader will not *go* very far—without a setting that has been meticulously crafted.

Readers want to know a few things right up front, like what the weather is like and the lay of the land, the color of that lake, or the steep pitch of that steeple. Now whether or not these things have one iota to do with your story doesn't concern the reader. And it shouldn't; that's your business as the writer. That generic reader out there, who my students and I call the guy in Sheboygan, expects a few details from the start as part of his due for sitting down to spend any time with you at all.

The location and time frame of your story is more than just a stage for your characters to tromp around on. In some cases, the setting becomes a character itself. And all of the attendant details—societal conventions, seashores, mountains, regional dialects—determine the overall tone. In fact, if you do it right, setting and description become essential in your fiction. They become the foundation for the rest of your story to build on.

Very few existing novels or stories would work as well as they do, or work at all, in completely different times and places. It might be argued that *To Kill a Mockingbird* could be set in Nova Scotia in the 1980s, provided there was discrimination of some sort there, which there almost certainly was, discrimination being an abundant commodity in most times and places. In that venue, the story might possibly do the transcending my old professor spoke of. But, though it may survive such a transplant, it certainly wouldn't be the same book, or even—almost surely—a very good one. Harper Lee set her tale in the Deep South of the early 1930s, fertile ground for bigotry and family oddballs kept hidden away in crumbling old houses, a perfect bedrock for her unique novel.

Your fiction has to have a setting rich enough to match the story you intend to tell. It must be believable and sufficiently described to be as real for your readers as the rooms they are sitting in when reading it.

It's a tall order. But it's one that you'll have to fill before your writing can work on any level. This book will show you, through the use of explanations, examples, and practice drills, how you can go about establishing realistic, believable settings and providing engaging descriptions that will allow your readers to see, when they read your story, what *you* saw when you envisioned it.

CRAFT AND VOICE

Whenever I meet with a new class, the first thing I tell them is that creative writing consists of two things: craft and voice. I pilfer pretty liberally here from William Zinsser's *On Writing Well,* but he wouldn't mind; writers are usually gracious sharers and universally proficient pilferers. Then I tell the class that I might be somewhat helpful to them regarding craft, which includes the tricks of the trade and various clever manipulation tools, like rabbits out of hats.

But when it comes to voice, the entirely individual way in which they spin their yarns, I admit that I'm not likely to be of any use whatsoever. They'll just have to dig around for that on their own. I can point them in the right direction, can show them examples of other peoples' voices, and can even tell them when they haven't found it. But *finding* it is a personal expedition.

This business of description and setting is rooted firmly in both craft *and* voice. The careful brush strokes that bring your story to life, the delicate tightrope walking between too little and too much, and the careful choice of a locale that makes your tale accessible to the guy in Sheboygan will require all of the tools in your kit and your ability to employ them. Jumbled in there—like screwdrivers and hammers—are metaphors, similes, sentence- and paragraph-length variation, onomatopoeia, allusions, flashbacks, and many more things. Your job is to lift each one out as it is needed and—in your distinctive voice—put it to work.

And while voice can't be taught—at least within the strictest definition of the word, by a teacher in a classroom or the pages of a how-to manual— it *can* be learned. The process through which it finally emerges is a refiner's fire of mystical components, made up of honing the basic skills of storytelling, devoting plenty of time to reading a wide assortment of talented writers who *have* found their voices and put them to good use, and then undertaking, meticulously and slowly, the ancient enterprise of wordsmithing: the careful selection of each and every word and phrase.

THE TRINITY

In each chapter, we'll look at various conventions and devices that undergird effective writing (craft), we'll dissect specific examples of how established writers have provided description and established setting (models), and we'll look at ways that you can go about the planning, writing, and fine tuning necessary to write quality fiction (wordsmithing).

Let's set some ground rules. Instead of dealing with craft and voice as two things, let's consider them from here on out as one. The tools and your unique use of them must be a single enterprise, the two fusing continuously into what will eventually be your finished product: a story or a novel. The same is true of our dual topics, setting and description. One depends entirely on the other, and separating them in our thinking or our treatment won't be helpful. For that reason, I've chosen not to break this book into two parts, one dealing specifically with setting and the other with description. They're going to have to work together in your fiction, so let's go at them as a single entity.

Finding and polishing the writing voice in which you will describe your setting is a solo voyage with you alone at the helm. But if you tinker sufficiently, using the many tools available to you, and pay attention to how other writers have used them, then your style will surface, like Ahab's white whale off there on the horizon. And it will get clearer and clearer as you row toward it. Here's a warning, however. This thing you are chasing is likely to give you as much trouble as the whale gave Ahab.

Good writing is hard work, any way you look at it, and not always a lot of fun. It's a lonely business and oftentimes a frustrating one. We might as well have our first bit of wisdom from Flannery O'Connor, and you should get used to it. Some of my students call her Saint Flannery since I invoke her words pretty often.

"I'm always highly irritated," O'Connor says, in *Mystery and Manners: Occasional Prose*, "by people who imply that writing fiction is an escape from reality. It's a plunge *into* reality and is very shocking to the system."

So prepare to have your system shocked. But prepare also to reap the rewards of your struggles. I'm not talking about a huge advance from a publisher and a national book tour and plopping yourself down opposite Katie Couric on the *Today* show. You can't be concerned with any of that just yet. What has to occupy you for a good while now is the actual writing of this piece that might or might not provide your deliverance. The rewards I'm referring to are more basic: the good feeling of having written well for a few hours and the satisfaction of crafting a piece of your story in your very own way, putting your own stamp on it.

Good, clear writing that has been sufficiently wordsmithed, that's what we're after. A solid, well-written work of fiction with your name under the title and your voice throughout. A story and a cast of characters that will make the guy in Sheboygan continue to think about them even after he's finished the reading.

Two of the most essential components are description and setting. Before you can work one bit of the magic in that story or those characters, you have to make your reader fully aware of the place and the time, of what the weather is like, what things look like, smell like, and feel like. All of these—and many more—are the details that add up to create the world that you're offering.

PUTTING THE READER IN THE SETTING

Saying that description and setting are important in fiction is like saying that an engine is important in a car. Other things are essential too, like a steering wheel and tires and dozens of other gizmos. The car won't do much without most of them. But it won't even *start* without an engine. Neither will your story really start until your reader is aware of the time and the place.

Here are several examples of how writers have chosen to introduce their reader to their setting. Consider these options, determine which might work best to draw your reader in, and place them where you want them to be.

Giving the Lay of the Land

Slapping the reader in the face with the setting in the first few sentences is not usually the best approach. The first image that you paint in his or her mind is enormously important; that image—that first taste of your story and your voice—will shade their impression of what you're up to. If the first paragraph is a straightforward description of a house or a city street or any other place, with nothing evidently happening there, then the reader might assume that nothing much is going to happen later, either.

That's not to say that it can't be done, and done effectively. Look at John Steinbeck's opening paragraph in *East of Eden*:

> The Salinas Valley is in Northern California. It is a long narrow swale between two ranges of mountains, and the Salinas River winds and twists up the center until it falls at last into Monterey Bay.

This is pure telling rather than showing, a topic that we'll take up in chapter four. It is reportage. But Steinbeck goes on to quickly establish that the place itself is essential to his story and to the narrator. Notice that we meet the place *before* we meet the narrator or any of the characters; such is its importance to the tale we're about to be told.

A first time novelist starting to write a story set in Bolivia would be ill advised if told to begin with a description of its topography, climate, and gross national product. What he's likely to end up with is a report about Bolivia and not a story about the elderly rancher who has his sights set on the pretty peasant girl who is in love with his son. The writer will eventually get around to all of that, but what readers are likely to have lodged in their minds is that little geography lesson. And it will be hard to overcome.

So, how did Steinbeck pull it off? His first two sentences work in *East of Eden* because he knew where he was headed and how he wanted to get there. He knew that the land itself would be a living, breathing character in the novel, as essential as any of the other characters. Look at his next paragraph:

> I remember my childhood names for grasses and secret flowers. I remember where a toad may live and what time the birds awaken in the summer—and what trees and seasons smelled like—how people looked and walked and smelled even. The memory of odors is very rich.

Now we have the narrator present and accounted for, looking around and beginning to tell us whatever it is that he wishes to impart.

So, while I would be hesitant to suggest that writers who are still finding their feet regarding craft begin their books with a geographical description of the countryside, neither would I tell them *not* to do it under any circumstances. As a writer, you have to put your readers exactly where you want them to be, seeing exactly what you want them to see. Or, more importantly, what you *need* them to see to establish the setting in their consciousness. If your setting is going to play a vital role in your story—which it almost certainly will—this may be the ideal approach for you. But don't decide until you consider others.

Using Intricate Details

Don DeLillo begins his novel *Underworld* with the famous 1951 baseball game between the Brooklyn Dodgers and the New York Giants. Here's his first sentence:

> He speaks in your voice, American, and there's a shine in his eye that's halfway hopeful.

Readers don't know who *he* is, not yet. They don't know why there's a shine in his eye or why it's halfway hopeful. They don't know that it's the famous baseball game—or any baseball game—that he's going to. But they are made aware in the fourth word that they are being spoken to directly.

DeLillo goes on, in the next fifty or so pages, to paint a picture, in present tense, of that game that plops readers down in one of the seats at the Polo Grounds on that long ago cloudy afternoon. He infuses those pages with detail after detail after detail that lay the groundwork for the larger part of

his story, set fifty years later, which plays out in the next eight hundred pages.
Listen:

> People stand in both decks in left, leaning out from the rows up front, and some
> of them are tossing paper over the edge, torn-up scorecards and bits of match-
> book covers, there are crushed paper cups, little waxy napkins they got with
> their hot dogs, there are germ-bearing tissues many days old that were matted
> at the bottoms of deep pockets, all coming down around Pafko.
>
>> Thomson is loping along, he is striding nicely around first, leaning into his run.
>> Pafko throws smartly to Cox . . .
>> Cox peers out from under his cap and snaps the ball sidearm to Robinson.
>> Look at Mays meanwhile strolling to the plate dragging the barrel of his bat
> on the ground.
>> Robinson takes the throw and makes a spin toward Thomson, who is stand-
> ing shyly maybe five feet from second.
>> People like to see paper fall at Pafko's feet, maybe drift across his shoulder
> or cling to his cap. The wall is nearly seventeen feet high so he is well out of
> range of the longest leaning touch and they have to be content to bathe him in
> their paper.
>> Look at Durocher on the dugout steps, manager of the Giants, hard-rock
> Leo, the gashouse scrapper, a face straight from the Gallic Wars . . .

Now notice what DeLillo is up to here. Having called out readers individually in the first sentence of the book (remember the "He speaks in your voice . . ."), he goes on to show them everything that's going on: people in the stands, the mannerisms of the players on the field, the texture of the napkins that come with the hotdogs. He points his readers in every direction that he wants them to go:

> "Look at Mays . . ."
> "Look at Durocher . . ."

In the wonderful flow of description that winds through the next many pages, DeLillo hovers over several characters at the game. The young boy who "speaks in your voice"—with the halfway hopeful shine in his eye—has snuck in without paying and is nervous, jumpy. The businessman in the seat beside him who buys him peanuts and soda is . . . "close-shaved and Brylcreemed but with a casual quality, a free-and-easy manner that Cotter the boy links to small-town life in the movies."

Suddenly we're in the radio broadcast booth with the announcer. Then, in one paragraph, we're in people's houses and in bars and stores across the several boroughs of New York, where they're listening to the game on the radio. Then we're in the stands again, with four men in the VIP section: Frank Sinatra, Jackie Gleason, Toots Shor, and J. Edgar Hoover. There are people we know, men we've watched on television or read about.

Gleason is playing hooky from the rehearsal of his television show, where he's supposed to be running through his lines for a new skit they're trying out this week called *The Honeymooners*. Hoover learns, during the game, that Russia has exploded an atomic bomb in their first rehearsal of an entirely different sort. Both of these anecdotes serve to anchor us securely into a particular era that is bigger than a baseball game and into a world that is wider than the Polo Grounds. Sort of the *thing* played out against the bigger *thing*, which we'll discuss throughout the book.

All of these characters—the ones we've never known and the ones for whom we have a preconceived mental image—are talking to each other and laughing and swilling beer and eating peanuts, and we are—through the courtesy of a gifted writer—right there with them. Sinatra, Gleason, Shor, and Hoover are all dead now. But here they are fully alive; their loosened neckties are as wide and colorful as all the other men's ties on that early 1950s afternoon. Little triangles of handkerchiefs peek out from the breast pockets of their suit coats. Cups of frothy beer are cold in their hands.

This detailed approach might be a good way for you to bring your reader into your story, to carefully paint a mental picture—down to the texture and shapes of seemingly unimportant things—and establish in the reader's mind an image as clear and focused as a good photograph. We'll deal with how to *look* for those details in the very next chapter. Then in chapter four, how to *show* them (rather than report them).

Let's go back for a moment to that business about the three approaches to finding your writer's voice: craft, models, and wordsmithing.

DeLillo uses most of his tools: a variety of sentence lengths, allusions, metaphors, similes, the five senses. His mastery of the craft is apparent. I've never met him, but I believe it's a pretty safe bet that DeLillo has read a novel or two, or—more likely—hundreds. And I suspect that most of them made some impression on him as a writer. He undoubtedly found in many of them techniques that he might employ, things that he might do, and plenty of things that he would make sure *not* to do. And all of it—the practice of the craft, the influence of models, and the fine wordsmithing—results in the sure, comfortable voice that makes the reader want to stay on board for another eight hundred pages.

We talked earlier about using a variety of writing approaches and techniques (the tools in your kit). In a passage like DeLillo's, where there are several paragraphs or maybe pages of details, you'll need to pay particular attention to this in order to keep the reader interested. So mix in metaphors and similes with strong, clever adjectives. Slip in a few sound-words (onomatopoeia) and maybe some pleasing cadence. We'll be looking closely at these devices and others later, and we'll practice using them. They are the basic building blocks of the craft of writing. These instruments of manipulation are trickery of the most devious sort. But that's okay. In a long passage like this one, such devices are the keys to keeping your reader on board.

This is a good spot for us to make a distinction between literary and popular fiction. Though the terms are too general—there is a wide middle ground where they bleed into each other's territory—we can at least try to pinpoint a place where they differ. The use of description will serve nicely. Readers of literary fiction, like the DeLillo novel we just looked at, will generally be more tolerant of long passages of description since they are as interested in the way the author unfolds the story as in the progression of the story itself. Fans of writers of popular fiction, like Stephen King and Belva Plain and Ken Follett, usually want escapism first and foremost. They want to be entertained, and one of the jobs of the writer is to *not* bog them down in what they might perceive to be too much detail.

The problem for the writer of popular fiction is to give sufficient description without giving too much. The best solution is to keep your type of reader in mind all the time, and follow what I call the clutter rule: If something isn't serving the advancement of the story, it needs to go. All writers have sacrificed some finely crafted paragraphs or complete chapters to the clutter rule. And while it's not fun to delete writing you've struggled with and polished, your story or novel will work better without it.

Another good idea would be to enlist a few of your friends who read the type of fiction you're writing. Ask them to read your manuscript with an objective eye, trying their best to imagine that they've never met the author—writing groups are enormously useful for this—and the feedback you'll get will help to guide you in your description.

Readers don't usually declare themselves as partakers of literary or popular fiction exclusively, like Democrats and Republicans attending caucuses. Many, many readers enjoy both. And many authors write both. In this book,

I'll use both types of fiction as models since each includes numerous talented wordsmiths in their ranks.

Sensory Description

Chapter five will deal specifically with using the five senses in all of your writing. But let's look here at how this approach might be a good way for you to get your story or novel going. Consider how Margaret George starts her novel *The Memoirs of Cleopatra*:

> Warmth. Wind. Dancing blue waters, and the sound of waves. I see, hear, feel them all still. I even taste the sting of the salt against my lips, where the fine, misty spray coats them. And closer even than that, the lulling, drowsy smell of my mother's skin by my nose, where she holds me against her bosom, her hand making a sunshade across my forehead to shield my eyes. The boat is rocking gently, and my mother is rocking me as well, so I sway to a double rhythm. It makes me very sleepy, and the sloshing of the water all around me makes a blanket of sound, wrapping me securely. I am held safely, cradled in love and watchfulness. I remember. I remember . . .

This is pure sensory description. Before we know the name of the body of water we're floating on or its location, we know what it feels and smells and looks like. Before we know who is telling us the story—though the title of the book would no doubt be helpful here—we know what is quite possibly her earliest memory. And we are experiencing it with her, rocking gently with her, the sloshing of the water and the movement of the vessel setting the tone that slides us gently into the novel.

So, here's another way for you to bring your reader in. Your beginning might benefit from the delicate brushwork of sensory description, letting the reader not only see what's going on, but feel, taste, touch, and hear it as well. In fact, this might be one of the best choices for beginning writers, since relating what things sound, look, feel, smell, and taste like might prove to be an easier chore, starting out, than some of the other approaches.

Setting the Tone

The tone, the pervading attitude or mood, will determine early on whether this is going to be a serious matter or a frivolous one. Funny or sad? Formal? Informal? Heavy or light? And a very good place to begin the establishment of the tone, to get a solid toehold into it, is in description in general and description of your settings in particular.

Steinbeck's tone in the first sentences of *East of Eden* is straight to the point, with no dillydallying. Here's where we are and here's the layout: mountains over here and a river over there. In *Underworld*, Don DeLillo works the tone like a musical instrument, hitting every detail just right, bringing the reader fully in. Margaret George's mood is peaceful, almost drowsy; but instead of rocking us to sleep, she's carefully positioning us closer to where she wants us to be. Now look at how Jack Finney starts his novella *The Night People*:

> The great bridge, arched across the blackness of San Francisco Bay, seemed like a stage set now. Empty of cars in the middle of the night, its narrow, orange-lighted length hung wrapped in darkness, motionless and artificial. At its center, where the enormous support cables dipped down into the light to almost touch the bridge, two men stood at the railing staring out at the black Pacific, preparing themselves for what they had come here to do.

There's nothing dreamy here; we're not being eased into this one. The night is dark. The ocean is dark. The bay is black. The bridge is massive and deserted, the support cables "enormous." The two men are dwarfed by the setting, and they have a mission. We don't yet know what it is that they intend to do, or why. But the tone is set. The game—as Sherlock Holmes used to mumble to Dr. Watson—is afoot.

The tone of a piece of literature is the overall mood. If you imagine your story being played out on a stage, the tone might be a combination of the backdrop, the set, and the lighting. The prevailing tone of *The Night People*, at least at the beginning, is gloomy and mysterious, maybe a little creepy. So far, it could be an Edgar Allan Poe story. And that gloom is exactly what the author wants us to feel as we start our adventure, whatever it turns out to be.

When starting your story or novel, pay close attention to the overall mood or feeling that you want to convey, then work elements of that particular tone into the opening lines. Carefully choose each adjective and image; in fact, each and every word should be the product of a meticulous selection.

DESCRIPTION AND SETTING THROUGHOUT THE STORY

We're running the risk here, when putting forth models of how writers begin their novels, of making the neophyte author believe that careful description of the setting needs to happen only on the first page or two, like tempting

It was a Dark and Stormy Night . . .

Don't hesitate to let the weather help you set the tone of your story or novel.

Often in good fiction what's going on outside is reflective of what's happening *inside* of characters and plots.

Here are some examples:

- *King Lear*: a raging thunderstorm during Lear's "Blow, winds, and crack your cheeks!" soliloquy.
- William Faulkner's humid, sweltering summer days mirroring his characters' lazy, apathetic attitudes.
- The hopelessness and desperation of a blizzard as the backdrop for the central character's escalating madness in Stephen King's *The Shining*.
- Though there are bits of humor and hopefulness and yearning in Edith Wharton's *Ethan Frome*, the persistent mood can be encapsulated as stark or bleak, like the harsh wintertime New England countryside that is its setting.
- Heathcliff, in *Wuthering Heights*, is as brooding as the windswept moors he wanders around on.
- The laid-back, bright sunshine lifestyle of a south Florida harbor community is reflected in the easygoing, but tough when it needs to be, narrator's voice in John D. MacDonald's Travis McGee novels.

The weather sometimes helps to determine *your* mood ("rainy days and Mondays always get me down," and all that), so let it do the same for your fiction.

bait impaled on stout hooks. The truth is that the description of time and place must be a sustained effort; it has to be continuously worked at, continuously painted in the reader's mind.

A short story makes enormous demands on description and setting, since everything has to transpire clearly and succinctly in not too many pages. A novel, on the other hand, being so much longer than a story, usually hundreds of pages longer, makes just as many demands and usually many more. Characters undergo big changes in those hundreds of pages, and their sagas are most often played out in a variety of places. And the description has to be as strong and as useful on page 201 as it is in the opening paragraph. Listen to E. Annie Proulx halfway through her novel *The Shipping News*:

> The hill tilting toward the water, the straggled pickets and then Dennis's aquamarine house with a picture window toward the street. Quoyle pulled pens from his shirt, put them on the dashboard before he went in. For pens got in the way. The door opened into the kitchen. Quoyle stepped around and over children. In the living room, under a tinted photograph of two stout women lolling in ferns, Dennis slouched on leopard-print sofa cushions, watched the fishery news. On each side of him crocheted pillows in rainbows and squares. Carpenter at Home.

Here's detail aplenty. The novel takes place in Newfoundland. But one chapter—chapter sixteen, titled "Beety's Kitchen"—takes place in one room, which has to be rich in its uniqueness. Thus: children that have to be stepped over, the tinted photograph of an odd tableau, the assortment of mismatched sofa pillows and cushions. Later, we hear water gushing into a kettle. We smell bread baking, yeasty and strong in the hot room. We watch one of those children eat yellow bakeberry jam (whatever *that* is) on a piece of the bread.

It wouldn't be a bad idea to post this little tenet over your monitor or at least in your brain: *My reader has to be there, too.* The fact that *you* have to be there is obvious; you won't be able to have your characters walk around and do things in your setting if you don't have a good idea of the layout. But the guy in Sheboygan's perception of it has to be just as clear. You have to take him there.

By the way, you might have noticed in the Proulx model that there are three sentence fragments. In fact, many of her strongest descriptions come in incomplete sentences throughout the entire novel. Here's a good place to say something about the canon of rules pertaining to writing. Namely, that it is sometimes a good idea to break some. What, in fact, is the use of fragments—which many fine writers employ to great advantage—but the violation of a steadfast decree that has been drummed into us since elementary school?

Fragments can often be the very best way for you to emphasize something. Because they are infractions, they stand out; so, if you *need* something to stand out, here's a good way to do it. But you might get a reprimand from your old English teacher.

The Shipping News, even with its abundance of fragments, won both the National Book Award and the Pulitzer Prize.

Thus endeth that lesson.

SUMMARY: SENDING THE INVITATION

If a novel works well, it's because the novelist has worked hard. How many times have you heard somebody say that this or that author's prose is so real and comfortable that he bets the words just poured out?

I'll take that bet.

The brutal truth is, when it comes to creative writing, words hardly ever just pour out. What has to happen is that you have to struggle and groan and write something any number of times so that, at the end, the finished product has to look like it took no effort whatsoever. The narrative has to be as easy and relaxed as an old uncle spinning a yarn on the front porch, as smooth as cold buttermilk easing out of a porcelain cup.

In other words, you have to work a little magic.

You'll have to do it other places, too. Remember the bit about good writing having to transcend place and time that we started with? That calls for magic, also. Making your setting accessible to a reader who has never been there, has never lived in that era, or maybe never knew of the place's existence or cared one way or another about it is going to be a tricky task. Here's Flannery O'Connor again: "The writer operates at a peculiar cross-roads where time and place and eternity somehow meet. His problem is to find that location."

The real problem is the eternity part. That's where the magic is required. The eternity that Flannery O'Connor is talking about is the much larger commonality that links us all together. It is—to risk sounding awfully philosophical—the vast human experience that all people share, the enormous connection that allows a reader removed from a setting by hundreds of years and thousands of miles to relate to the story, understand it, and enjoy it.

Adequate use of description and an adequate rendering of time and place in a novel will allow your readers to have *some* access to your story. *Good* description and a carefully crafted setting will make them *want* to be there. This significantly more precise and polished effort will make them want to settle in and stay a while, to get to know the characters and their situations, to see how your characters get into moral dilemmas and out again. They want to see how they end up surprising him, or how they misbehave. With good description and a believable setting, your readers will have a front-row, center seat, as opposed to one in the back of the third balcony.

The difference between just being in attendance and *wanting* to be there starts with an invitation. Good, clear writing has to, first and foremost, lure the reader in. Think of the examples we just looked at, at how Steinbeck, DeLillo,

George, and Finney began their novels. Here are four distinctively different styles and settings, four very different voices. Yet what they all have in common is that they were carefully written to entice readers to step right up into the vehicle and, once in, to look around and wonder where they're off to.

Novelists usually have to be stealthier than poets, who can get away with a beckoning as straightforward as Robert Frost's in "The Pasture," which is usually the opening poem in collections of his work:

> I'm going out to clean the pasture spring;
>> I'll only stop to rake the leaves away
>> (And wait to watch the water clear, I may):
> I shan't be gone long.—You come too.

You come too.

That's what your writing has to say to your readers. Something in the situation you are presenting, in your characters and in your writer's voice, has to be compelling enough to bring them on board. And two of the very best places to issue your summons, and to keep on issuing it page after page, are in your description and your setting.

In this book, we'll look at various ways to bring the magic about: techniques and examples and devices and blatant trickery, all aimed toward that moment when your readers will connect so strongly with something you've described, or have such a realistic sense of the place where you want to take them, that they hear your invitation: You come too.

EXERCISES

Throughout the book, there will be several exercises in each chapter to give you the opportunity to try your hand at specific approaches and techniques. I encourage you to do these, so that you can get some hands-on experience. For the introductory chapter, we'll try three ways that might help you ease into this overall process of providing your readers with a believable setting in particular and description in general.

EXERCISE 1

In the next chapter, we're going to look at the importance of gathering details and then working them into your writing. Let's get a little head start. For this exercise, look back at the several paragraphs from *Underworld* on pages 10 and 11. The author piled detail on detail to firmly entrench his reader in the setting.

I suspect one of the first things that Don DeLillo, the author, did was make a list of the details that he wanted to include. In all likelihood, his list contained many more details than he ended up using when it came time to write the text.

Make a short list of ten or so details or items that you might include in a good description of at least one of the following topics:

- a trip to the dentist
- a farm
- riding mass transit (bus, train, subway)
- Saturday chores
- A busy city street

There's no need to incorporate your details into any lengthy writing; as I said, we'll go into this in much more detail in another chapter. But, at least do this: Think about how you *might* work them in, in any way other than simple statements of fact. Then, select one or two of your choices and write a sentence that will bring the detail to life for your reader.

EXERCISE 2

Look back at the bit from *The Memoirs of Cleopatra* on page 14. Look at how the author conveyed the five senses in that one scene. Think of the list that she might have made before she tackled that paragraph.

Now, choose one of the following topics, and make a list of the five senses, leaving enough room beside each one to come up with several possibilities for description. Then get down at least one example of each sense.

I know. The list looks awfully familiar. That's not because I'm too lazy to come up with another one, but these same five topics can be approached from several entirely different directions by a good writer. This time, instead of coming up with a collection of details or things, focus on the five senses.

- a trip to the dentist
- a farm
- riding mass transit (bus, train, subway)
- Saturday chores
- A busy city street

EXERCISE 3

Think of five books or short stories that you've read and enjoyed. Now, try to come up with a few words (maybe just one) that convey the overall mood, or tone, of the work. Moods certainly change throughout stories, but you should be able to pinpoint a prevailing tone for each title.

When you've completed your list, it might be interesting—and certainly instructive—to pull those books and stories down from the shelf and dig around in them looking for examples of how their authors went about setting the tone. Searching for ways they worked the magic that you will work in your own writing.

EXERCISE 4

Using one of your manuscripts, look at how you introduced the setting. You might have used one of the approaches discussed in this chapter—giving the lay of the land, using sensory detail, tone, etc.—or you might have used a combination. Now, try bringing the setting in using another strategy and see what works best.

chapter 2

[LEARNING TO PAY ATTENTION]

Anyone who spends any time at all at baseball games will immediately understand the phrase "Heads Up!" It is to a baseball fan as instantly recognizable as "Batter up!" and "Two over here, with mustard."

Heads up means, clearly and succinctly, pay attention. It literally means, at the ballpark, that a baseball is currently in flight and you would be well advised to seek it out, and, if need be, get out of its way, lest it plow into your noggin with the velocity of a missile.

To a writer, heads up should mean something less dangerous, but not less important. As a writer, you have to pay attention, too, constantly, not just when something appears to be coming your way. For a writer, something is *always* coming your way. You just have to be alert.

To be a good writer, you have to be a persistent and meticulous harvester of detail. To put it less politely, you have to be a thief, pure and outright. Some of your best dialogue will come from people in the line with you at the grocery store or from the teller at the bank or from conversations at other tables that you aren't intended to hear. Then if you're smart, you'll write the details down, preferably in a pocket notebook but saving that, on a napkin or a deposit slip or a business card. You must gather seemingly unimportant minutiae from the world around you and then carefully place them in your writing, like perfect stones in a garden wall.

Morley Callaghan in *That Summer in Paris: Memories of Tangled Friendships With Hemingway, Fitzgerald, and Some Others* remembers the time that F. Scott Fitzgerald came to his flat and was intrigued by freshly washed handkerchiefs spread out on the windowpanes to dry quickly in the sun. Fitzgerald watched Callaghan's wife peel one off and fold it then asked if he could do one. Here's some of what Callaghan recalls about Fitzgerald's reaction:

Fresh little details. That's what you'd better be on the lookout for. Because all those fresh little details will finally blend together to make your fiction accessible to your reader.

In this chapter, we'll look at ways for you to pay much closer attention to all manners of things out there in your world, in your daily life. So that when you undertake the important business of establishing your setting and describing it, you'll have—if not a veritable cornucopia—at least a wider selection of possibilities than if you hadn't looked around and taken notice in the first place.

Then in the rest of this book we'll use our trinity of approaches (craft, models, and wordsmithing) to find the best ways for you to infuse some of that detail into your setting and your story or novel as a whole.

CREATING A WAREHOUSE OF DETAILS

When you begin to look at everything with a stronger magnification, you'll end up with more bits and pieces of data than you'll ever use. Your journal or file or shoe box or brain (not your best choice here; bits and pieces stay put much better in a shoe box than they will in your brain) will finally become like that crate of old record albums in your closet. You'll never need most of them, but if you *should* happen to want to listen to a Roger Miller tune that you've taken to humming, you'll know where to look.

This constantly growing collection of observations and discoveries will serve you well. Because the details that will eventually work their way into your setting and description—the characters that will people your story, the words they will say, the clothes they will wear, the rooms where they will wear the clothes—all have their genesis in the world around you, the writer. What you have to do is have your antenna up, and when you find the details, catalog them in some way, tangibly or mentally. Trust me on this: Tangibly is better. Then, you can dip into your warehouse of details whenever you need to and use some of them in your writing.

But what you have to do first is hone your sense of perception and power of observation.

PAYING ATTENTION TO EVERYTHING AROUND YOU

When my wife and I visited Ellis Island one cold January day, we had lunch in the snack bar. The snack bar offered typical snack bar fare, and we settled down to our burgers and fries and steaming coffee in a high-ceilinged, drafty big room that might have once been a holding area or examination room back when shiploads of immigrants still docked outside. I looked around— I cased the joint, to use a crime writer's idiom—and made little mental notes of my surroundings. About the texture of the walls. The exposed pipes that gurgled and groaned. The frosty condensation on the windows. These are the kinds of details that you should always be on the lookout for as a writer, just in case you might be able to work some of them into your writing.

Then I noticed an older couple sitting at the table nearest us. I had seen them on the boat ride over, standing close together at the rail, their overcoat collars pulled up high at their necks. Now they were still in their coats but had taken off their gloves and mufflers. The small man said a few words to his small wife in a distinctly British accent. High British, not Cockney. The Queen's English. Hugh Grant English. They fidgeted with the little packets of salt and pepper; they smiled at them. Then they carefully unwrapped their packets of plastic cutlery and began to eat their hamburgers and fries with knives and forks, the forks never leaving their left hands, the knives never leaving their right.

My attention was entirely on them now. I lifted out my pocket notebook and scribbled a few words about the man's pencil thin mustache, their white hair, the way they sat up straight at the table, like our mothers used to tell us to do. I noted the way they both lifted up the tops of their burgers with their plastic knives to peek at what exactly it was they were eating.

My wife and I have promised ourselves another trip to Ellis Island. Her because she had so looked forward to it. She's a third grade teacher and does an immigration unit, but she took too strong a motion sickness pill prior to riding the boat and was doped up for the whole experience. And I want to go back because my attention was riveted the entire time on that little couple from England, on their mannerisms and their dialect, on their reactions to the exhibits. On the way they held on to each other when they stepped back on the boat at the end, so neither of them would stumble.

Now, let's put you in this scenario. You're out there on Ellis Island instead of me, and your writer's radar has locked unto this couple. How do you go about the task of gathering some useful information that you might actually end up using?

First, I'd advise against following around behind them with your pocket notebook open and your pen scratching like that of a cub reporter in an old movie. But you do need to pay careful and close attention. To you, that little couple has to become *possibilities*. Think about who they might be in a story. You might imagine them as high society, having asked the concierge at the Plaza to book them an outing at Ellis Island and the Statue of Liberty. They'd had all their New York meals in fancy restaurants, at Tavern on the Green and the Four Seasons. Out on the island and feeling a mite peckish, their only option was the strange snack bar cuisine and plastic utensils. So, not used to eating with their hands, they made the best of it.

Then mystery and irony may lift their sinister heads. Now you might see them as a couple of spies blending in quietly on a tourist outing. The crisp, British accent has been polished to perfection, the ritual with the knives and forks worked out nicely. Or maybe he's on the lam—has been since the sixties—living on the money he embezzled in Geneva.

Then, in a softer mood, they may become a retired tailor and his wife of fifty years from Liverpool, on the vacation they've been saving for since they started watching American shows on the telly. Maybe one of them is sick, and this trip is the big splash before the darkness, before the other one is left alone in the small house on a narrow street where they've lived since Queen Elizabeth was a young girl.

If you end up using this pair in your fiction, you're going to have to eventually describe them so well that your readers will see and hear them as surely as if they were watching them in a movie. If your story takes place at Ellis Island, you'll have to do the same thing with the setting. So, here they are, the couple in the flesh and the place spread out around you laden with details. If you intend to ever use them, what you need to do is come away from that outing with a notebook full of snippets that should soon become more legible entries in your journal. Then, who knows? They might just become a story that college freshmen will grapple with a century from now.

Or—more likely—some of the snippets will work their way into several pieces of your writing, into several of your characters. This encounter needn't have only character possibilities; you might end up using some of these details to describe how an entirely different elderly couple interacts or how foreigners behave in unfamiliar territory.

Now, here's the point. In order to come up with something that you can use in your writing, you have to glean many, many details, most of which you will probably end up not using at all. You have to know how these people stood and walked and sat and waited in line. You have to know how they moved their hands around when they talked to each other or how they kept their hands perfectly still. Beyond the people themselves, you need to know what the place looked like, what it smelled and sounded like, and even what it felt like.

In short, you have to have a complete sense of it, whether you use the details in a story about that particular time and place or completely different ones—down to seemingly unimportant details—if you stand any chance at all of taking your readers there.

SCAVENGING FOR DETAILS

The best way to become more proficient at anything is to practice; just ask any athletic coach or piano teacher. And that certainly holds true for writers. The more times you revise something, the better it's likely to get; the longer you write fiction, the better *you're* likely to get. And the more time you spend searching for details, the more interesting and useful details you're likely to come up with.

There will be some specific practice exercises at the end of the chapter. But for now let's look at a couple of ways to get better at paying attention to details.

Focus on the Past

Pick a time and a place in your past that you remember reasonably well. You shouldn't pick an episode when you were an infant or a very small child, since you'll be fabricating almost everything. Fabrication is fine and proper for a writer, but the purpose of these practice field trips is to hone your powers of perception, not your imagination. Neither should you to pick a monumental or life-changing event, like the day your father died or the day you became engaged or became a parent for the first time. The enormity of such an experience will tend to overshadow what you're trying to do, which is mine for particulars.

Here are two more rules for these practices: The time has to be more than ten years ago (readers less than sixteen years of age may modify that to five), and the place has to be one that you haven't seen for quite a while. That's important; this won't be a helpful practice if you had the experience recently or if you see the place often. Your grandmother's kitchen might work, when you were, say, ten or eleven, or a girlfriend's or boyfriend's living room when you were in high school. Maybe a place where you went on a family vacation many years ago would be a good choice.

Once you've settled on the time and a place, make plenty of notes. Don't worry about sentence structure at this point; in fact, don't worry about writing sentences at all. A list might work better for you, or some sort of diagram. Get down everything that comes to your mind about both the time and the place: what the weather was like on that day, who else was there, what the landscape was like—if you were outside—and what kind of furniture there was—if you were inside.

Then move on to the nitty and the gritty: the sensory details. What did the furniture *feel* like? Exactly what *color* was the sky? Just blue won't do. Maybe a metaphor will work better for you, or a simile. Maybe just a darned good adjective will suffice. Adjectives are one of the real workhorses of good writing, the salt and pepper that perk things up, but sometimes carefully chosen nouns and verbs can eliminate the need for them. When you're practicing, just spill out a bunch of words and phrases that capture the place and time you are remembering for *you*. When you're done, write a rough draft that will capture the moment for your *reader*.

These needn't be lengthy sagas. Something around one typed, double-spaced page ought to do it, or two or three pages in the journal that I'm going to strongly suggest, a few pages from now, that you never let get very far from you. And these *shouldn't* be stories with conflicts and rising action and suspense and resolution and all of that business. Trying to write a story will just defeat your purpose. Just compose a clear first draft describing that time and place. Be a wordsmith. Choose each and every word carefully so that the finished product will actually take your reader there. It's a good idea to start doing some of that wordsmithing in your notes; that way, a little of your most important work is done before you even get to the writing. When something that smells good pops up on your list, you might go ahead and write down *aroma* and *drifts*, since these are better words than *smell* and *approaches*. Or when you first imagine clouds in a light blue sky, you might write *stringy wisps in a robin's egg sky*, since this is an image you might end up using.

Each time you start one of these practices you must remember an essential step: As you make your notes, think of that time and that place in *present tense*, not past. The events of that day should be happening right now. In our pigeonhole brains, past tense means over and done with. It means been there, done that. Present tense means something is playing out as we watch it. Even when you write a story in past tense, the events *still* have to play out as the reader watches them. So you had best do all of your imagining in present tense if you intend your story to come to life for your reader.

Try this and see what you come up with. I think you'll be surprised at the details you'll unearth that have been buried for a long time. By practicing this over and over, you'll become accustomed to spotting—and creating— the small, often unnoticed fine points that will craft rich descriptions and settings in your stories and novels.

Focus on the Present

Another way to practice allows you to give your memory a rest. Settle comfortably into a fairly interesting place that is quite real and in the here and now. It should be an active place where something is happening—preferably where people are coming and going—so that you can describe them. Notice how they're dressed, the pitch of their voices, their mannerisms. Pick a place where you don't know the people, so that your descriptions won't be based on preconceived notions but on what you actually see and hear.

Plop yourself down with pad and paper on a bench in a busy park or in a shopping mall. Maybe you're waiting for your flight to be called at the airport and you need something to do anyway; airports and bus and train stations are wonderful arenas for people watching. Try a coffee shop, a museum, or outside your office building at lunch hour. The possibilities are endless.

As with the practice from memory, pay close attention to the physical surroundings, to smells and textures and sounds. Look for little things that you might very well have missed if you weren't tightening your focus. See how perceptive you can be when you don't have to remember a thing, when all you have to do is pay close attention.

When practicing in the present, your subject is hustling and bustling all around you—not in the foggy recesses of your brain—so you might dispense with taking notes and just *write*. Freewriting is useful for practicing your thinking *and* your writing. With freewriting, you don't worry about syntax or spelling or maybe even punctuation. You just spill out ideas as they come to you and images as you see them.

But as you freewrite, again practice wordsmithing, choosing just the right words and phrases. Once you've come up with a paragraph or two, look back over it and circle words that might have better possibilities. For instance, if somebody you are watching is walking, consider the kind of walking they are doing. Walking is generic and dull. It hardly ever tells your reader enough. Watch your subject closer and determine just exactly what sort of walking she is up to. Is she ambling? Strutting? Meandering? Strolling? Promenading? Is she traipsing or tiptoeing or tromping or bounding? Something that makes a person unique can very often be conveyed in one word. But it has to be just the right word. So choose carefully.

When you're choosing, be careful with the thesaurus. It's an extremely useful tool when used correctly, as simply a list of *possible* replacements, but very few words are exactly interchangeable. Look back at all those walking words; each one means a distinctly different action. Each one carries with it a reflection of the walker's attitude. So you can't very well slap one in place of any other one and expect to come up with the precise image you want to convey.

As an example, let's say you settle into a comfortable chair in a large bookstore a few days before Christmas. What you come up with might start something like this:

> The Christmasy sweater on the plump fellow in the chair across the table from me has seen more than a season or two. Its turtle neck has drooped a bit; the holly and berries are less vibrant than they must once have been, the white background more a dull gray now. Still, 'tis the season, and this guy's sweater is more of a celebration of it than I am currently providing. He's flipping through a computer manual that is thicker than a Bible. But he's not really looking at it. He stares at his watch every minute or two. Waiting for his wife to finish her shopping, I'll wager.
>
> Two old friends run into each other in the aisle between Christian Inspiration and Poetry. They are in late middle age and are either pleasantly surprised or act sufficiently so. One of them has a granddaughter of seven or so with him. She is restless and wants the little reunion to adjourn. She begins to kick one small foot back and forth and then the other. Now the kicking becomes a rhythmic enterprise, the upper half of her body not moving at all. She's taken clog dancing, this one.

Now, what can you make out of this hodgepodge, or any hodgepodge that you put together? Probably nothing. Remember, you're doing these exercises simply as practice, to hone your powers of observation and your wordsmithing.

Look at a few of the details and word choices. *Christmasy* is more unique than *festive* or *holiday* when referring to the man's sweater. *Thicker than a Bible* offers a more concrete visual image than just *thick*.

A freewriting exercise like this—in addition to giving you practice at locating and polishing details—might also provide you with some story ideas. Even the beginning of this one has possibilities. Maybe the two old friends bumping into each other is the starting point for an interesting backstory that involves both of them and the woman that they both loved long ago. Maybe the clogging girl standing anxiously by is the granddaughter of that long ago love. Maybe, in fact, she is the spitting image of the man who just ran into her grandfather.

For a writer, the world is made up of *maybes*. And they're all in the details. What you as a writer have to do—all the time—is pay attention to the grand parade that is constantly passing in front of you.

TAKING NOTES

Now that we've established the importance of digging up details, let's look at some useful ways to remember them.

The best chance I have of remembering anything is writing it down. Whether it's groceries that need to be bought, dry cleaning that needs to be picked up, a phone call that needs to be made, or whatever, if it's going to get done by me it needs to be on paper.

Note taking—the filtering down of lots of stuff to not very little, the focusing on the most important components—is a skill that too many high school students get to college without knowing how to do. Their freshman fall semester grades are often evidence of this.

For you as a writer, note taking is as essential as it is for those college freshmen. Being a keen observer of human nature and architecture and cloud formations and everything else that constitutes the big, wide world that is your database is one thing. But *remembering* any of it is quite another.

I see more and more people poking away at their Palm Pilots with little probes, and that might work just fine. Except that I don't have a Palm Pilot. What I *do* have is smaller, considerably less expensive, and—from the looks on the faces of those Palm Pilot pokers—less aggravating. Of course, you should use whatever works best for you.

A TRUSTY NOTEBOOK, CLOSE AT HAND

I suggest you keep a pad or a small notebook in your pocket or purse. Keep another one in the glove compartment of your car and one more in your desk at work.

Who knows when you'll hear a nice bit of dialogue that is worth remembering or see a particularly pretty sunset whose mixture of colors needs to be recorded? You'll most probably never again see that odd pair of children skipping stones across a lake—better get down the details while you have them.

Don't think that you have to be only on the lookout for unusual or ironic things, like the couple eating their burgers and fries with knives and forks on Ellis Island. You should be looking for ordinary things, as well. Remember, everyday life is made up mostly of ordinary things. And if your fiction is to be reflective of everyday life, it had better contain plenty of the same.

If you're afraid that that will make for boring fiction, I suggest you read John Updike's classic story titled "A&P." It's set in a suburban supermarket, and the central character—a high school grocery checker—and his daily surroundings are as ordinary as things can get. "A&P" is anthologized in hundreds of collections. It's taught in high schools and colleges. It will outlive Updike by many hundreds of years. I don't know about you, but I'll take the risk of dealing with ordinary things if any of that is even a remote possibility.

Plenty of words and snippets about commonplace things and people find their way into my pocket notebook. Then the little torn-out pages collect on my desk like autumn leaves, until I think better of their usefulness and throw them away or transcribe them into my journal or work them directly into a manuscript.

The leaves should start piling up on your desk, too. They might be the sparks that get your writing started and the twigs that keep it burning. Your fiction will be made up of ideas and details, and it's more than just a clever plan to jot them down as you find them. It's absolutely essential to your craft.

In addition to scraps of dialogue that either get spoken by real people or that you (or your characters) dream up, and notations of details that you notice all over the place, the following are a few things that might end up in your notebook.

Maps, Floor Plans, Schematics

When I decided to write my first book—a memoir about growing up in a small East Texas town—I needed a more exact perception of that town than the almost thirty years separating it and me left intact. I remembered my parents well enough, and my sisters; our house was sufficiently clear. And I had photographs and some old letters and school yearbooks to help me. But what I didn't have was a focused, visual layout of the town itself, in 1962. What I needed was a map. What I needed was Jonnie Hodges.

Jonnie and I have known each other all our lives. And one of the things that I've known best about him is that he has one heck of a memory. I hadn't seen or heard from him in a long time, but I was betting that he still had it.

He did. I gave him a call, visited a few minutes, learned that Jonnie had become Jon about the same time that, in my case, Ronnie had become Ron, then told him my predicament. Several days later, a large brown envelope showed up in my mailbox; folded into it was a big piece of butcher paper, maybe two and a half feet by four. And on that paper, in careful pencil markings, was my old hometown. To say it was detailed would be an understatement. It was as much a bird's eye view as it was a map, and it even had trees—duly noted as "pecan" or "elm" or "hard to climb"—in the correct locations in yards. Jonnie had penciled in little notes and arrows, like this one that hovers over the corner of the sidewalk at Bobby Stroud's hardware store: "Narrow here. Hard to turn on a bike."

That map became one of my most valuable sources for *Into That Good Night*. It provided me with detail after detail that I would have never been able to remember for myself. So I was smart, I think—and certainly fortunate—to tap a resource in the person of an old friend that could remember things better.

When you're concocting your setting, be it real or imagined, it might prove useful to come up with a map of your own—or maybe a floor plan— showing how furniture is arranged in a room. If an important scene (and if you're going to be any good at this, *all* of your scenes will be important) is to be played out in a park, or on a city street, draw a schematic of where things are—of where your characters will be standing or sitting or running or dying.

The guy in Sheboygan might not want to know where absolutely everything is located. Let's face it, often he doesn't *need* to know. But *you* do, if you're going to write the scene well.

We'll be spending lots of time later on how you can best describe settings that are real and settings that are not. But here's the deal: They *all* have to be real for you.

Details From Movies, Television, and Radio

The world around you is filled to brimming with images and details and people that you can draw from as a writer. Now let's get a little more specific and look at three resources for your note taking that you probably spend a lot of your time with anyway.

When I wrote *The Windows of Heaven*, a novel that is set in Galveston in 1900, I must have watched the videotapes of two old movies, *O. Henry's Full House* and *A Tree Grows in Brooklyn*, at least a dozen times each. They are both set in the same era as my story and both have similar specific settings, like city streets and restaurants and front rooms and butcher shops. Obviously, careful attention was paid in the production of each film to the accuracy of historical detail. And that was precisely what I needed. I needed to *see* somebody sit down in a fancy eatery in 1900 and order a meal. I needed to *hear* horses clip-clopping on brick streets and delivery wagons clanking along behind them and organ grinders on the sidewalk. Much of the description of the setting in my novel came directly from those two movies, and others.

When you write your story or novel, don't overlook this readily available store of information. Watch a movie or television program that might be helpful to you with a pencil and pad in hand. You'll be surprised at how many nuggets of details you'll come up with that will find their way into your settings and descriptions.

One more thing: DVD copies of movies often provide an "added features" selection on their menus. These are usually directors and/or screenwriters sharing why they chose to keep or delete or lengthen or shorten entire scenes in the film. They offer a unique insight into the way the story has been developed, and it will almost certainly be useful to you as a writer, because you'll be constantly making exactly the same sorts of decisions in your work. These artists' philosophies regarding the way they told their stories might very well influence how you will tell yours.

Most of your readers grew up watching television, and almost all of them watch it on a regular basis. Much of what they know about how stories work is from the programs they see on the tube, so—since you intend to tell them a story—you'd better log a little time watching also. That's certainly not to suggest that you should pattern all that you write on television scripts, but here's an advantage to doing so at least some of the time. Scripts written for television—especially those of the half-hour situation comedy variety—have to conform to very precise time limitations, so they must be free of everything that doesn't have to be there. And guess what: so should your fiction. A careful analysis of how a writer introduces situations, moves conflicts along, and then resolves them in short order will benefit you greatly when you have to do the same thing in your writing.

Now, let's move to the radio. Listen to National Public Radio (NPR) in your car, and in their wonderful interviews with writers and newsmakers and movers and shakers in society, you'll hear uniquely turned phrases and clever manipulation of syntax that you should try to remember to jot down when you get where you're going. NPR also broadcasts lots of writers reading their essays or portions of their stories, novels, and poems. We can learn more about the economy of language, the untainted essence of wordsmithing, from good poems than from just about any other place. Hearing the poet read her words—emphasizing what she wants emphasized, whispering what she wants whispered—is pure magic to a writer and can be enormously useful to you when you sit down to write words of your own.

The Engines of Our Ingenuity, a program on NPR, is a daily essay read by its author, Dr. John H. Lienhard, a retired professor of engineering at the University of Houston. I've listened to hundreds of them, all finely written little stories about how human beings down the centuries have made things work or have made them work better. The stories are always interesting and enjoyable, but their greatest value to me has been the crafting of them by Dr. Lienhard. I hear the program on the way to work each morning, and many days the first thing I do when I get to my desk is download and print out the text of that day's essay. Then I read it over and marvel at its wordsmithing. I owe Dr. Lienhard a debt of gratitude; his fine phrasing and sense of drama have been particularly beneficial to me as a writer. Listen in sometime—or find another good essay program—and see if this method helps your writing, too.

Noting Other Wordsmiths

An important component of our three-way approach to description and setting—our trinity that we will use in every chapter after this one—is modeling. That means careful examination of how published writers work their magic. Most of our models will come from novels and short stories, but don't overlook the many talented, skillful writers that appear in magazines and newspapers.

I have favorites among columnists, who I look forward to reading. Each has his or her own individual style that, more than likely, has affected *my* style, *my* voice. I enjoy crusty conservatives like Bill O'Riley and fiery liberals like Molly Ivans equally well, since the one thing that they *do* have in common is that they are both skilled manipulators of the written word. And what wordsmith worth his stripes hasn't marveled at the pieces by William Safire—the syndicated king of all wordsmiths—who provides interesting and useful insight into the origins and history and changing meanings of words and phrases.

When I wrote a novel set in northern Ohio where I've never been, I needed help regarding topography and climate and trees and such things. A friend who lives in Cleveland proved useful, as did a couple of reference books and the Internet. As odd as it might sound, my clearest, strongest *sense* of the place came from a pair of small spaces I've visited daily for years: *Funky Winkerbean* and *Crankshaft*. They're both comic strips set in—you guessed it—northern Ohio.

All of these—movies, television, radio, columnists, even the comics—offer visual and mental images and unique phrasings that transport you somewhere else. Pay close attention to them, so that you can do the very same thing for your reader.

SURPRISE, SURPRISE

Remember the small irony of the British couple I watched eating their hamburgers with knives and forks? Very likely, I would never have dreamed that up on my own. But once I saw it, I remembered it. It was a nice, little surprise on a cold winter's day.

One of your best tools in your writing will be the use of irony, and sometimes it comes in small doses, in details. So be on the lookout for surprises; readers like to be surprised. Everybody likes a bit of irony worked in, if not in his or her own lives then certainly in fiction. The fact is that we get plenty of irony in reality—things that don't work that should, people who let us down, situations that turn out all wrong or, happily, right for once—so we expect it to be there in stories and novels.

Look a little closer at things, people, and places to spot anything that might be amiss. Like ivy that has woven its way through the framework and wheel sprockets of a bicycle that has been left much too long beside a flowerbed. Or the Baltimore Colts coffee mug that is never very far away from the security man in your office building, even though Baltimore hasn't had a team called the Colts in years. What a fine little telling detail that would be to help establish one of your characters, whose loyalty to a team has outlived the team itself.

Be on the lookout for surprises.

KEEPING A WRITER'S JOURNAL AND/OR A DIARY

You've been expecting this, I suspect, since I've mentioned it more than once.

In my creative writing classes, I require my students to keep a writers' journal, a binder of blank pages on which I want them to record—on a daily basis—reactions to how stories work (or don't) in books and movies. I want them to make notes about things they see or hear or taste or smell or touch, unusual word combinations, ideas for stories or poems. And I encourage them to scribble down pieces of scenes from whatever they are currently writing.

We're not talking about a diary here. A writer's journal shouldn't be made up of secrets. Neither should it be rantings about how you've been mistreated. We all get mistreated from time to time, and if you intend to wade into the publishing world one day, you'll get mistreated again. Fret over it quietly, or howl at the moon, but keep it out of your writer's journal. It should be reserved for the notes and sketches and observations of someone who is serious about the business of writing. It's a fine place to embellish those maps and floor plans that you scribbled into your notebook and to record treasures you pick up in columns and interviews.

What if one of your characters in your story starts talking in your head? They do that, you know. Well, you'd best write that down. Because you won't remember it long, and they more than likely won't say it again.

I use a loose-leaf binder for my journal, so that I can insert tabs in an attempt at categorizing the contents. I can toss what proves on second thought to be chaff while keeping the wheat. But use whatever format works best for you. Try a few different ways until you find the right fit.

Journaling is an essential component in writing fiction. And, if I could believe that you will actually *do* at least some of the things that I suggest, I hope that keeping a writer's journal will be one of them.

My new students balk at the prospect. Many of them are veterans of teacher-imposed journaling. But once they see how their journals can benefit them as writers, most of my students come onboard as believers, and I hope you will too. Here's proof that journaling is effective: When I announce to my classes that they aren't responsible for journal pages over the Christmas break, my really dedicated writers do it anyway. In fact, they almost always have many more pages filled in their journals on due dates than I assigned. That's because, early on, they stopped writing the entries for me and started doing it for themselves. More specifically, they started doing it for their fiction.

Any writing that you do helps you to become a better writer. Writing is like that, like playing the piano and driving a car and tap dancing. The more you do it, the better you get at it.

When you set aside enough time to write a page or two—or more—in your journal every day, you'll be surprised at how much of that seemingly

Some Things to Keep in a Writer's Journal

- outlines/planning
- observations on how elements of storytelling work (or don't) in movies, novels, plays
- borrowed (stolen) dialogue and dialect from the world at large
- situations that you observe that might be worked into a story
- physical characteristics of people that you might end up using to describe your own cast of characters
- floor plans, maps, schematics for possible settings
- title ideas (pilfer profusely from the Bible, the works of Shakespeare, and poetry, historically the three most fertile sources for titles)
- story ideas
- possible first/last sentences
- interesting, uncommon words
- words that might not exist at all, but need to
- a cliché count (every time you come across one, in print, in conversation, on television, movies or over the radio, jot it down. Then avoid it like the plague)
- life's little ironies (things that are not as they should be; people who should not be where they are)
- general notes regarding your fiction
- lyrics to songs that catch your fancy
- Details! Details! Details! that you might use in your description and setting

unimportant stuff works its way into your fiction. And at how much better you become at hooking words to each other to convey images, which is wordsmithing at its most fundamental level.

Now this, please, about diaries: Even though I may never be able to convince some of my students to maintain one, they may wish they had. A well-kept diary is a lucrative source for all manner of practical information concerning exactly when the diarist was at a particular place or event, whom she was there with, and what was done there.

My diary, rather than my journal, is where I *can* vent on occasion about mistreatment. It's where I jot down a little summary of each day's proceedings, oftentimes nothing more elaborate than "Rained in the morning. Graded short stories. Meat loaf for supper." Other times they run to a page or two. Nothing, I assure you, that will keep a reader on the edge of their seat a century from now.

When I wrote that memoir about growing up in the little East Texas town, every other chapter was the story of my father's Alzheimer's experience, his stroke, and, finally, his death. My diary became an essential tool when it came to logistics, to specific dates and the general progression of his illness. It was also very useful in helping me recall my own feelings about Alzheimer's. And revisiting those emotions in the pages of my diary have helped me to develop characters in my fiction that are going through similar circumstances. A day's events could wind up as the basis for a scene in one of your stories, or even as the major plot line.

You might be wondering why a journal and a diary can't be kept as one volume. Many people do it that way. I use them as two very different tools and have determined that for me they work better as separate units. Each succeeding volume of the diary I *keep* ends up on the closet shelf. The journal dies in stages. Those things that I will only need for a particular story or novel get tossed when the work is done. But some of the other things that didn't get used this time around I hold on to. They may be used later, or maybe not. But—like that crate of old record albums—I know where to find them if I need them.

SUMMARY: THE LITTLE WORLD IN THE WRITER'S MIND

Wherever you go searching for the details that might be helpful to you, wherever you locate them, and however you choose to preserve them, remember this: Your job as a writer is to ultimately weave some of them into a piece of writing that will lift your readers up and situate them in a place and a time of your choosing.

In this chapter, we've looked at the importance of paying close attention to details—in your writing and in the world around you—and ways to hang onto them. Look for ideas and particulars everywhere, in places that you see every day and places that you've never seen before, in movies and television and radio programs, in conversations among people around you, in the published work of good writers, even in the most unlikely places, like comic strips. And don't forget to look in one of your best resources: your own memory of times and things past. Then get those things down, first on anything close at hand—like a pocket notebook—and later in a writer's journal or a diary.

Once you've sharpened your observation skills and taken notes about what you've seen, you're ready to get down to the matter of telling this story you want to tell. And the first order of business is to create the little world in your own mind in which that story will take place. Because if it doesn't exist there, it won't stand a chance of existing in your reader's mind. Two of the most essential elements of that world—of your access and eventually your reader's access to it—are your treatment of setting and use of description.

EXERCISE 1

Think of five places you have visited for which you had a preconceived notion or expectation before arriving. Think harder, now, and recall something in each place that blew that preconception away. Write down your preconception and the detail that shattered it for each.

EXERCISE 2

Try this: In that pocket notebook you're going to start carrying around, make it a point to jot down at least one thing that you wouldn't have expected to be where it is, or there at all, in several places that you go every day, or every week. Check out the lawns in your neighborhood on your way to work or to the market.
At least one of them will hold a surprise that you've overlooked, because you haven't been looking closely. Now you are.

Here are a few categories of things to look for to start you on your quest:

- useless things
- outdated things
- flawed (or broken) things
- things you hadn't expected
- the absence of things you *had* expected
- things (or people) completely out of their element

We've spent most of this chapter talking about how to look for details in the world around you. Sometimes the best place to look is at the holes in your existing drafts that are begging for more elaboration.

Sit yourself down with a printed copy of several pages of your manuscript and a pencil. Read over your work, paying particular attention to your inclusion of details in your setting and overall description, or—as might be the case—to your *absence* of details. Draw circles or arrows or frowning faces. Use whatever code that best suits you, but find places that would benefit from better details and better description.

Perhaps the best way to practice paying better attention is to do the two things we discussed earlier in this chapter:

- Close your eyes and remember a place that you haven't seen in a long time and get down as many specific details as you can.
- With pen and paper in hand, closely observe what is going on around you in an active place.

In both exercises, make sure you find things you wouldn't normally pay close attention to. Write rough copies full of the things you found, practicing wordsmithing as you write.

chapter 3

[USING ALL THE TOOLS IN YOUR KIT]

Just because you might have a kitchen cabinet absolutely overflowing with spices and flavors and various sundry things from the specialty foods market, and a drawer brimming with gadgets and utensils and cutlery and racks of shiny pots and pans, you would be foolish to try to use all of those doodads and ingredients when preparing every recipe. As foolish, in fact, as if you tried to use *none* of them.

Cooking is a process of using what you need in order to come up with what you want.

So is writing.

The crafting of fiction is, as I've said before, a slow and deliberate undertaking, in which you should use all of the magic that you can conjure up to tell the best story that you can. It will call for good ideas and planning, believable and interesting characters and settings and situations, and many other things. But, at the bedrock of its foundation, it will require a set of useable tools.

In this chapter we'll look closely at just a few of the many devices and approaches available to you. Some of them are purely utilitarian and serve a single purpose; others encroach on bigger ambitions, like moving the story along or calling attention to a character or a theme. A few are out and out trickery, ways to influence your readers without them catching on. We'll look at several that will be particularly useful to you when tackling description and setting.

37

MODIFIERS

When I say modifiers, I'm referring specifically to adjectives and adverbs whose functions are most often to more specifically define nouns and verbs. You've relied on them all your life; you use them countless times every day.

You tell the kid at the drive-through window that you want the *big* order of fries. You urge your children to speak *quietly* on the phone while you grab a nap. So, none of this will be news to you. But paying careful attention to the selection and use of these two essential parts of speech that are often taken for granted will make an enormous difference in your fiction, especially in regards to setting and description.

Adjectives

People who attempt to replicate the sparse, clean writing style of Ernest Hemingway—and it's become quite the vogue (they even have a festival in Key West that has a contest)—sometimes assume that his unique voice emanates from the almost absolute absence of adjectives. Following that template, some would-be Hemingways have produced some really ghastly narratives.

But they miss the point. Hemingway did indeed use fewer adjectives than many authors. But when he used them—much, much more often than his imitators seem to realize—he did it in pure Hemingway fashion: the best that it could be done.

Here's a morsel from *For Whom the Bell Tolls*:

> There had still been snow then, the snow that had ruined them, and when his horse was hit so that he wheezed in a slow, jerking, climbing stagger up the last part of the crest, splattering the snow with a bright, pulsing jet, Sordo had hauled him along by the bridle, the reins over his shoulder as he climbed.

Jerking, climbing, bright, and *pulsing* make up an active little covey of adjectives, especially coming from a man who is widely believed to have shunned them. More importantly, they are each perfect defining words that were selected carefully and well.

Adjectives, along with other modifiers, are the spices that good writers use to flavor their writing. A serving of scrambled eggs is okay all by itself, but it's much more appetizing, in most peoples' opinion, with salt and pepper sprinkled on and even more so—depending on personal taste and inclination—with paprika or garlic or rosemary or Tabasco sauce. Eggs are good with a little spice or a lot. So is fiction. But remember, food that is not flavored at all might be bland, but when spices are poured on like mad it becomes inedible. So strike a balance between too little and too much, in your cooking *and* your description.

Look at how Robert Cremins uses adjectives in a couple of places in his novel *A Sort of Homecoming*:

> I laugh, a little hissy laugh, and that breaks the heavy spell I've been under for the past few minutes.

Then, a few pages later:

> I woke up feeling grotesque, unbelievable, bizarre, unprecedented.

The first time around, he relies on one small adjective—*hissy*—to "break the heavy spell" and, in the second piece, he lays it on thick, putting forth a group of heftier modifiers, like defensive linesmen on a football team, to show that the spell has returned. Determining how little or how much you want to describe is a decision that you will have to make constantly in your writing. The answer, of course, depends on how much you *need* to describe. *Hissy* is a modifier that nails a particular, singular attitude, and does it well. That thundering quartet of adjectives in the second example makes a stronger impression—each word packs more muscle than *hissy*—that leaves no doubt about what sort of mood this guy woke up in.

Cremins uses the four adjectives to drive home his point, not because he thought of four good ones that would work. He most likely could have thought of dozens more, but those dozens wouldn't make his description any clearer or stronger; in fact, the effect would be diminished with each new one he tacked on. When using modifiers, don't get so carried away that you let the adjectives become the focus of what you are doing. Never let *any* of the tools become more that just that: tools. The important thing—from start to finish—is your story. In the Cremins model the use of an uncommon, unexpected word like *hissy* is effective, as is the piling on of the four stronger ones later on. But all of them do exactly what the author intended and needed them to do: They paint a clearer picture of a situation or a character within the larger context of the tale he is telling.

The use of any of these tools, as well as everything else that you do in your writing, must pass the clutter rule, which stipulates that anything that is not directly serving to move the story along is clutter and must go. Test your adjectives and adverbs constantly. If you've written something about a large, ferocious, gigantic dog terrorizing a neighborhood, you'd best lose either *large* or *gigantic*, since they both mean the same thing.

Also, be on guard against falling into a pattern of using similar modifier structures, like teams of adjectives, over and over.

Listen:

> At the last of the hectic, exasperating day, the small, tired man approached the crowded, frantic train station with trepidation.

Each of the coupled modifiers—hectic/exasperating, small/tired, and crowded/frantic—is a fine describer. But what is likely to happen is that your reader will pick up on the repetition of the pairs and that will be what he focuses on, rather than on the action that is important to your story. Then the adjectives will be working against you, and, as with all of these tools, you want them working *for* you.

Adverbs

As you know, adverbs serve a triple function; they can modify verbs (he *slowly* chewed the apple), adjectives (the *overly* attentive man became a bore), as well as other adverbs (she ran *very* quickly). Because of this, you will use them very, *very* often. But beware; they can, like all of their fellow tools, be used badly, to the detriment of your fiction.

One way to use them badly is to work them into your tag lines—speaker identification lines—in fiction.

Consider:

"Oh, my," Ellen sadly replied, "it's not even worth getting up today."

If it's not even worth getting up today, then we hardly need to be told that Ellen replied *sadly*. Her own dialogue describes her as sad, and that is altogether more effective description than providing constant little instructions in modifiers.

This isn't meant to imply that adverbs are evil and should never be used at all. They *should* be used—even occasionally in tag lines—but they should be, when you use them, the best choice available to you. "Leave me alone," she said, defensively," might be the most effective way for you to show that a speaker is defensive. Having her cringe and bare her teeth would be a little over the top, don't you think? And using the one word—*defensively*—is a much more delicate approach.

Here's one more point concerning adverbs: Since so many of them end in *-ly* make sure that you don't overdo it, lest you end up with *eagerly*, *charmingly*, *angrily*, and *cleverly* in the same sentence. After wading through all of those, your reader might just put your story aside, vehemently.

PUNCTUATION

We could get awfully technical here and trot out the several rigid grammatical rules regarding punctuation usage. But for our present purpose regarding description and settings, let's bypass all of the procedural guidelines that you can dredge up out of style manuals and grammar texts and get to the point of what these little devices can do for you when writing fiction.

In a nutshell, exclamation points, periods, commas, colons, semicolons, and dashes are road signs for your reader, put there by you throughout your fiction to show them where to pause, where to continue, where to speed up, and where to stop.

This requires that you *listen* to your story or novel, both while you are writing it and when you revise. Not necessarily reading it out loud, or having somebody else do it, but actually striving to hear the words and phrases and sentences as you want your reader to receive them.

Sometimes more of your story can be told in a pause, either in narration or in dialogue, than in a paragraph or a page. And your readers won't make that pause unless you tell them to.

Periods and commas carry most of the workload, and their placement is usually so predetermined that you don't have much flexibility in their usage, but you have more options with exclamation points, colons, semicolons, and dashes.

Exclamation Points

If your characters bellow at each other from time to time, that's fine, and that's when you'll need to use exclamation points. But *your* voice, the hopefully dependable and comfortable voice in which you tell your story, shouldn't depend on such shenanigans as shouting. Horde these useful little devices in the corner of your kit, and use them only when you really need them, as Luanne Rice does in her novel *The Perfect Summer* to emphasize the absurdity of a concept:

> The other parents would be smiling at her father, giving him thumbs-up for her excellence in—Annie cast about, searching her mind for the perfect sport—field hockey!

In your fiction, determine when your characters need to be loud and when they need to be quiet. By the same token, determine when *you* need to be loud and quiet in your telling of the story. Sometimes an important moment in your plot will demand some noise, thus requiring exclamation points, but other times the point will be better made by a different approach. Listen:

> "I hate you so much I could *kill* you!" she yelled.

It certainly gets the point across. If somebody yelled that at me, it would get *my* attention. But in a story or novel, something like this might create a stronger image:

> She locked him into a frigid gaze, the hate welling up in her eyes along with the tears. "I could kill you right now," she whispered.

There's no yelling this time, so there's no need for an exclamation point. People who are angry often yell, which carries with it all of the fly-off-the-handle, heat-of-the-moment, sorry-about-that business that whispering hardly ever involves. People who whisper things usually have thought things through, and mean every word of what they say. Your readers know that, because they have both yelled and whispered. So the quieter treatment of this little scene—the one with the whispering and the tears—will deliver a more vivid image.

When writing your fiction, consider each and every scene and decide how it will best be played out—loud or quiet, long or short, light or heavy—in order to serve the bigger story.

Colons

This fellow (:) is so regularly confused with its cousin the semicolon (;) that some writers use them interchangeably, and in doing so they commit a cardinal sin. The use of a colon gives the reader some warning. Here comes something of importance, it says.

The most common task of a colon is to introduce a list, and this can be one of the best ways to describe a character or a situation in your fiction.

Here's Edward Rutherfurd, in his novel *London*:

> There had been three candidates for King Henry's vast inheritance: Richard, his brother John, and their nephew, Arthur.

Remember, your job is to convey information and images to your reader. And, sometimes, things are made clearer when methodically laid out—one, two, three.

That information doesn't *have* to be a list. It might be a definition, like this one, again from *London*:

> Ned was a good dog: medium size with a smooth, brown and white coat, bright eyes, and devoted to his cheerful master.

Or it might be an example or a clarification:

> The patriots of the Revolution fought for one thing and one thing only: freedom.

Whenever you use a colon, you're setting your reader up for something: for a description, a clarification, an idea, a list. It's one of the best ways for you to call attention to something important in your story.

Semicolons

While colons can be used in several ways, semicolons have only one function. But it's a very important one. They connect two otherwise complete sentences without resorting to conjunctions like *and* or *then*, thus letting you avoid two unforgivable offenses: (1) run-ons and (2) an overabundance of short, choppy sentences that bump along like a rocky road.

Consider these three sentences, all of which are complete (subjects and predicates in attendance) and all of which are clearly stated:

> The Hens continued laying.
> It was a miracle of sorts.
> As a boy he'd not eaten a fresh egg from November until the spring.

Taken together, the sentences dovetail into a particular image, that of a boy who hadn't expected a thing to happen and saw its occurrence as a sort of a miracle. If you wanted to convey this image in your fiction, you could line the sentences up just like that and be done with it. But look how much nicer the image works when configured in another way, as Jeffrey Lent does it in his novel *In the Fall*:

> The hens continued laying. It was a miracle of sorts; as a boy he'd not eaten a fresh egg from November until the spring.

Varying the lengths of your sentences is an effective tool that we'll get to in a few pages, and the best way to create longer, more flowing ones is to use semicolons to tie short sentences together. Be on the lookout in your manuscripts for places to do this.

Dashes

Dashes do almost exactly what commas do; they set things off from the rest of a sentence. But the use of dashes comes much closer to establishing your unique voice. Everyone must use commas in exactly the same way; they fall into the province of the immutable rules of the language. But dashes are freer spirits than commas and offer you more leeway. Look at how Clare Francis uses them in two places in *Night Sky*:

> He wondered what time it was—probably after four. Still too early to go out.

And later:

> Soon—by tonight—he would have enough money to buy a D8SS.

In both examples, the author uses the words set off by the dashes to more clearly define something mentioned in the main bodies of the sentences. In each case, she could have used commas, but, by using dashes, she focuses the reader's attention more closely on the details they enclose.

Dashes everywhere will become old fast. But using them sporadically, along with the more conventional commas, or *instead* of them in many cases, will add a little spice to your description.

Parentheses

Don't get dashes and parentheses mixed up. Anything set off by dashes is still a part of the ongoing story, but if it's set off parenthetically, the reader is being told to assume that it isn't there at all. It's like an *aside* in a play, where an actor turns away from the drama and explains something to the audience. It's like a jury being told by a judge to disregard something said in the witness stand. Of course, the jury can't *really* disregard it, since they heard it. Neither can a reader separate it fully from the tale, which you don't really want him to do anyway, or you wouldn't have put it in.

Using parenthetical material throughout a manuscript is a way to carry on a running conversation with your reader, as if you're sitting beside him while he plows through your story or novel, offering little comments along the way. Charles Dickens did it regularly, as did Victor Hugo; both were of that era of literature where a phrase like "And now, gentle reader, let us continue" popped up pretty often.

Chit-chatting with your reader in modern times isn't likely to be the best of ideas, unless you've decided to use a correspondence or a diary motif in which to tell your story. But adding little snippets of information in parentheses occasionally can add flavor to your work. Here's an example from *King, Queen, Knave*, a novel by Vladimir Nabokov:

> Somewhere a door closed softly, and the stairs creaked (they were not supposed to creak!), and her husband's cheerful off-key whistle receded out of earshot.

If the parenthetical information was lifted out altogether and tossed away the rest of the sentence would still convey the image that needs to be conveyed.

But the slipped-in bit—almost like a secret being shared—adds much to the description, especially since it is followed up with that dramatic exclamation point.

WAYS TO SHOW RESEMBLANCE

One of the most effective ways to convey a particular image to your reader is to show him something that it is similar to. Metaphors, similes, analogies, personification, symbolism, and allusions are all ways to nudge your readers toward making the connection that you want them to make. The first three differ in what they do only by degrees; a metaphor is an implied resemblance, a simile a stated one, and an analogy is a detailed one. Each of them will be useful to you, depending on how broad or how slight you want a particular resemblance to be in your story or novel.

Metaphors

A metaphor is an implied analogy; it suggests a similarity without actually saying that the similarity exists. It literally makes your reader think of a thing or an action that is *not* the thing or the action that you are describing. The end result of which is—you can only hope—that the reader will see the thing or the action that you are pointing her toward more clearly.

Look:

> Winston Churchill, a proud statesman, led England through the war.

It isn't quite as catchy (or as effective) as this:

> Winston Churchill, that proud English lion, led his nation through the war.

The second sentence isn't meant to imply that Mr. Churchill was an animal. Only the most literal of readers would get that out of it. Metaphors help your reader to see how something that is in your story is like, in some way, something that is not actually *in* the story at all, so very literal readers will just have to make the little leaps of faith that metaphors require. It's very much like a wine expert saying that a particular vintage has hints of berries or melons or pepper. These things aren't actually *in* the wine, but they help the listener imagine what it will taste like.

In *Roots*, Alex Haley did not mean for his readers to believe that big carpets sometimes fly around when he wrote this description:

> . . . a great beating of wings filled the air and a vast living carpet of seafowl—hundreds of thousands of them, in every color of the rainbow—rose and filled the sky.

In your fiction, you'll want to use this tool pretty often. If you have a burglar in the process of burgling, and you want the reader to see him as catlike, you can simply tell him he's catlike, or you can have him move around on "little cat's feet" (to steal a line from Carl Sandburg). Now you're not telling the comparison; you're implying it.

We need to call attention now to the greatest and most constant danger of using metaphors, namely mixing them. We've all come up with these rascals. My most recent faux pas of this particular variety was in the first draft of the first chapter of this book. I originally wrote this sentence:

> Finding and polishing the writing voice in which you will describe your setting is a solo flight, with you alone in the cockpit.

Then, a few sentences later, I referred to your style surfacing, like Ahab's white whale off there on the horizon. So I had, in one paragraph, both aeronautical and nautical imagery and, almost certainly, a very confused reader. So when I revised, I changed that first sentence to this:

> Finding and polishing the writing voice in which you will describe your setting is a solo voyage, with you alone at the helm.

After the alteration, my images are completely nautical, with no mention of airplanes or pilots. I hesitate to say we are, to use a common metaphor, all on the same page now, since pages have nothing to do with ships. So I'll just say we are all steering in the same current.

If you want to see mixed metaphors used pretty often, read the comic strip *Crankshaft*, part of the humor of which rests on the central character's frequent use of them. In one strip, somebody tells the old man that his granddaughter has really grown up. "Yep," he responds. "Pretty soon she'll be spreading her wings and walking out the door."

Mixed metaphors come off as comical when you have a character use one. But it's not one bit funny when *you* let one slip into your writing.

Similes

Similes do exactly the same thing that metaphors do, except the similarity is prefaced by *like* or *as*. So it's not quite as subtle. This time, Mr. Churchill might roar *like an English lion*, or be *as proud as an English lion*.

Here are a few examples of how authors use similes (the italics are mine):

Aidan Chambers uses one to express movement in *Postcards From No Man's Land*:

> To one side of the theater, facing in to the rest of the plein *like an auditorium facing a stage*, was a mini-square crammed with tables served by waiters who fluttered in and out of canopied cafes *like birds from nesting boxes*.

Ken Follett, in *The Hammer of Eden*, uses a simile to portray a lack of action:

> As the light strengthened, they could distinguish the dark shapes of cranes and giant earthmoving machines below them, silent and still, *like sleeping giants*.

When some of my writing students first stumble onto the fine things that similes can do for them, they tend to *over*do, like young girls dipping for the first time into their mother's makeup drawer and globbing it on too thick. Some of the students are apt, in their stories, to trot similes out one after another, like ponies in a parade.

I overdid the similes myself in that last paragraph. The cosmetic laden girls are *like* writers using too many metaphors; so are ponies in a parade. But to use both in one paragraph is a bit much. But, not overdone, the simile will be one of the most effective tools in your fiction.

You'll use similes in many of the places were you might have otherwise chosen to use metaphors, but now they will be stated resemblances rather than implied ones. This time, your burglar will not move on little cat's feet but will move *like a cat*, or as silent *as a cat*.

Analogies

While metaphors are more delicate than similes, analogies are at the other end of the spectrum and make no attempt whatsoever at understatement. They are carefully laid out comparisons, hitting on how two things are similar in at least one way. Here's a short one from *When Kambia Elaine Flew in From Neptune*, a novel by Lori Aurelia Williams:

> The bayou was to me like hot-water cornbread was to Mama.

This one is in the exact format of all those analogies that used to give you fits on standardized tests in high school—you remember: *card is to deck as month is to year*—but don't think you have to work your brief analogies into this precise wording. Yours might go something like *The bayou was as important to me as hot-water cornbread was to Mama* or *Hot-water cornbread was the epitome of goodness to Mama; just like the bayou was to me.*

Sometimes in your fiction a short analogy won't accomplish everything you need it to. Then you'll need to work it into something longer.

The subjects of James Michener's *The Eagle and the Raven* are Santa Anna and Sam Houston, so he decided to begin with an extended analogy, linking them metaphorically with the two birds that symbolize them in the title and throughout the book:

> It was as if two powerful birds had entered the sky within a single year, The Eagle in the south, The Raven in the north, each circling and gaining strength, each progressing in the consolidation of its own powers. For forty-two tempestuous years the adversaries would fly in ever-widening orbits until confrontation became inevitable. They would meet only once, a clash of eighteen culminating minutes in the spring of 1836 which would change the history of the world.

In your own fiction, short descriptions of similarities will work best as metaphors or similes, and more elaborated juxtapositions that compare two characters or things should be treated in a brief or an extended analogy.

So if you choose to use an analogy in your burglar saga, you would go into some detail about just *how* he is like a cat.

Allusions

Since we're already on the subject of cats, let's look at how Kurt Vonnegut begins his novel *Cat's Cradle*:

> Call me Jonah. My parents did, or nearly did. They called me John.

The "Call me Jonah" part is an allusion, a figure of speech that makes reference to a famous person or event. In this case, the author is referring to the first sentence of *Moby Dick* ("Call me Ishmael."), just as I alluded to that novel a few pages ago when I mentioned Ahab and his white whale.

Using an allusion is a great way to describe something or someone by calling attention to something else, but you must remember this (which is an allusion to the song in the movie *Casablanca*): The key word in that definition is *famous*. The allusion will fall flat if the reader doesn't make the connection. So, while your Uncle Elmer out there in Flagstaff might be the epitome of thrift, saying that a character in your fiction is as cheap as your Uncle Elmer isn't likely to work for anybody outside of your family.

So, when using allusions, you want to make them wide enough for the reader to get. Neither should they be a puzzle that you've designed. I was given a novel a few years ago in the introduction of which the author let us in on a little game that she had devised. She said that those readers who, like herself, had "been happy enough to have had a classical education" should look for allusions to works of art and literature that she had planted in the text: words or phrases or dialect that would ring a bell (a silver one, no doubt). She gave the exact number of the precious nuggets and sent us on our way, like well-scrubbed children after Easter eggs. She said, in that introduction, that none of the allusions were essential to any understanding of her novel, and that neither disregarding them nor being unable to decipher them would alter a reader's perception.

And here is where I disagree with this classically trained scribe. Allusions that are not perceived with at least some ease are useless. They slow down the pace at best, or, at worst, they offend. I don't know if I would have picked up on any of her little gems or not, since I slammed her tome shut before even getting to her story.

The purpose of using allusions is not to drive your readers away, but to bring them more completely *in*, by reminding them of similar situations or events that they know something about. And, by the way, this author was wrong in thinking that allusions don't have to add to the story. If you choose to use them, they should have a purpose beyond giving your reader a chance to identify them. They should—as everything you write should—add value to your story.

Here's how Tony Kushner alludes to the movie *The Wizard of Oz* in his play *Angels in America* by having a character wake up from a serious illness and point to some of his friends. "I've had a remarkable dream," he says. "And you were there, and you . . . and you. And some of it was terrible, and some of it was wonderful, but all the same I kept saying I want to go home. And they sent me home." This is exactly what Dorothy says at the very end of the movie. It's an obvious allusion to a film that long ago established itself as an American icon, so most readers will recognize it.

Much less obvious is the short sentence "Then I defy you, Heaven!" in Anne Rice's *The Tale of the Body Thief*. Which is awfully close to Romeo's "Then I defy you, Stars!" in *Romeo and Juliet*. The character in the Rice book is going through a Romeo-like moment, so his shouting of the similar line reinforces its meaning.

Allusions, either strong or subtle, will work well for you in your writing, as long as you make them broad enough so that just about everyone will get it. You're on solid ground calling a little boy's dash on his bike

Lofty Language Indeed

Literary tools that show resemblance have been used in the world's religions for centuries.

Consider a couple of the hymns that are sung each Sunday morning. "A Mighty Fortress is Our God" is not proclaiming that the Almighty is, in fact, a fortress, but that He is *like* one. In another one, we sing of Christian soldiers, marching as to war, not *off* to war, or *into* war, which would be the thing itself. *As* to war means that these soldiers are not soldiers in the literal sense, but are similar to them in their commitment.

Sacred texts are filled with metaphors, similes, and symbolism. What are parables but stories whose only function is to make their hearers think of other things than are *in* the stories? And while debate rages on regarding the literal, historical truth of many biblical or sacred text events, most of the debaters would agree that, whether Noah actually floated an ark or not, the symbolic lesson is the most important thing: that people better behave.

Think of how many times characters in sacred texts allude to characters that came before them, to prophets and kings and rascals and rogues. And if a group of listeners are referred to as sheep, or lambs, then you can bet (or hope) a metaphor is being employed.

If literary devices like symbolism, similes, metaphors, and allusions have helped countless generations to see something as mystical and lofty as divine nature and eternity, just think how useful it will be in your fiction, which will more than likely focus on characters and settings and situations that are tethered more securely to the here and now.

through town to alert the population to a fire a "Paul Revere's ride." But leave your Uncle Elmer at home.

Personification

Let's consider another couple of lines from *Romeo and Juliet*, at the very end:

> A glooming peace this morning with it brings;
> The sun for sorrow will not show his head . . .

Here, Prince Escalus is lamenting the two dead lovers sprawled out before him and numerous other deaths in the play (Shakespeare liked to bring his tragedies to a close with high body counts). He is implying that the very sun in the heavens—the gaseous star itself—is remorseful and hides behind clouds. And though even the most literal of readers will know that this can not be (it just happens to be a cloudy day in Verona), it works well as personification, a figure of speech that bestows human actions or sensibilities on inanimate objects and ideas.

Here's another literary element that you already use constantly, both in your thinking and in your speaking. Who hasn't been *slapped* by a wave or *kissed* by the wind? Who hasn't heard the wind *singing* in the trees or a last slice of pie in the fridge *calling* your name?

You can take your time with personification in your writing, working it meticulously along, as Ann Packer does in her novel *The Dive From Clausen's Pier*:

> The silk was like nothing I'd ever worked with before, slippery and so fluid it was almost as if it were alive, slithering from my table onto the floor, sliding off the deck of my sewing machine if I was careless when I pulled the needle out, if I didn't have my hands right there to coax it to stay.

Or you can pack the personification into one short image, as J.K. Rowling does in a single word (swam) in *Harry Potter and the Goblet of Fire*:

> They set off across the deserted moor, unable to make much progress through the mist. After about twenty minutes, a small stone cottage next to a gate swam into view.

The use of personification is an excellent opportunity for you to make clear in your reader's mind an action that is important in your story. It is a dull description indeed to say that the warm water of a swimming hole touched a character's arm, and extremely more effective to say that it *caressed* it.

Symbolism

Too many people, I fear, come away from their high school and college English courses thinking that literature is composed almost completely of symbolism. This is because teachers pay a great deal of attention to what characters and things and situations stand for or, more specifically, to what they *think* or the textbook or the study guide *says* they stand for. So their students sometimes get the notion that the heart and soul of the works they are told to read are the various symbols their teachers point out, often to the exclusion of other important elements in the stories; too often, in fact, to the exclusion of the meanings of the stories themselves.

Though symbolism isn't the alpha and omega of literature that your high school teacher might have thought it was, it *is* an essential tool in your kit. Aaron Elkins in *Fellowship of Fear* describes some sculptures that are obviously intended to be symbols, things that represent other things or ideas:

> The great stone eagles on either side of the entrance had once gripped laurelled swastikas in their talons, but those had long ago been chipped away by young GIs laughing into the newsreel cameras, so that now they did duty as American eagles, guarding the headquarters of USAREUR—United States Army Europe.

In this example the symbolism is as heavy as those stone eagles. Almost always in fiction you will need to be more understated than that when using this tool.

It's a good idea to refrain from intentionally building symbols in, unless you're up to something as obvious as Elkins was with his eagles. The most effective symbols occur naturally in the story and float effortlessly to the surface, like cream in milk.

When I wrote the memoir about my father and his Alzheimer's ordeal, I mentioned, several times, a navy surplus clock that he had bought before I was born and attached to the wall in our kitchen. It is a great, heavy thing, with a glass face that tilts up on a hinge; I grew up watching my father wind it with a key each morning, and even learned to tell time on it (unfortunately, it is a twenty-four-hour contraption and I had to be retaught on a traditional twelve-hour clock in elementary school). When my father died, I unscrewed the clock from his wall and moved it to my house, where I took over the winding duties.

I honestly never intended that clock to be representative of anything or anybody in my book, but more than a few readers perceived it as symbolic— of my father, of their fathers, of *all* fathers, of the inevitable passage of time (the classic symbol called a *memento mori*—a reminder of death). So, the fact is that my inherited clock is indeed a symbol, no matter what I think about it. And it's a symbol because it *works* as one, in the natural progression of the story, and not because I planted it there to *be* symbolic.

What you're probably asking yourself right about now is how the heck you're supposed to use symbolism if you're not supposed to put symbols in your text. Here's my answer: Write your story or novel the best that you can—write it truly and well, as Hemingway might have said—and don't worry about what will be symbolic and what won't be. Let things and characters that turn out to be symbolic simply materialize.

That's not to say that you won't write characters that personify goodness or evil or love or vindictiveness or any number of other things. But they should personify those qualities because of things you have them say and do in the story, not because your intention was to set them up as symbolic. What you'll likely end up with—if your overall intention is to create a symbol—is what some critics call cardboard characters, people who are so one-dimensional that they resemble cutouts that are propped up to look like real folks. In short, let your characters *be* real folks, and if they end up being symbolic, then so much the better.

The same holds true for things and places. You don't want your setting to be just a backdrop that thumps down on the stage when a scene changes. You want it to be a vibrant, believable *place*. And if your only goal for it is to stand for something, like Maple Street being a slice of apple pie America right out of a Norman Rockwell painting, that's likely *all* it will be, and not a street where real people with real problems live.

Now, how about the names of the people that live there? Long ago, very obviously symbolic names could be used to great effect. Like the hero who made his hard journey through life in *Pilgrim's Progress* being named *Christian*. But now we have to be considerably quieter about it. So quiet in fact that my first inclination is to persuade you not to make your characters' names stand for things at all. But if you do, make sure you are as inconspicuous as Harper Lee was in *To Kill a Mockingbird* when she named the central character Atticus Finch. A finch is a songbird that doesn't cause anybody any problems, just like a mockingbird, and just like Atticus himself, and Tom Robinson, another character in the novel.

Perhaps the best use of symbolism, when it comes to names, will be in nicknames. In *The Windows of Heaven*, I had the children at an orphanage call a nun with a large birthmark that covered much of her face Sister Blister. And symbolic nicknames can be ironic, as when naming a slow thinker Einstein or a bumbling lady Grace.

In your manuscripts, stay on the lookout for characters or situations that might make the natural progression to symbolism. Then you might very well want to do things that emphasize the resemblance. Let's say it becomes obvious that an old homestead in your setting begins to represent a years old crime and the guilt that a character feels because of it. That means you'll need to come up with a backstory, a few red herrings (false clues), a few foreshadowings (real clues), and a good many other things. The homestead, in the midst of all that literary commotion, becomes finally a bona fide symbol. And your story becomes the richer for it.

ONOMATOPOEIA

Many first-time writers want to begin their stories with onomatopoeia, words that sound like the actions they describe. Or they want them to stand alone in their texts. So words like *Bang! Pow!* and *Slam!* pop up as one-word sentences all over the place and, before long, it's like we're back in an old *Batman* television episode, where such things frequently splashed across the screen. *Splashed*, by the way, is an example of onomatopoeia.

Ring! Ring! all by itself is one way to show that a phone is ringing, but it's almost never the best way. Even resorting to reporting that the phone rang is preferable. But much better yet is something like this:

> He picked up the receiver and said hello.

Give your reader a little credit. Surely she knows, if a character picks up the receiver and says hello, that the phone rang.

Instead of using onomatopoeia all by itself, weave it into the fabric of your sentences, letting the sound words work their magic in little doses. Like Zane Grey does in the opening sentence of *Riders of the Purple Sage*:

> A sharp clip-clop of iron-shod hoofs deadened and died away, and clouds of yellow dust drifted from under the cottonwoods out over the sage.

Clip-clop sings out to readers from within the sentence, not set apart as a sentence of its own. We hear it, and then we move on to the next bit of business, just like we do hundreds of times every day in real life.

Make sure that your use of onomatopoeia occurs as naturally in your story or novel as it does in the real world. Let what things sound like work toward the bigger description that you are after, rather than be isolated little descriptions of their own. If your scene is set on a beach where some gulls are squawking and the waves are sloshing against a piling, steer away from coming up with something like this:

> "Squawk! Squawk!" sang out the many gulls. Slosh! The water met the piling.

As a matter of fact, steer *far* away from something like that, because it's absolutely abysmal.

> "Squawk! Squawk! Slosh." The sounds of seagulls and the waves filled up the
> morning.

Now that's a little better. But you'll fare better yet with something like this
instead:

> A congregation of gulls squawked as they floated through the gray morning;
> uninspired waves sloshed against a concrete piling.

Squawking and *sloshing* are fine sound words that will help your reader imagine the setting you are offering, but the words will be much more effective
when worked into the overall framework of your description, not standing
outside of it calling (squawking) attention just to themselves.

CADENCE

Here's a mantra that you might consider chanting from time to time while
writing: *Cadence is good; repetition is bad.*

Cadence is when you employ a measured, lyrical movement, often repeating words and phrases for rhythmic effect. Repetition, on the other hand, is
when you botch things up and repeat a word or a phrase too soon. Believe
me, your reader knows the difference and so should you.

Cadence is a wonderful way to describe something in your writing, all
the while letting your reader glean the information in something akin to
hearing it in a melody. John Grisham uses a brief cadence in this segment
from his novel *Bleachers*. He uses the same word—*our*—and the same verb
structure—*were waiting*—in a pair of sentences that describes a situation:

> We ran two plays until all eleven guys got everything perfect. Our girlfriends were
> waiting. Our parents were waiting.

And in *Provinces of Night*, William Gay establishes a longer cadence by giving
a pleasing cluster of descriptions of the setting:

> The citrusy smell of the pine woods, the raw loamy earth smell of a field turned
> darkly to the sun by Brady's tractor, the faint call of distant crows that was all
> there was to break the silence.

If you come to a place in your story where you want your reader to have no
doubt that one character is deeply in love with another one, you might just
say that this is the case: He loved her very much.

There. That should do it, don't you think? Well, it does accomplish what you set out to do: to relate that he was deeply in love with her. But if you want to *prove* it, do something like this, using cadence to get the point across:

> He thought of her all the time. He thought of her when he got out of bed in the morning and when he rode the subway to work. Thought of her all day long, as he went about his dreary job, and when he rode subway home again. Thought, during his nightly dinner of meat and cheese from the corner deli, of how beautiful she would be standing on the platform at the train station on the weekend. And he thought of her, finally, when he closed his eyes to go to sleep each night.

All of those *thought of*s aren't repetition at all (remember: repetition is bad). They make up a carefully choreographed melody that should bring your reader fully on board with the fact that this guy is head-over-heels in love.

Using cadence is one of the best ways to utilize and call attention to the essential beauty of language. It is pleasing to your reader's ear and—being that—it provides you an excellent opportunity to not only convey important parts of your story but to help establish the unique voice in which you are telling it.

FLASHBACKS, BACKSTORIES, FUTURE STORIES

A flashback is a sudden, brief relocation to a previous time and then, just as suddenly, a return to the present story. A backstory is a longer trip (in fact, sometimes backstories make up *most* of a story or even a novel). A future story is a glimpse of what is to come after, sometimes long after, the present action.

In a flashback, a character is usually reminded of something or someone from his past. The smell of cabbage cooking might cause him to see a kitchen that he hasn't actually seen in years. Or you might have a character who looks over at his wife of fifty years and, in just the right light, sees her as the teenager he married.

Flashbacks come in handy when you need to infuse a clue or two into a mystery story or when some character trait needs to be enhanced or explained. Let's say you have a fellow in your story that doesn't like dogs. Your reader wants to know why this is the case, so you lead her along for a while and then give her a nice little flashback, in which the man recalls being bitten by a dog as a child.

Flashbacks are quick. Backstories, because they drag in the baggage of a character or a situation, are longer. Here's how William Styron begins the fourth chapter of *Sophie's Choice*:

> "In Cracow, when I was a little girl," Sophie told me, "we lived in a very old house on an old winding street not far from the university."

Thus begins the backstory that becomes the heart and soul of that novel. It goes on to play itself out in many scenes that are built into the framework of the present story.

A less frequently used vehicle to wander away from the present story is the future story, which can be nothing more than a glimmer into the future, like this from M.M. Kaye's novel *The Far Pavilions*:

> Years afterwards, when he had forgotten much else, Ash could still remember that night. The heat and the moonlight, the ugly sound of jackals and hyenas quarreling and snarling within a stone's throw of the little tent where Sita crouched beside him, listening and trembling and patting his shoulder in a vain attempt to smooth his fears and send him to sleep.

Flashbacks, backstories, and future stories are good ways to establish setting and provide description. Diverting your readers' attention away from the here and now allows you to focus on times and places that give deeper insight into a character or a situation.

FORESHADOWING

Foreshadowing gives the reader a clue—a taste of what is to come—like a formation of geese ahead of an approaching cold front. Listen to the first sentence of Alice Sebold's *The Lovely Bones*:

> My name was Salmon, like the fish; first name, Susie.

The word that is most packed with foreshadowing is the verb *was*. Why, most readers will want to know, isn't her name *still* Susie Salmon? The very next sentence answers that one:

> I was murdered on December 6, 1973.

Now the readers' inquiry changes; now they want to know how and why she was murdered. That, and what the heck is going on here? They won't get all of their questions answered for several hundred pages. But their interest is stirred in the two opening sentences.

That's what foreshadowing should do for you. And that is also exactly what first sentences should do: make the reader keep reading.

Little harbingers of what's to come are wonderful carrots to dangle in front of your readers. They are the cold wind against the windowpane, the giddy step along the lane, the money buried in the backyard. They are some of the things that keep your readers reading. So they are very important bits of business.

SENTENCE AND PARAGRAPH LENGTH VARIATIONS

Sometimes you can impress your reader with the *arrangement* of your sentences and paragraphs as well as with the fine wordsmithing that comprises them. Consider these sentences from Patricia Cornwell's novel *From Potter's Field*:

> One bullet had entered through his right cheek, and as I compressed his chest and blew air into his mouth, blood covered my hands and instantly turned cold on my face. I could not save him.

The point here—that this unfortunate fellow's a goner—is made as effectively by the structuring of the two sentences as by the words contained in them. Your reader may not realize this when reading them; so in a way this is a form of manipulation. But it is also a darned effective way to convey what you want the reader to know.

Look at this passage from Shelley Mydans's novel *Thomas*:

> Baldwin sat back and looked at him. In Eustace's mind, a thought was forming; he looked at Thomas, then to his brother, then at Thomas, breathing as though he might soon speak, but he said nothing.

She begins with a short, nonelaborated sentence and then gives us a much longer, more involved one that builds on the first. It makes for a fine description of a scene. You'll do well to pay attention to sentence length variation in your own writing, and the best way to do it is to fiddle with your sentences constantly, either in your mind or on the monitor screen. Consider several configurations, then choose the best for what you're trying to show.

Imagine for instance that you wrote this paragraph, which is really from *Miss Buncle's Book* by D.E. Stevenson:

> Sarah looked up at the clock; it was midnight and John had not returned. She
> hoped there was nothing wrong. It was a first baby, of course, and first babies
> were apt to keep people waiting.

The sentences work fine as they are, but they will work a little differently when reworked. How about this, starting with a shorter sentence and following it up with a pair of longer ones:

> Sarah looked up at the clock. It was midnight and John had not returned, and
> she hoped there was nothing wrong. It was a first baby, of course, and first
> babies were apt to keep people waiting.

Neither is inherently better than the other, and your decision should be based on the meaning you are attempting to convey.

Pay as much attention to the *structure* of your sentences as to their length. Many times I find myself falling into a pattern of using the same sentence framework one after another. A prepositional phrase followed by my subject followed by my verb followed by one more prepositional phrase felt right the first time, so why not do it again? You know the answer to that one: because it becomes repetitive quickly. So mix your structures up; move things around. Flip-flop phrases and clauses and adjectives and adverbs as regularly as you shorten and lengthen the sentences themselves. Word processing programs are real blessings here. Just think: Shakespeare and Jane Austen and Hemingway had to do all of this tweaking in their heads or with lots of scratch-throughs and little arrows. We can do it with a few clicks of a mouse (a phrase that would have baffled those three writers mightily).

This same advice applies to the lengths of paragraphs. Some authors are of the opinion that starting a work of fiction—or anything else—with a long paragraph is counterproductive to enticing the reader to come onboard. And it's a valid argument that goes along with another one concerning long chapters as opposed to shorter ones. As a reader, I can tell you that, if I am getting tired and contemplating turning off the lamp and going to sleep, I am much more likely to read one more short chapter than a long one. But I'll leave psychology to people who know considerably more about it than I do. Varying the lengths of paragraphs has little to do with psychology, and much to do with creating a user-friendly format. Readers get weary of long paragraphs, and they get just as weary of paragraphs of the same length being lined up like a freight train. So vary the length; write a long paragraph followed by a very short one.

It's quite effective.

SUMMARY: PULLING IT ALL TOGETHER

In this chapter we've rummaged around pretty thoroughly in the set of tools available to you as a writer. We certainly didn't lift each and every one out and look at it, but we focused on several that will be particularly useful to you when writing description and settings.

Instead of recapping all of the approaches and devices, let me leave you with some good advice: Let moderation and balance weigh heavily when selecting the tools and using them. You won't use all of them in any one story or chapter; you'll employ them as you need them, given specific scenes and characters and situations. In one case an extended analogy will work better than a metaphor or a simile. Sometimes a trio of adjectives will work better than one; other times no adjectives at all will be needed.

Think of these tools as the spices and ingredients and utensils that we started this chapter with. Use each one carefully and well, sparingly at times and in abundance at others. Then, when you're done, look at the end result as one thing, not as all of the little things that went into it or were used to prepare it. Then you will almost certainly have to go back in and make some changes (that's where you're better off working with writer's tools than with kitchen utensils and spices; when you cook a meal that turns out badly, you're pretty much stuck with it).

After several revisions, and reusing the tools and tinkering and maneuvering, you'll finally come up with a story or a chapter that works for you. And that's the most essential criteria that it must meet in order to eventually work for your readers.

EXERCISE 1

Using one of your manuscripts, circle verbs that might work better if you substitute onomatopoeia (sound words), like replacing *fell* with *splattered*, *pounded* with *thumped*, and *hammered* with *ratatattatted*.

EXERCISE 2

Using random paragraphs from published stories and novels, practice restructuring sentences and paragraphs. Remember to vary the lengths; chop long sentences into shorter ones and make choppy ones into longer ones to see how the reorganization might produce a different effect.

When you've played around for a while with other people's writing, turn your attention to your own. Dig out one of your manuscripts and go to work on revising sentence and paragraph variation and structure; you'll be surprised at how much better (and clearer) some of your passages will end up.

EXERCISE 3

Using one of your manuscripts, try this: Circle every adjective and adverb. Then, for each one, ask these four questions:

- Is it essential to have it here?
- Is it the best word choice for this context?
- Is the description you're trying for already made somewhere else in the text?
- Can the modification be made stronger in some way (i.e., additional modifiers, more elaboration, use of Italics for emphasis)?

If the answer is no to one or both of the first two or yes to the third or fourth, then you have some work to do.

chapter 4

[SHOWING, TELLING, AND COMBINING THE TWO]

Showing versus telling is a constantly waged war in creative writing. And some of the battles have been fought in my classroom.

My students come to me from years of composition assignments in which they were not only expected, but required, to tell everything. And show nothing. So when they wander into Creative Writing, I have to attempt to pound into them many of the basic essentials of writing, one of which is to do exactly what they've been trained not to do. If I'm not successful, what I'll get for their first assignment will be a thinly disguised term paper, or a report.

Or I'll get a five-paragraph theme, that tired old plow horse that is fine when used for its intended purpose: to line up pieces of information and trot them out systematically. But it is a horribly ineffective structure for writing fiction.

The reason it doesn't work for creative writing is that it is pure reporting, which is almost completely made up of telling. Reporting is a fine mission, if you work for *The New York Times*. But, when you're writing your story or novel, you don't want to be a reporter, you want to be a storyteller.

It's time for another little dose of Flannery O'Connor here. "Fiction writing," she tells us in *Mystery and Manners*, "is very seldom a matter of saying things; it is a matter of showing things."

Let's go back for a moment to *To Kill a Mockingbird*. Never on any page in that novel does Scout, the narrator, tell us that Atticus Finch, her father, is a good man. But throughout the novel, we know it; at the end, one of the strongest images is his goodness. The author, Harper Lee, carefully gives us scene after scene in which Atticus' actions speak for themselves. She *shows* us his goodness constantly, and *tells* it never.

So you might expect the absolute rule to be *Show, Never Tell!* Always and forever. No exceptions.

The trouble is that for a writer there aren't as many absolute rules as one might think. There are certainly a few, like run-on sentences never being acceptable, and subjects having to agree with verbs (though even that one can be broken when writing dialect). But this matter of showing and telling refuses to be governed so strictly.

Once you locate that voice that we've discussed, or more correctly when you've polished the one that is already in residence, you'll be constantly determining when to show things and when to tell them. As your voice becomes more distinctive and your powers of description better, you'll show more than you'll tell. But—believe me—you will do *both* if your fiction ends up being any good. Remember, Flannery O'Connor didn't say that fiction writing was *never* a matter of saying rather than showing, she said it *seldom* is. O'Connor was a wordsmith of the highest order; she wouldn't have used *seldom* if she had meant anything else.

In this chapter, we'll look at several examples to see how other writers have primarily shown or told or—more commonly—used a combination of both. We'll dig into the examples to see exactly what they did to make them work, and we'll pay special attention to the fine-tuning they employed to bring them fully to life. Then we'll look at a few ways that you can sharpen your skills, when tackling description and setting, at combining showing and telling.

But, first, let's determine the distinction between the two.

THE DIFFERENCE BETWEEN SHOWING AND TELLING

Consider this statement:

> A good time was had by all.

Now, spend a moment with this paragraph from Toni Morrison's novel *Sula*:

> Old people were dancing with little children. Young boys with their sisters, and the church women who frowned on any bodily expression of joy (except when the hand of God commanded it) tapped their feet. Somebody (the groom's father, everybody said) had poured a whole pint jar of cane liquor into the punch, so even the men who did not sneak out the back door to have a shot, as well as the women who let nothing stronger than Black Draught enter their blood, were tipsy. A small boy stood at the Victrola turning its handle and smiling at the sound of Bert William's "Save a Little Dram for Me."

A question: Which of the two descriptions on page 63 does more for you as a reader?

I'll bet you chose the longer one, unless you're one of those people who likes to be different just for the heck of it—one of those go-against-the-grain sorts.

But the point is this: In terms of what we end up knowing about this celebration, they both do exactly the same thing. We end up, both times, realizing that a good time was had by all.

So, why should we opt for the longer one when the snippet fills the bill?

Because brevity doesn't usually fill the bill for a writer or—much more to the point—for a *reader*. The guy in Sheboygan, unless he's addicted to condensations of novels, wants elaboration. He wants to know about those feet-tapping church women and that jar of hooch that got poured into the punch to help things along.

The big difference between these two examples isn't that one is considerably longer. It's that the most essential image, a sense of universal enjoyment, is not specifically mentioned at all in the longer one.

The first version is telling, the second is showing. We know that all of the participants in Morrison's paragraph are enjoying themselves because we watch them doing it.

Showing rather than telling is part of the magic that you have to work as a writer; in fact, it's one of the most vital parts. Your reader has to make his way through your story or novel—and then finally come away from it— with a sense of the characters and the settings and the situations that must have seemed to occur naturally. To use a sewing metaphor: You have to stitch your images together so meticulously that the seams are invisible.

One of the most effective ways to pull that off is to let your reader experience things rather than be told about them, to feel them rather than have them reported to him.

In *Black Rain*, Masuji Ibuse's novel about the dropping of the atomic bomb on Hiroshima, Japan, this sentence does not appear:

> The city suffered significant damage in the blast.

But this paragraph *does*:

> Among the ruins, the reflection of the sun on the pieces of broken glass on the road was so strong that it was difficult to hold your head up as you walked. The smell of death was a little fainter than the day before, but the places where

houses had collapsed into tile-covered heaps stank vilely and were covered with great, black swarms of flies. The relief squads clearing the ruins seemed to have been joined by reinforcements, since I saw some men whose clothes, though bleached with frequent washing, were not soiled with sweat and grime as yet.

Again, as in the example from Toni Morrison's novel, we get the pertinent information in the first version. But we see and hear and touch and taste and smell the experience in the second. The difference between the two accounts is something like the difference between an accident report that a patrolman would write and the sensation of being in the accident itself. If you've ever been in one, you know that the curt, factual summary is worlds away from the reality of experiencing it.

"The city suffered significant damage in the blast" is too cold, too distant, and too all-inclusive. So what Ibuse does is drive home the image in small details, one after the other, throughout the novel. Pay attention to the delicate pictures here, almost like miniatures arranged on a wall: the reflection of the sun on the pieces of broken glass, the collapsed houses, the smell of death. The swarms of flies. All bits and pieces of wordsmithing that add up to an inevitable conclusion: that the city suffered significantly in the blast.

In short, the second piece is considerably better. And it's better because it brings the reader more fully in.

Now, this is important—so heads up, please. The longer version is not better because it is all showing and no telling. It's better because it is both showing *and* telling.

Look back over it; "the reflection of the sun . . . was so strong that it was difficult to hold your head up . . . ," "The smell of death was a little fainter . . . ," and ". . . were covered with great, black swarms of flies" are all telling. But the overall effect of the paragraph is that it shows the reader how badly the city had suffered. And it makes much, much more of an impression than simply reporting it.

Your fiction has to be a balanced blend of both approaches. Just remember this: Your story shouldn't come off as a report, or a summary. Think about that car accident we envisioned a few moments ago. Would your reader benefit most from the patrolman's efficient, curtly worded account of the wreck or from the driver's or the passenger's emotions and sensations as it happened?

You know the answer to that one, even if you're the gotta-be-different, go-against-the-grain guy.

Actions Speak Louder Than Words

Remember the television preachers who could deal out fire and brimstone from the pulpit, holding themselves up as paragons of virtue? Then remember how we read about the escapades and scandalous behavior of some of them in the newspaper.

They didn't practice what they preached.

They didn't *show* what they *told*.

Take Reverend Dimmesdale in *The Scarlet Letter*, who had no trouble presenting himself to the community as pious and stainless, all the while letting poor little Hester Prynne catch all that Puritan flack for a transgression of which he was equally guilty, or even more so.

Dimmesdale and those television preachers didn't remember something that you—as a writer of fiction—must never forget: Showing carries greater credibility than telling. And not just in your actions, but in your writing. Particularly in your descriptions.

The best way to keep your tale from emerging as a report is to mostly show, and, when you tell, to make the telling as carefully wordsmithed and polished as the rest of your writing.

WHEN TO SHOW; WHEN TO TELL

We'll spend some time now with a variety of writers, looking at how they used this combination in their work.

In her novel *The Book of Mercy*, Kathleen Cambor could have written this:

> In addition to the potential risk and the possibility of notoriety, one reason he chose to become a fireman was that he liked the uniform, which his mother also admired. But his father was against the whole idea.

Which would have gotten the point across. But not nearly so effectively as what she *did* write:

> He liked everything about the idea of being a fireman. The excitement, the danger, the chance to be a hero or a prince. The dress-blue uniform, dark serge, a knife-like crease down the center of each pants leg, patent-leather visor on the cap,

> in which a man could see himself reflected. "Very fancy," said his mother. His
> father's eyes were wells of rage and disappointment. He spit onto the floor.

The short one tells us pretty much what we need to know to understand this part of the story. But the longer one—the *real* one that Ms. Cambor actually did compose—does far more than that. It takes us into the attitude of the character, into his sense of values. It shows us how he feels about becoming a fireman rather than telling us. And there is more drama and description in those last two sentences, about his father's reaction to it, than the author could have conveyed in a page or more of explanation.

Look a little further along at a bit more about how the character feels about his new job:

> He learned to smell the smoke from blocks away, he watched for the sky to begin
> to lighten, as if from the tip of a rising sun. Each time, he felt his heart pound,
> his own heart filled his chest, it echoed in his ears until they made the final turn
> into the red-hot stunning light.

Here again the writer could have told us what we needed to know in fewer words. "His job was exciting" might suffice. Or if you want a little more detail: "His heart rate elevated when his truck approached a fire." But the point is that your reader wants, in fact he demands, a *lot* more detail, not just a little.

Your characters, their situations, the basic logistics of your plot—how characters move from Point A to Point B and the chronological order of their actions—are all important to your story, essential in fact. What brings the story to life, and makes it all as real as seeing it happen for the reader, is your description. Showing these things, as opposed to simply reporting them, will be what finally makes the whole thing work.

Dig back into that last piece. Note the strong images of the lightening sky and the pounding of the fireman's heart. That's fine stuff that drives home to the reader exactly how this fellow is feeling at that moment, in that place. Because the reader has probably felt that way, too. Maybe when a family member was in an accident and he was rushing to the scene. Maybe in a war. Maybe when his teenager was three hours late coming home from a party and dozens of possibilities—all bad—had galloped through his mind.

In your story, you need to plug your reader into images like that—to situations and emotions he can relate to. That's difficult, maybe impossible, to do when you are telling the thing. But your images can ring soundly and true when you are showing.

Here's a smidgen of *Cold Mountain* by Charles Frazier, where Ruby, a mountain girl, has first arrived to help Ada, one of the central characters, on the farm she has inherited during the Civil War:

> Ruby's recommendations extended in all directions, and she never seemed to stop. She had ideas concerning schedules for crop rotation among the various fields. Designs for constructing a tub mill so that once they had a corn crop they could grind their own meal and grits using waterpower from the creek and save having to give the miller his tithe. One evening before she set off in the dark to walk up to the cabin, her last words were, "We need us some guineas. I'm not partial to their eggs for frying, but they'll do for baking needs." Even discarding the eggs, guineas are a comfort to have around and useful in a number of ways. They're good watchdogs, and they'll bug out a row of pole beans before you can turn around. All that aside from how pleasant they are to look at walking around the yard.
>
> The next morning her words were, "Pigs. Do you have any loose in the woods?"
>
> Ada said, "No, we always bought our hams."
>
> "There's a world more to a hog than just the two hams," Ruby said. "Take lard for example. We'll need plenty."

It is made abundantly clear, in this passage, that Ruby's knowledge of farming and farm life is extensive. And, at the end, it is just as obvious that Ada doesn't have a clue about such things. The author could have just told us that and been done with it. *Ruby understood everything about the workings of a farm, about which Ada knew absolutely nothing.* That's what the reader needs to know.

But what she wants to know is more than that basic fact. She wants to know more about the uniqueness of these two women and their situation that can never effectively come through in just the telling. This flowing catalog of the things Ruby knows slowly paints a picture of her in the reader's mind, one that the author continues to add to as the novel progresses.

Look at how Ruby uses words like "partial" and "discarding," and the phrase "in a number of ways." If we are paying sufficient attention, we begin to see that she's not your average bumpkin that wandered down out of the holler. Probably she's had some education; probably she's done some reading. And those possibilities add an interesting aspect to a character that could have been one dimensional, and stereotypical.

If the reader ends up liking Ada and Ruby, and if she ends up pulling for them in their struggles, it will be because the characters and the struggles have been adequately shown to her, not reported.

Notice, too, that all of this attention to corn crops and guinea eggs and tub mills and pole beans goes a long way toward establishing the rural, historical setting of the story. Remember, it is easy enough to tell your reader that we're on a farm during the Civil War. But it isn't enough if the reader is going to actually feel like she is there. You're going to have to work considerably harder than simply telling her. You're going to have to show her hundreds of little details, all of which finally add up to what an 1860s era farm looked and smelled and sounded like.

By the way, you might have noticed that Frazier plays loose and easy with old, established rules regarding quotation marks in particular and dialogue in general. For which we'll forgive him, as the National Book Award judges obviously did, when they gave him their award.

Look at how John Gardner first shows, then tells in *Grendel*:

> No use of a growl, a whoop, a roar, in the presence of that beast! Vast, red-golden, huge tail coiled, limbs sprawled over his treasure-hoard, eyes not firey but cold as the memory of family deaths. Vanishing away across invisible floors, there were things of gold, gems, jewels, silver vessels the color of blood in the undulant, dragon-red light. Arching above him the ceiling and upper walls of this cave were alive with bats. The color of his sharp scales darkened and brightened as the dragon inhaled and exhaled slowly, drawing new air across his vast internal furnace; his razorsharp tusks gleamed and glinted as if they too, like the mountain beneath him, were formed of precious stones and metals.
>
> My heart shook. His eyes stared straight at me. My knees and insides were so weak I had to drop down on all fours. His mouth opened slightly. Bits of flame escaped.
>
> "Ah, Grendel!" he said. "You've come."

The first longer paragraph shows us much about this dragon and his lair. In fact, if I asked you to make a list of every detail covered in that paragraph, it would take you a while. Then, in the second paragraph, Gardner curtly reports Grendel's reaction to it. The first paragraph floats along like a river of nicely wordsmithed images; the second is five short, to the point statements of fact—some more of that sentence length variation I pointed out earlier. Taken together, the paragraphs work very effectively to convey the horror that Grendel feels in the confrontation. It's a good example of showing *and* telling, from an author who knew when to do each.

Here's another example that effectively uses both showing and telling. Consider these two paragraphs from Ray Bradbury's *The Martian Chronicles*:

> Mr. and Mrs. K were not old. They had the fair, brownish skin of the true Martian, the yellow coin eyes, the soft musical voices. Once they had liked painting pictures with chemical fire, swimming in the canals in the seasons when the wine trees filled them with green liquors, and talking into the dawn together by the blue phosphorous portraits in the speaking room.
>
> They were not happy now.

Notice that the word *happy* is never used in the first paragraph, the obvious intention of which is to convey that Mr. and Mrs. K *are* happy. In a mellow flow of pleasing, futuristic images, Bradbury shows us that this is the case.

Then, in the second paragraph, the image is brought to an abrupt halt with five words.

Bradbury, like Gardner, knows when to show and when to tell. Often, as in this example, the carefully constructed, elaborately detailed showing is the perfect setup for the sucker punch—for the change-up pitch. In baseball, a good pitcher will lull the batter into expecting the same offering every time, maybe one fast ball after another, until he throws a change-up—say, a sinker—to catch the batter off his guard. Good writers do that, too. The buildup calls for showing; the change-up is most effectively told, in the shortest, most matter-of-fact manner.

Let's look now at how Bradbury crafted that overall sense of happiness in the first paragraph before he negated it in the second. Consider the physical description of the couple, detailed images like fair, brownish skin and yellow coinlike eyes. We get a good glimpse of them, even of their natures (soft, musical voices), in less than twenty words. Then we see the things they once enjoyed: the strange (to us earthbound folk) Martian things like painting with chemical fire and visiting in a speaking room with phosphorous portraits.

We are told these things, you might be thinking—and you are correct. But remember, the prevailing image that the paragraph gives us is that they were happy. And we are not told that. It is shown to us.

What we *are* told—in no uncertain words—in the second paragraph, is that they are no longer happy. The harshness of the fact is equal to the harshness of its telling. And while the author could certainly come up with a paragraph or two to illustrate their discontent, this blunt statement of it works much better.

Remember this technique when you're writing. There will be places in your story or your novel where careful, intricate showing will best be followed by rapid telling.

I'll bet good money that Bradbury didn't spend all of his time while writing *The Martian Chronicles* thinking "I believe I'll tell this" and "I think I'll show this." Neither, certainly, did he flip a coin (a yellow one, like Martians' eyes) to determine whose turn it was: showing or telling. He instinctively knew when to do one and when to do the other. And so will you. As your story unfolds, both in your thinking and your writing, you'll find yourself making the show or tell decisions almost subconsciously, based on the particular need or circumstance.

But remember: show more than you tell.

DON'T TELL WHAT YOU'VE ALREADY SHOWN

The student manuscripts that make their way to the critique table in my classroom often contain something like this:

> Martha Louise considered the three large teacakes in her hand. She thought of the yeasty sweetness of them, and how they would feel as she slowly chewed them, how they would taste, like sweet cream and butter and cinnamon. She even thought of the crumbling bits of them that would trickle down her face and the front of her dress.
>
> Then she considered this pair of barefooted girls, standing beside the wagon. Their dresses had obviously been handed down through many children before them. Their big eyes were as empty as their stomachs surely were.
>
> Martha Louise sniffed at the teacakes just once, then handed them to the girls. She was a generous child.

Here, the writer shows us how important these cookies are to this particular little girl, and how much of an impression is made on her by the two unfortunate children. The writer then hints at the internal dilemma for the girl as she sniffs at the teacakes, "just once," before sacrificing them. Good job, all around.

But then the writer blows it.

If the reader doesn't understand—after all of that showing—that this kid is generous, then he just isn't paying attention.

That last sentence in the example is pure telling, and the difference between it and the bits of telling at the ends of the Gardner and Bradbury examples is that, this time, we've already been *shown* what is now being told. In good writing, that should never, *ever* happen.

The last sentence is clutter, which William Zinsser in *On Writing Well* calls the disease of American writing. And he's right; it is a human tendency to tell more than is needed. Specifically, in creative writing, to tell when we've already shown.

The best way to assess how you're doing in this regard is to ask yourself—every time you convey a new image or situation—if you have already shown what you are now telling. If the answer is yes, then you've got yourself a piece of clutter that needs to be disposed of. The delete key (or a good eraser) is close by, and it should be one of the most frequently used tools in your kit.

SUMMARY: A LAST WORD ON THE SUBJECT

What we've discussed in this chapter are ways to go about blending showing and telling in your descriptions and settings, in fact, in all of your writing. We'll look at using sensory description next and then many other things. But showing and telling will weave their way into most of what we talk about.

Deciding when to show and when to tell will become an instinctive process, if it hasn't already for you. But that doesn't mean that you shouldn't stop pretty often when you're writing and ask yourself if a particular passage or image would work better in another way. And that other way, usually, is showing rather than telling, or vise versa.

Before we close, let's look at one last example, this time from a movie rather than a book or a story. Good movies tell their stories in images, too, just like good writing does.

There's a wonderful moment at the end of *Out of Africa* where the narrator, an old woman, looks back at her long-ago love affair with a fellow who died young. She wants to tell us, near the end of her long life, that she believes in the existence of heaven, of an afterlife.

But she shows us instead. Here's how:

She hears from an old friend back in Africa, where she has never returned after moving far away from there, that lions often go to her old sweetheart's grave on a hillside that overlooks vast plains. The lions lie on the grave, the friend reports, sometimes for several hours. Her sweetheart, dead for many, many years, had loved and respected lions.

"He would have liked that," she tells us, in her old, tired voice.

"I'll have to remember to tell him."

How insufficient it would have been for her to announce that she believes in heaven, and intends to see her lover again, probably soon. How wonderful to casually let it slip its way into her narration, as if she hadn't meant to tell the thing at all.

Which is, almost always, the precise difference between showing and telling.

Choose a verb. Any *action* verb, that is. Make a list of several common verbs that are generic in their meanings. Words like walk, talk, and hit. Then take a few moments with each word and write down as many verbs or phrases that you can think of that are more specific. Your goal is not to create a catalog of more precise descriptions; instead, practice refining an action down to its clearest description.

By the way, after admonishing you regarding the use of the thesaurus earlier, I encourage you to use it here. Many of its offerings will be what you're looking for. Some won't. And you'll come up with some of your own.

Think of some ways that you could show the things that are told in these short statements, then jot down a few notes on how you might go about it.

- The man is nervous.
- The pocket watch is a very old keepsake.
- The lawn has been recently mown and the hedges trimmed.
- The cruise ship is considerably larger than the sailboat docked beside it.
- The student is ready for the final bell of the day to ring.
- The old woman in the bus station is waiting for someone.
- The larger of the two dogs is arrogant.

Think about this statement: She told me about how wonderful Paris is.

I think you would agree that this, alone, doesn't go very far in describing someone's perception of Paris. And if you've got a good story churning along that has arrived at a point where one of your characters tells another one about Paris, "she told me about how wonderful Paris is" just isn't going to cut it.

So grab your journal and a pencil, and redo it. Elaborate. Turn this sow's ear into a silk purse. If you've never been to Paris, that can't be your excuse for not attempting this. I'm pretty sure that Ray Bradbury never went to Mars either. But that didn't keep him from writing beautiful, believable passages about Martian cities and landscapes and Martians themselves.

Take your image of Paris and put it to work. Put it into words.

EXERCISE 4

Here are some other telling statements that you might try to work into short compositions that show. Remember, avoid using *telling* words and phrases like *feels*, *hears*, *sees*, *felt like*, and *smelled like*.

- Sunsets are nice at the beach.
- A housewife's work is never done.
- He had never looked closely at his father-in-law.
- It seemed that the mail would never come.
- The park is interesting at daybreak.

You can, of course, come up with plenty of statements of your own. Try this. It will make you a closer observer of details and encourage you to show things to the guy in Sheboygan rather than report them to him in little summaries.

chapter 5

[SENSORY DESCRIPTION]

Twenty or so years ago, I attended the dedication of the planetarium at the arts and sciences center in the town where I live. James Michener was the speaker. He had moved to Texas to research and then write the novel of that name, and his novel *Space* had recently been published, so his public blessing of a planetarium was altogether fitting and proper. And quite a crowd gathered. He packed the house.

That night, Mr. Michener talked about his long career as a novelist, about some of the fascinating places he had lived in and written about, and even about what he considered to be his strengths and weaknesses as a writer. His place in literature was secure by then—his many long sagas in their millions of copies—and he seemed satisfied with what he could do well and with what he couldn't.

I don't recall what he said were his failings, but I remember exactly what he said he believed was his great strength as a writer. He said that he could imagine a chair, carefully write a paragraph or so about it, and his reader would know precisely what it would be like to sit in *that* chair. To not only visualize it, but feel it. To hear it creaking under his weight and to smell the oil that was used to polish it and the old cloth of its cushion.

And he was right. James Michener was quite often letter perfect when it came to using the five senses to describe.

In fact, he hadn't come to my part of Texas to dedicate that planetarium at all. That arrangement got cooked up when the committee had learned that he would be in the area. What he had come for was to spend a couple of days with a local water well digger that he had heard of, that, most probably, one of his research assistants had dug up (no pun intended). Michener was an absolute stickler for accurate detail, and a researcher of the first order.

The digging of a well certainly plays no great part in *Texas*, and the author could easily have told one of his minions to just look up the procedure. But he intended to watch the location of a site and then observe the actual digging, noting every detail, missing nothing. A couple of chapters ago remember how much emphasis was put on the importance of paying attention to everything and collecting details? Michener's work is the perfect example of how details can make an important difference in engaging readers.

Michener told us that night that he was off to the frozen North soon to research his next book *Alaska*. He intended to stand somewhere in the Arctic Circle, outside, for long enough to truly know the effect of that frigid temperature, and at the coldest time of the year. Most writers—myself included—would be content to just imagine how darned cold that would be. But not Michener. He had to feel it, taste it, touch it, hear it, and smell it, so that his readers could, too.

That's the important business we'll undertake in this chapter. Because, as I've said all along—and you're no doubt tired of hearing it by now—the success of your story or novel will depend on many things, but the most crucial is your ability to bring your reader into it. And that reader will be most completely *in* when you deliver the actual sensations of the many things that comprise your story.

USING THE FIVE SENSES TO PAINT A PICTURE

Have you ever stood in front of a painting in a gallery and gotten hungry? You've looked, perhaps, at one perfect peach in a still life, with just a glimmer of morning sunlight falling on it, its delicate fuzz caught in the muted illumination, its plumpness attesting to the sweet nectar and meat inside. You hadn't been thinking of eating a peach before you came across the painting, but now you're giving serious consideration to stopping at the market on the way home and picking up a few.

You can blame the artist for that. With a mixture of just the right colors and tones, and the careful application with the brush, the artist made you realize what that peach would feel like if you could actually touch it, what it would smell like if you could lift it to your nose. And—this is what will cost you the trip to the market—what it would *taste* like if you could bite into it. In short, the artist has given you a mental perception of a peach. The better the artist, the better the perception.

In your writing, you have to do exactly the same thing. You have to describe places and things and people and situations so completely that you actually give them to your reader. If you're good at it—and you'd better be *very* good at it if you want your fiction to work—then you, like the painter of that peach, might also be responsible for a little inconvenience. A fresh batch of chocolate chip cookies in your story, their aroma wafting through the house like sweet perfume, might just send the reader off to the bakery in search of a dozen.

The way to do this is to make use of your readers' five physical senses, and sometimes even that mysterious sixth. When they can relate to the tangible nature of things and places and characters, then you, the writer, have taken a giant step toward bringing them fully on board.

Let's briefly review two important distinctions again—the difference between showing and telling and between literary and popular fiction—before we look at ways that you can work sensory description into your story.

Showing and Telling

First, think back to the preceding chapter, to all that we talked about regarding showing and telling. Nowhere will all of that be more important than in the use of sensory description.

Saying that something *smelled like* or *tasted like* or *felt like* is always telling. Sometimes that's fine, like following up a long description of a slaughterhouse with a curt proclamation like this: *It smelled like death.* But to simply blurt out that something smelled like death, without somewhere showing why, is ineffective.

Having a rich aroma wander in is better than saying that it smelled like coffee, just as showing why a person's feet hurt is preferable to saying that they do.

Nowhere in your writing would I encourage you more adamantly to show more than you tell than when using sensory description.

Your Audience

You might recall that I said readers of literary fiction will usually be more tolerant of long passages of description, since they are as concerned with how the author is working her magic as with what's going on in the story. Readers of popular fiction want the magic worked, also, but they want it done more quickly. The plot and its various twists and turns are more important to them than how the story is being unfolded.

Look at a couple of examples—one from a literary novel and one from a popular one—to help illustrate how to work description into different types of stories.

Here's William Goyen in *The House of Breath*, a novel that is something of a literary classic of southwestern prose:

> A fragile, melodious Oriental language blew in on the wind like the odor of a flower and we saw the string of smoke from a gypsy camp somewhere in the woods. The sliding of our feet in the road flushed a flutter of wings from the bush. The fields were alive with things rushing and running; winged and legged things were going where they would, no engine or human to stop them. Out in the fields under the thick brush and in the grass and green were myriad unseen small things that were running and resting from running.

Now compare that to Joy Fielding's *New York Times* bestseller *Whispers and Lies*:

> I unlocked the kitchen door and tiptoed outside, the grass cool on my bare feet. A sudden rush of nausea almost overwhelmed me, and I gulped frantically at the fresh air until the feeling subsided. I took several long, deep breaths before continuing toward the cottage door. It was then I heard the sound of laughter from inside the cottage. Clearly, Alison wasn't sick. Nor was she alone.

The reader of literary fiction is as interested—in the first piece—in what the character is seeing and hearing, the intricate details of the sensations, as in where he is going. In the second piece, the character sees and hears and feels things, also. But the emphasis this time is on what Alison is up to in that cottage.

The reader of popular fiction doesn't mind at all that the narrator tells her outright that she hears laughter. Someone used to reading literary fiction might want to know what that laughter sounds like.

One of your first jobs as a writer is to determine which of these audiences you're aiming for and craft your description accordingly. When writing popular fiction—for readers who want that story fairly zipping along—you'll need to keep detailed description to a minimum.

EACH OF THE SENSES IN THEIR TURN

You will, of course, use sensory description many, many times in your fiction, and the employment of one or another of the senses will be dictated by the plot and the setting. Never feel compelled to use *all* of them. The crafting of fiction is not like coaching Peewee League Baseball; you don't have to get every player into every game. Determine in a particular scene or circumstance which image you most want to convey, what *exactly* you want your reader to experience. Then you will know which of the senses to use. Let's say a child

Titles With Sense and Sensibility

Your title is your very first offering to your reader. In many cases, its appeal will determine whether or not she will move on to the first sentence and paragraph. So you need to craft precisely the right few words—or sometimes just one—that will stand above your name.

It might be a good idea to appeal to one or more of the senses in the title, before you do it continuously in your text. Here's how some writers have worked sensory description into their titles:

- *The Touch* by Colleen McCullough
- *If You Could Hear What I See* by Kathy Buckley
- *Snow Falling on Cedars* by David Guterson
- *A Stone in My Hand* by Cathryn Clinton
- *The Smell of Apples* by Mark Behr
- *A Knife in the Back* by Bill Crider
- *A Distant Trumpet* by Paul Horgan
- *Night Scents* by Carla Neggers
- *Strangled Intuition* by Claire Daniels
- *Roll of Thunder, Hear My Cry* by Mildred Taylor
- *Hungry for Home* by Cole Moreton
- *Cat on a Hot Tin Roof* by Tennessee Williams
- *A Fair Wind Home* by Ruth Moore
- *Too Loud a Solitude* by Bohumil Hrabal
- *Bitter Medicine* by Sara Paretsky
- *Death Is Lighter Than a Feather* by David Westheimer
- *The Sound of Waves* by Yukio Mishima
- *Scent of Danger* by Andrea Kane
- *Wolf Whistle* by Lewis Nordan
- *In Plain Sight* by Carol Otis Hurst
- *The Whisper of the River* by Ferrol Sams
- *A Taste of Blackberries* by Doris Buchanan Smith
- *When the Wind Blows* by James Patterson
- *All Quiet on the Western Front* by Erich Maria Remarque
- *Hard Rain* by Barry Eisler
- *Echoes* by Danielle Steel
- *Light on Snow* by Anita Shreve

in one of your stories receives a new puppy. Now you need to decide how to describe it: by how it feels, smells, sounds, or looks. Maybe—if the child you have created is particularly curious—even by how it tastes. If the old curmudgeon that lives upstairs gets angry about noise, then what the dog sounds like will be most important; if the child has allergies, then smell will move up on your agenda list. You might end up using a combination of the senses. And you might end up using none of them. Maybe this gift is not at all important to the larger story that you are building, and it will suffice for the reader to know that the gift was given and received. Use the senses as you need them or, more precisely, as your reader needs them to get a more detailed, personal conception of whatever it is you are describing.

Don't hesitate to let the senses overlap. For instance, you might want to let what something *looks* like describe what it *tastes* like. You do this all the time (remember that peach in the painting), so let it happen in your fiction, also.

Let's consider each of the senses now, looking closely at how you might use them effectively in your fiction and how other writers have done so.

Sight

This is the one you'll use most often, since showing what things and people and places look like is the most common sort of description. The inherent danger in using this sense is to use it too often, to the exclusion of all the others. But when you use it, pay close attention to what you're showing the reader, and how you're doing it.

The trick is not simply reporting what you want the reader to see. It's using your wordsmithing to full advantage, filling your writing with words and images the reader can't predict. Surprise him. Look at these two snippets from Cormac McCarthy's *Cities of the Plain*:

> Billy peered out at the high desert. The bellied light wires raced against the night.

And, a little later:

> Billy sat watching the night spool past. The roadside chaparral, flat black scrim of the mountains cut into the starblown desert sky above them. Troy smoked.

Before I first read that passage, I never thought of the sagging lines between utility poles as *bellied,* but now I do. Neither did I perceive them as racing against the night, which gives the image of a vast, seemingly endless landscape, reinforced in the next section by the night *spooling* past. I doubt if *scrim*—a light, transparent fabric used mostly for window curtains—had ever before been used to describe a mountain range, but McCarthy wants us to see these mountains as distant and hard to detect, as almost not there at all. The stars, on the other hand, he wants to be there in abundance, so he makes the desert sky *starblown*.

He uses unexpected images—uncommon phrases and adjectives—to paint precise images in the reader's mind.

This is an effective approach that you will want to make use of in your own writing. Describing something or someone in an unusual way—like this writer calling the power lines "bellied"—makes the reader pay a little closer attention and remember the image better. It also makes her remember the *writer* better, which is what that elusive voice is all about.

Avoid giving your reader the overused clichés that she's read time after time after time. Like a startled character being caught "like a deer in the headlights," or one gazing intently "staring daggers." Those have been done to death. But they are resurrected by far too many authors.

A warning here: while uncommon, unexpected bits of description will serve you well, they will probably only do so *once* in a single story or novel. A uniquely turned phrase is delightful the first time around, but goes stale quickly if used again.

In your fiction, you might want to use description to do more than simply describe. It's also a good way to establish the tone you are seeking or to call attention to the time period. If your story is set in London in the late nineteenth century, then you should pay careful attention to the description of things Victorian, like horse-drawn cabs and gentlemen's walking sticks and ladies' parasols. If your plot involves the Jack the Ripper murders or some other mysterious doings, then come up with plenty of dark alleys and a pea soup fog hugging the river.

Sometimes, even the types of words you choose will bring your readers closer in to where you want them to be. Consider how Walter M. Miller employs unusual imagery to convey another desert landscape in his science fiction novel *A Canticle for Leibowitz*:

> A sky-herd of cumulus clouds, on their way to bestow moist blessings on the mountains after cruelly deceiving the parched desert, began blotting out the sun and trailing dark shadow-shapes across the blistered land below, offering intermittent but welcome respite from the soaring sunlight. When a racing cloud-shadow wiped its way over the ruins, the novice worked rapidly until the shadow was gone, then rested until the next bundle of fleece blotted out the sun.

Here the writer infuses his tale set in the distant future with a descriptive device pulled from ancient literature. *Sky-herd, shadow-shapes,* and *cloud-shadow* are modern day kennings, hyphenated metaphorical compounds that you might not have dealt with since you read *Beowulf* in high school. *A Canticle for Leibowitz* is set in a world that is reorganizing itself after devastation, so this use of an antiquated descriptive device is very much in keeping with the primitive, back to the basics tone of the novel.

Don't be afraid to try something as unusual as this in your fiction. The figures of speech and other approaches you'll use—like adjectives and metaphors and all the rest—are the common tools of all writers, but the unique manipulation of them can be quite uncommon.

Occasionally you will need your reader to detect only slight differences between things in your story, like the almost imperceptible disparity between two shades of the same color. Here's one way to do it, from William Martin's *Cape Cod*, a novel that begins with the pilgrims coming to the new world on the *Mayflower*:

> Jones raised his newfangled and most expensive spying glass to his eye and studied the horizon. Smoke gray sky sat atop slate gray sea, and beyond the line that divided them lay America.

Here, the reader needs to know that there is only a slight disparity, or none at all, between two shades. The easier task for the writer would have been to tell it: "The sky was a slightly darker gray than the sea." But the descriptions of colors do more than *just* describe, they serve to move the bigger story along by showing that a destination, hopefully bright, lies wedged between those two gloomy hues. Sort of a light at the end of the tunnel, one of those clichés you should avoid.

You must keep pointing at things that you want your reader to see. Many times, it will be a big, blaring thing that is hard to miss. Other times it will be so tiny that he might otherwise have overlooked it altogether, like the slight differences between these colors.

Remember, you'll call upon the reader's sense of sight much more often than his other senses to anchor him in your time and place, and keep him there. So pay very special attention, always, to what everything *looks* like, so that you can show it in your writing. Focus on the fine points of colors, lighting, shadows, shapes, and textures as closely as you note the bigger aspects of what will end up in your pages.

Remember, too, that there are at least four other senses to appeal to. Too many writers make the mistake of packing almost all of their description into showing what everything in the story looks like, bypassing more effective senses.

Smell

I heard or read somewhere that the sense of smell is the most nostalgic of the five senses. And I believe this to be true. Every time I smell diesel fumes from a bus or a truck my mind's eye goes quickly back over thirty years to the large army motor pool shop in Germany where I was the clerk. If I'm ever around where butter beans—perhaps they're called lima beans in your part of the world—are being boiled, I am instantly back in my grandmother's kitchen, where she cooked them nearly every day. I'm sure there are certain scents that you, too, can identify because of the memories they evoke.

The fact that your reader's olfactory memory is laden with treasures is reason enough for you to take full advantage of it. If this truly is the most nostalgic of the physical senses, then you should draw on it like a bank account, tapping it often to engage your readers more fully. You have to be generic enough for everybody to make the connections you need them to make, however. Not all of my readers served in motor pools, I suspect, or had butter bean-cooking grandmothers, so I can't use those continuously and get away with it.

You can use smell to, among other things, kick your character's memories into gear, to symbolize something else, to describe something that is difficult (or impossible) to describe, and to help build your setting. Let's look at how a few writers did these things, and at how you can do them, also.

Gore Vidal lets a certain aroma trigger a memory in one of his characters in his novel *Washington, D.C.*:

> "There you are! But get away from those gardenias. I can't stand the smell. They make my head ache. I don't know why Mother's so keen on them. They remind me of dancing school! Remember Mrs. Shipman's? When each boy had to bring his date a corsage consisting of two wilted yellow gardenias. My God, it's hot in here."

When using a scent to remind a character of something in your fiction, you have to first decide—in addition to what the memory will be—if it will be a pleasant memory or a bad one. Happy or sad? Frightful or hopeful? The overall tone of the thing will color the tone of the remembrance of it.

Here, the recognition of a particular smell makes a character recall something unpleasant. So gardenias, which give off a pleasing smell to most people, make this woman want to get completely away from them. Using scents in this way allows you to enlarge your story and, more specifically, your backstory.

In Marly Youmans's *Catherwood*, a smell becomes symbolic of something being given up:

> The smell of the sea grew in intensity as the last glimpse of Ireland fell into the mist. The rich odor of the Irish coast, a fragrance of turf smoke and soil, dropped away.

Sometimes it's a good idea to let something that defines your character—like loyalty or honesty or, as in this case, devotion to a particular place—be triggered by something she smells. A long lost love might come to mind when a woman detects a particular brand of cologne, or the fragrance of fresh lemons might unlock a clue in a murder mystery.

The use of symbolism can be a tricky business for a writer and can quickly go over the top. Modern-day readers aren't as a rule very tolerant of blatant symbolism, where great white whales stand for vengeance and fallen young women walk around with scarlet letters on their chests. But even the pickiest of symbol hunters will accept subtle ones. And some of the most subtle reminders in the world are aromas. In the two sentences from *Catherwood*, the smells of the sea, the coast, the turf smoke, and the soil are mentioned only once, and quickly. The words are barely there, like the scents themselves, and they are receding, like the place they represent.

There are as many times to be quiet in your writing as there are to be loud. And I'm not just referring to having your characters bellowing out at the stars or whispering sweet nothings in each others' ears. Loud and quiet in regard to using the senses really means blatant and subtle, and all the stations in between. The overpowering stench of stockyards in Upton Sinclair's *The Jungle* is one thing; the delicate hint of Ireland in *Catherwood* is quite another. Both are extremely effective. In your fiction be prepared to be quiet as often as you are loud in your descriptions, for the quiet, subtle approach is often the most effective.

One or another of the senses can even be used on occasion to describe the indescribable. As the sense of smell does in *Montana 1948* by Larry Watson:

> Because Daisy kept the curtains drawn and windows closed to keep the heat of
> the day out, the McAuley house was dark and stuffy. The house always had a
> strange smell, as though Daisy had found some vegetable to boil that no one
> else knew about.

A lesser writer might have gone to great lengths to describe this completely indistinguishable odor, or might have finally resorted to letting the narrator conclude that he doesn't know *what* the heck it smelled like. But you have no intention of being a lesser writer, so learn a valuable lesson here from this author: When you've got a particular thing to do, be clever. Turn a phrase. Invent a word. Give the guy in Sheboygan what he's not expecting. Remember those bellied light wires in Cormac McCarthy's novel? Your only limit is your own imagination. Your readers have been seeing things from their vantage points all their lives; let them have a taste of yours.

As with the sense of sight, the description of what things smell like can help you establish the setting in your fiction. Look at how Patrick Suskind in his novel *Perfume* captures the city of Paris in the eighteenth century by focusing specifically on what it smelled like:

> In the narrow side streets off the rue Saint-Denis and the rue Saint-Martin, people
> lived so densely packed, each house so tightly pressed to the next, five, six
> stories high, that you could not see the sky, and the air at ground level formed
> damp canals where odors congealed. It was a mixture of human and animal
> smells, of water and stone and ashes and leather, of soap and fresh-baked bread
> and eggs boiled in vinegar, of noodles and smoothly polished brass, of sage and
> ale and tears, of grease and soggy straw and dry straw. Thousands upon thou-
> sands of odors formed an invisible gruel that filled the street ravines, only seldom
> evaporating above the rooftops and never from the ground below.

Notice that the author uses the word odors, but not aroma. These are words that are at different ends of the olfactory spectrum. Aroma is positive, indicating a scent that is pleasing, and odor is negative, pinpointing something that stinks. Though there are some pleasing smells in his "invisible gruel"—like fresh-baked bread—they are mixed in with significantly more displeasing ones, so the overall balance is tipped decidedly toward *odors*.

This catalog of odors should take the reader directly to the grimy streets of Paris of two centuries ago, where Suskind's tale takes place. But remember, *Perfume* can be considered a literary novel, so the author has the luxury of heaping detail on detail to paint his picture. In popular or commercial fiction, we might need to cut to the chase here and winnow all of this down to a couple of well-crafted sentences that show that Paris contained an abundance of scents.

Let's say you have two of your characters taking a walk on a nice spring day. On the soft breeze they can detect several things at once: the fragrance of wild onions from a field beside them, the odors from a factory not far away, and the pleasing scent of a bakery in town. Now, you have two choices here. You can build your details slowly, layering them like bricks in a wall—like Suskind does in *Perfume*—or you can come up with a nice sentence or two that will do the job more succinctly.

If you choose the more meticulous approach, you can move the tangy presence of those onions across the landscape toward the walkers; you can have multicolored smoke belching out of the smokestacks of the factory (tapping home a bit of environmental criticism into the bargain). And you can have a field day with the enticing fragrances emanating from that bakery.

But if you are aiming toward an audience that reads popular fiction, then you might make do with something like this:

> Zach and Noah stopped for a moment and took in the fine day. The sweet, yeasty aroma from Mulligan's Bakery blended with the harder presence of the tire factory. Something sweet and pungent on the gentle breeze told them that old Wilson's big field was teeming with wild onions.

And that's not just making do at all. It's a perfectly fine way to describe that setting, that moment. Your shorter approach can't *just* be shorter. It has to paint a picture in your reader's mind, just like the longer, more detailed one. So what you have to do here is select the very strongest images, the best ones.

Touch

The sensation of what something *feels* like is used in fiction to describe everything from sensual pleasure to pain and torture. It's a wide range, and your readers have actually experienced only some of those feelings. So your job is to either make them recall exactly what it feels like when something occurs in your story or, if they haven't experienced it, what it *would* feel like if they did.

Let's start with the pain and torture, and get them out of the way. We'll save the sensual things for later, sort of like delayed gratification.

One of the very best portrayers of physical pain is Dick Francis, the retired jockey turned suspense novelist, who must have taken more than a few tumbles from his mount to glean such eye-squinting detail. Here he places his narrator in a particularly unpleasant situation in *Longshot*:

> I put both palms flat on the decaying undergrowth and tried to heave myself up unto my knees.
>
> Practically fainted. Not only could I not do it, but the effort was so excruciating that I opened my mouth to scream and couldn't breathe enough for that either. My weight settled back on the earth and I felt nothing but staggering agony and couldn't think connectedly until it abated.
>
> Something was odd, I thought finally. It wasn't only that I couldn't lift myself off the ground but that I was stuck to it in some way.
>
> Cautiously, sweating, with fiery stabs in every inch, I wormed my right hand between my body and the earth, and came to what seemed like a rod between the two.

As it turns out, this fellow has been shot by an arrow. Now, I've never been shot by an arrow, but I can imagine how painful it must be. And part of the reason for that is Dick Francis's description. Look at some of his wordsmithing here: *practically fainted, excruciating, couldn't breathe, staggering agony, sweating, fiery stabs.* All of which leaves little doubt that this experience is downright painful.

Description of pain in your story or novel might call for such elaboration, but sometimes you can drive the image home with a single sentence, as Chuck Palahniuk does in *Invisible Monsters*:

> "A headache, I get the kind of headache God would smote you with in the Old Testament."

Now *that's* a headache. The severity of which is confirmed by the verb *smote* and the reference to the Old Testament. I think you will agree it is light years better than "I have a bad headache."

When you describe pain in your fiction, remember that the level of the pain (for your character) should correlate with the level of your description of it. A headache, even an Old Testament one, should usually be mentioned and then you should move on. If the headache gets progressively worse, and impacts your character's actions and your story, then you'll want to describe *how* it is getting worse. Maybe throbbing becomes pounding.

You want to give your readers an accurate depiction of what the character is going through, but you don't want to lose them—the readers, not the character (maybe both)—in the process. Graphic breaking of bones and twisting of sinews is usually not a great idea. Give a good sense that something bad and painful is happening, but don't overdo it. Look again at one of the phrases that Dick Francis uses: *staggering agony*. He could have gone into much greater detail here. I, for one, am thankful that he didn't. I don't know about you, but when a writer tells me that a character is in staggering agony, I'm prepared to believe him.

Remember this: When it's time to inflict a bit of pain and suffering in your fiction, put more emphasis on your character's reaction to it than on the actual description of it. In the Francis piece, what this guy is going to do about his situation is the important thing, both to his survival and to the story.

When using the sense of touch, you won't always be describing what a character feels. Sometimes you'll be nudging your readers toward what you want *them* to feel when they read your fiction, so they can associate a feeling that they might never have experienced with one that they probably have.

Here's an example of how something as simple as rubbing dried flowers between fingers can be used metaphorically for something as lofty as the reshaping of politics and governments. It's from *The Poisonwood Bible* by Barbara Kingsolver:

> Languidly they bring their map to order. Who will be the kings, the rooks, and bishops rising up to strike at a distance? Which sacrificed pawns will be swept aside? African names roll apart like the heads of dried flowers crushed idly between thumb and forefinger—Ngoma, Mukenga, Mulele, Kasavubu, Lumumba. They crumble to dust on the carpet.

The overwhelming odds are that your reader has never restructured governments, but it's a safer bet he has rolled the heads of dried flowers into dust. So here is a small action, which he has experienced, being used to describe a much larger one, which he hasn't.

As with the other senses, let touch sometimes serve more of a function in your writing than to just convey what things feel like. When I was writing my novel *A Place Apart* I needed to reemphasize the emerging relationship between the narrator and a girl. So in the midst of a description of Paris, I slipped in a bit about her fingers moving like ivy might grow. That way, the intimate touching of fingers to the back of his hand, which is a small thing by any standards, calls attention to the bigger story, which is their budding romance:

> She would tell me about Paris. About the Boulevard Saint Michel that she loved the best, and its sidewalk cafes. And how the tall, curved buttresses of Notre

> Dame rose up over a steep wall just across the Seine from the Shakespeare and
> Company Bookshop. Ivy spills out over the wall, she said, and wanders down to
> the river. And her long fingers would make little journeys along the back of my
> hand, as ivy might grow.

This device, using something seemingly small to enlarge or call attention to the bigger story, will serve you well time after time. Be on the lookout in your manuscripts for places where you can work in bits of sensory detail that will help establish the setting and the tone. In this paragraph, the girl's description of the ivy is sufficient to let the reader know that there is, indeed, ivy there. But the reinforcement of her fingers moving—like ivy might grow—not only calls more attention to it but points the reader in the direction of the more important part of the story: the romance.

Taste

Not long ago, a writer for the *Houston Chronicle* named Jessica Danes did an article about tea. She included a few of its medicinal values, brief allusions to its place in—and sometimes alteration of—history (remember the Boston Tea Party), and, since it ran in the food section, several of its various types that her readers might like to try.

She could have started it out like a term paper:

> The world of tea is wide and varied.

Or she could have kicked it up a notch (to use a phrase not uncommon in food lingo these days) and come up with something like this:

> One of the world's oldest foods is also one of the most interesting.

Which is certainly better than that first offering of drab reportage, but not nearly so fine as what she *did* write:

> It tastes like the earth. Pungent and loamy and more real than anything you've
> tasted in a while.
>
> A sip and the daydreaming starts—of high-peaked mountains and the tender
> plants the prized leaves were plucked from.
>
> Tea can do that to you.

When I thumbed through my morning paper, I hadn't been looking for a piece on tea, which was just about the furthest thing from my mind. In fact, I hadn't intended to read anything in the food section at all. First the illustration that accompanied the article caught my attention. Then that first sentence hooked me and reeled me in. I read every word, learned a few things, and enjoyed it immensely. To paraphrase the author: *Wordsmithing* can do that to you.

Now let's consider the bait that she used to attract me: "It tastes like the earth." It accomplishes two important things very quickly. First, it evokes the sense of taste, which is perhaps the most reliable of all the senses. The others can sometimes be deceptive, but what something *tastes* like is usually quite simply the pure essence of the thing. Second, this sentence does exactly what a first sentence *must* do in order to be effective: It makes the reader read the second one. Sensory description is one of the best ways to do just that. In this case, I wanted to know *what* tastes like the earth.

The word *taste* has evolved into a universal barometer of our personal likes and dislikes. "I have no taste for country music," someone might say, or "Her tastes run to the abstract." And society has long labeled certain types of people by using the sense of taste. A bland, boring person is a milquetoast; a feisty girl is a hot tamale.

Don't overlook this sense to describe things and people in your fiction, and not just in telling what something tastes *like*; you'll run out of steam pretty quickly if that's all you're after. "It tastes like chicken" only works once, and not very well then.

Use it to help develop a character, as Gore Vidal does in this scene from his novel *Washington, D.C.* set during World War II. Here is a soldier who is much more interested in the food being served at a tea than with anything else, including the war. He's especially infatuated with anything made with butter, which is rationed and very scarce. Notice how Vidal keeps the character's attention on the food, thereby keeping *our* focus on his priority, which becomes important in the story:

> Life was good. He asked for tea, devoured a chicken sandwich, and said that he had not seen much of Enid lately. "They keep me pretty busy down at the Pentagon," he invented. The chicken sandwich needed salt, which meant the butter was fresh. He tried a hot rolled cheese sandwich: superb. Butter had been used to glaze the toast; cayenne gave definition.

And later, after some more offerings (probably butter-free) that don't impress him, this:

> But the main course was splendid: breast of chicken folded to make a cutlet. As his fork speared the browned surface, hot butter spurted from the interior.

This gradual playing out of little details, in the form of what the food tastes like to the character, moves the reader closer and closer to seeing who this guy is and what is really important to him. It's subtle.

Remember what I said a few pages back about being loud and being quiet? That goes for taste, also. There will be times when you want to quietly work in how something tastes—like this fellow's appreciation of butter. Not calling great attention to it, but letting it slowly help to define the character.

Then there will be times when you will want to be loud. When you'll need to not equivocate, but tell your readers straightforwardly what you want them to know. In *The Agony and the Ecstasy*, Irving Stone uses the sense of taste to show us the nature of a character:

> Bertoldo loved only two things as well as sculpture: laughter and cooking. His humor had in it more spice than his chicken *ala cacciattra*.

No beating around the bush there; this guy has a boisterous sense of humor. Period. Remember the balance of showing and telling you've got to maintain; the Vidal example works best as showing, the Stone as telling.

Just as you can let how something tastes help to establish your characters, let it do the same thing for your settings. If you have a story set in New Orleans, try something like this:

> She could taste the sugar-sprinkled beignets from the Café DuMonde before the plane even touched down on the runway.

The reader of that sentence may never have been to New Orleans, and may never have eaten a beignet. But if this lady is imagining eating one before she even gets there, than the reader must know that they taste good. The idea of New Orleans being a good place to be—at least for this character in this story—gets a toehold into the readers' perception before the tale even gets underway.

Sometimes in your fiction showing what something *doesn't* taste like is effective. In *Girl With a Pearl Earring*, Tracy Chevalier's novel, the central character is considering the food in one household as opposed to that in another:

> When we ate dinner I tried to compare it with that in the house at Papist's Corner, but already I had become accustomed to meat and good rye bread. Although my mother was a better cook than Tanneke, the brown bread was dry, the vegetable stew tasteless with no fat to flavor it.

Here, focusing on what things taste like—more specifically, on their *lack* of taste—serves to empower the much larger story that is running its course in two very dissimilar houses. The families that live in those houses differ in many ways, in religion, politics, and affluence, to name just a few. And those differences are at the heart of the novel. So the author uses a variety of ways to call attention to the disparities.

You can use taste in your fiction just as effectively as these authors have. Remember to let it do more than what it usually does, which is to report what something tastes *like*. Let a character's preference for one taste or another make him clearer in your reader's mind. Let the particular taste of something represent a place (like lobsters in Maine or barbecue in Texas or apples in Washington) or a time (like roasted chestnuts in Victorian England or honey-mead in the middle ages) or a character's mood (like the taste of bile when he thinks of his mother-in-law).

Hearing

Those of us old enough to remember the *Gomer Pyle* program on television recall that Gomer's drill sergeant used to get in his face and bellow out "I can't *hear* you!"

You don't want your reader having that same reaction to your fiction.

The reader needs to hear not only your characters speaking to each other, but countless other things as well. Like the cacophony of sounds that usually infuses a setting. Like the absence of sound on occasion. Or like something that only one character hears, like Edgar Allan Poe's murderer in "The Tell-Tale Heart."

Let the sounds that surround you all the time work their way into your stories and novels. Your readers hear them, too, every waking moment of their lives. And they will feel more comfortable in your settings if the hustle and bustle (and sometimes the quietness) of life are there with them.

Listen to this short scene from *Guns of the Timberlands* by Louis L'Amour.

> A clatter of running hoofs sounded on the loose planks of the bridge at the far end of town, then the rattle of a buckboard. It rounded into the street and a couple of fine blacks brought it down toward the riders at a spanking trot.

There's a lot going on here, and the author uses sound as his primary tool to convey it. Remember, one of the best ways to get your readers into a scene is to let them hear everything that's going on. Not all of these noises are important to the story, but they do help to establish the setting quickly, and not in such elaborate detail that the story has to slow down for it. Look for places in your fiction where you can do this; where you can use a short burst of several sounds—or smells or tastes or feelings—that will more clearly define the setting.

When applying the clutter rule about anything not serving to move the story along having to go, you might be inclined to delete good passages like Louis L'Amour's. But remember, even though the loose planks of that bridge and that rattling buckboard might not be greatly significant in the story, they do serve the essential function of bringing the reader more fully in. So they pass the test, and need to stay.

Onomatopoeia is an excellent way to let the reader hear things. In that last example, L'Amour works plenty of effective auditory details in, and then makes them even stronger with words like *clatter*, *rattle*, and *spanking*.

In most cases, as in the last one, you will show what things sound like, but sometimes it will be even more effective to emphasize the absence of sound. Sometimes you'll want to focus attention on something more important than the sound, as Robert Frost does in his classic poem "Stopping by Woods":

The only other sound's the sweep of easy wind and downy flake.

Frost hits upon one of the great ironies of nature and weather here: While most meteorological events—like storms and rain and wind—are noisy, snow falling is usually the opposite. It is quiet. Thus the adjectives *easy* and *downy* and the noun *sweep*, rather than *swoosh* or *boom*.

Sometimes things in your fiction will sound like almost nothing, like the easy wind and downy flake in Frost's poem. But usually they will sound like *something*, like being met by a fast-moving automobile in Robert Penn Warren's *All the King's Men*:

But if you wake up in time and don't hook your wheel off the slab, you'll go whipping on into the dazzle and now and then a car will come at you steady out of the dazzle and will pass you with a snatching sound like God-a-Mighty has ripped a tin roof loose with his bare hands.

Whenever I read that description—about the tin roof and the bare hands of God—I always think: Now that's *exactly* what being met by a speeding car sounds like. And that's the sort of reaction that you want your reader to have to your descriptions. The way to pull it off is to listen more intently than you probably have before. To anything and everything, but especially to specific sounds and noises that you know will play a part in your story or novel. Then take it a step further: When you pinpoint a sound—like seagulls squawking at each other on the beach—think of what all of that racket sounds like. Good writers spend much of their time thinking in metaphors. Those seagulls might remind you of a congregation of angry stockholders or of electricity zipping through wires or of Chatty Cathy dolls running amok. One or more of your metaphors regarding the seagulls will more than likely find their way into your writing, making the noise come more fully alive on your pages.

Whenever possible, go to a place that is similar to a setting you are using and listen. Just *listen*. Then write down what you heard in your writer's journal. You might be surprised by what you hear, and what you don't hear. Make sure you really know what an airport terminal sounds like before you describe one. Or a busy restaurant. Or a country road. This exercise might help you avoid using clichés, too. You might just discover that a beauty shop doesn't "sound like a hen yard" at all. But it has a dozen or more other sounds, most of which you probably never paid attention to before.

In your writing, perhaps even in your titles, you might call the reader's attention to what things *don't* sound like, to vast panoramas that are silent (like *Snow Falling on Cedars*) or to people or things that are quiet when they shouldn't be (like *The Silence of the Lambs*). Sometimes the absence of something is the most effective description of all. Let's have a word now from Flannery O'Connor, who we have neglected for too many pages. She defended creating her particularly unsavory characters by maintaining that often the best way to show God's grace was to convey the total lack of it. That opposite approach works with sensory details as well.

On now to something that most of us spend a lot of our time listening to: music. Don't overlook showing the effects of hearing certain songs or tunes on your characters. They might mean entirely different things to different people. Take "As Time Goes By," the song in the movie *Casablanca*. The Ingrid Bergman character wants Sam, the piano player, to play it again because hearing it takes her back to happier times. Rick, the character played by Humphrey Bogart, forbids him to play it because it reminds him of his lost love.

One excellent way to help describe your characters is to let the reader know what kind of music they listen to, maybe even what their favorite songs are. The lyrics in many songs, especially ballads, are little stories in themselves. Why not let one or two of them serve to empower your own story, or characters?

Look at how a melody serves to define a particular character in James Baldwin's story "Sonny's Blues":

> One boy was whistling a tune, at once very complicated and very simple, it seemed to be pouring out of him as though he were a bird, and it sounded very cool and moving through all that harsh, bright air, only just holding its own through all those other sounds.

The author uses this tune to help establish his character *and* his setting. It is both complicated and simple, most likely like the boy himself. And it comes out of him into the brightness and other noises of the surroundings.

Use sound—or one of the other senses—occasionally to make your reader curious. Remember, you've got to keep your story moving all the time. If it starts to sputter or stall out, then your reader might just put you aside and find something better to do. So keep him guessing. Consider how Wallace Stegner begins with a mysterious melody and uses it to solidify his setting in his novel *Crossing to Safety*:

> Then what was I hearing? Holding my breath, I listened. *Tick-tick-ticket-tick-tickety-tick-tick,* not one clock but many, unsynchronized. I brought my watch to my ear: inaudible an inch away. But the faint, hurrying, ratchety, dry ticking went on.
>
> Folding back the covers, I went to the French doors, opened one, and stepped out onto the roof terrace. The night was lighter than the room, and the ticking was much louder, hastier, its rhythms more broken—such a sound as several children might make running sticks at different speeds along a picket fence a block away. I went to the balustrade and looked down into the street, and *ecco*, there it came, a bobbing line of lanterns that curved off the Vittoria Bridge and came on up the Lugarno toward the city. Every lantern swung from a two-wheeled cart, and beside every cart walked a man, and drawing every cart was a donkey whose hasty feet ticked on the pavement.

Stegner could have just told us what the source of all that ticking was, as he finally does near the end of the passage. But making us wonder about it—maybe even speculate about it—anchors us more firmly in the time and the place, keeps the story moving along, and hopefully keeps the reader reading.

The Sixth Sense

I'm not talking about seeing dead people here, at least not exclusively. Sometimes sensory description comes down to something more than the five senses can convey. Something not concrete at all. You've had intuitive feelings in your life about something being wrong, or right, and you haven't had a single tangible or logical fact on which to base that feeling. So your characters will have those feelings, too.

This sixth sense becomes important in fiction quite often, especially so in mysteries, like Patricia Moyes's Scotland Yard detective Henry Tippett, who is famous for his "nose," which is another name for his intuition. That intuition will need to come into play whenever one of your characters suspects something or someone, and that will happen in all types of fiction, not just who-done-its. So let's look at a couple of examples.

John D. MacDonald relates his central character Travis McGee's feeling about a house he steps into for the very first time in *The Deep Blue Good-By*:

> It was one of those Florida houses I find unsympathetic, all black tile, glass, terrazzo, aluminum. They have a surgical coldness. Each one seems to be merely some complex corridor arrangement, a going-through place, an entrance built to some place of a better warmth and privacy that never was constructed. When you pause in these rooms, you have the feeling you are waiting. You feel that a door will open and you will be summoned, and horrid things will happen to you before they let you go. You cannot mark these houses with any homely flavor of living. When they are emptied after occupancy, they have the look of places where the blood has recently been washed away.

The message that McGee gets from this house is not anything that he can see or hear or touch or smell. It's something he *senses*.

The same is true for this morsel from Mary Higgins Clark's novel *Stillwatch*:

> The place seemed peaceful enough. Christmas trees and Hanukkah candles stood on card tables covered with felt and make-believe snow. All the doors of the patients' rooms had greeting cards taped to them. Christmas music was playing on the stereo in the recreation room. But something was wrong.

The something that was wrong was the thing that can't be depicted through the use of any of the other senses. It is intuition; it is something akin to magic, or prophesy. It is what causes that little "pricking of my thumbs" by which we know—according to Shakespeare—that "something wicked this way comes."

The use of this sixth sense can like everything else be overdone. A character who bases everything on what she *feels*, and nothing on what she gleans from the other senses, will lose credibility quickly. Use intuition when you need to focus attention on a particular detail that will make the reader wonder what's going on, like the unfriendly house and the nursing home where something was wrong. These premonitions come about rarely in real life, so use them rarely in your fiction.

SUMMARY: LOOKING BACK AT SENSORY DETAIL

Showing your reader what things look, sound, smell, feel, and taste like represents some of your most crucial tasks as a writer. And the essential word here is *showing*, because it will almost always be a more effective way to convey one or more of the senses than telling.

When using sensory description, recall the points covered in this chapter. Determine early on which audience you are primarily aiming for: readers of literary or popular fiction. Use unexpected, unusual ways to convey images to your reader, like Cormac McCarthy's "bellied" light wires. Don't rely too heavily on only showing what things *look* like; make sure you use the other senses, too. Employ the smallest, most intricate details as often as you use the glaring ones, like the almost imperceptible difference between two shades of the same color. Sometimes, emphasize the total absence of one of the senses, like sound. Quiet places are often louder in terms of mood and tone than noisy places. Perhaps most important, use sensory description to do much more in your fiction than to simply report what things look and sound and feel and smell and taste like. Let them help build your settings, characters, and situations.

In closing, let me try to reinforce just how important the five senses are to good writing by offering this anecdote that recently happened in my classroom.

A student was having her assignment—a story set in San Francisco—critiqued by the other members in her class. I required, for this piece, that the author/narrator situate herself in one place and show us what is going on in her field of vision. This student had chosen for her specific setting a tour boat making its way under the Golden Gate Bridge. So she had a lot of real estate from which to choose: the Presidio, the bay, the hills and buildings of the city proper, the mammoth bridge rising above her, even Alcatraz off in the distance.

We always start with positive comments in our peer critique sessions, so several students mentioned her good descriptions of some of those places. Others pointed out how nicely she worked in a few details about history and local customs. Somebody said her dialogue was right on target. Somebody else said that those seals swimming beside the boat must have been cute.

Then the group fell silent, until the author herself identified the problem. "It's missing something," she said. "Isn't it?"

Another student got to the root of the dilemma. He said that he could see everything clearly enough, but that he couldn't smell or taste or touch or hear anything at all.

He was right.

This very good writer had loaded all of her sensory description into only one of her five options. She conveyed only what things *looked* like. And someone standing in a boat in San Francisco Bay is privy to a much wider array of sensations: the rocking of the boat itself, the barking of those seals, the squawking of seagulls, the smell and taste and feel of a salty mist, the tolling of bells throughout the city, to name just a few.

Once she did her revisions, she turned in a story that was abundantly rich in details. One that plopped her readers right down in that boat under that bridge. Where they could—via her wordsmithing—experience everything with her.

EXERCISE 1

Make yourself a chart or a spreadsheet. Create six columns (up and down) and ten rows (across).

Label the columns *Sight, Smell, Taste, Hearing, Touch, Intuition*.

Label the rows:

- an approaching cold front
- pizza
- the seashore
- the mountains
- lunch in a cafeteria
- a city street
- a country road
- a mall
- the interior of an airliner
- your kitchen

Now, come up with at least one thing or action or feeling that can be described with the sensory description in each column. Feel free to repeat yourself; you might very well use *leaf* for sound and sight and touch. But don't hinder yourself by focusing too tightly. Though pizza might not actually make a sound, the pizza box being opened does. Fill in every space on your chart.

EXERCISE 2

Make another chart just like that one, with the same labels on the columns and rows. This time replace the things and actions and feelings with words or phrases that show how the sense of each one might be conveyed. For example, for that leaf, you might put *rough* or *raised veins* under "Touch," or *spiraling down* (maybe *helicoptering down*; remember it's okay to use uncommon images) for "Sight," or *wispy* or *swoosh* (practice using onomatopoeia) for "Sound."

The little boxes on your chart might not be big enough for all the wordsmithing you will come up with. Good! Spill over into your writer's journal.

EXERCISE 3

Choose one of the ten topics and, using the images you came up with and all the tools in your kit, write a page or so in which you take your reader to that place, making them see, hear, touch, taste, and smell what is there, even sensing something that is *not* there (extra sensory perception). Here's a rule: Try not to use the actual words *see*, *hear*, *touch*, *taste*, or *smell* (or any variations of them). In other words (quite literally), no *looks like . . .*, *smells like . . .*, and such reporting.

Show, don't tell.

EXERCISE 4

Using one of your manuscripts and a pencil, circle places that would benefit from more description of what things feel, taste, smell, sound, and look like. I'll bet you've packed most of your description into what things or people or places *look* like. So pay close attention to how you might use one or more of the other senses to provide clearer description.

chapter 6

[DESCRIPTION OF CHARACTERS]

The characters who become the inhabitants of your fiction are the actors that will take to the stage in your reader's mind. They are the channels for the fine dialogue you'll write and the players in your conflicts and resolutions. You'll have to conjure up all manner of folks to get the job done, and one of the very first decisions you'll need to make when a story is forming is how you'll go about describing these characters, especially central characters.

Let's say your protagonist, a woman of thirty or so, arrives at a party in your first scene. She might gravitate toward the safe harbor of a corner, losing herself there in the dull pattern of the wallpaper. Or she might stride purposefully in and guffaw loudly, planting her feet wide: a force to be reckoned with. More than likely, her conduct will fall somewhere between these two extremes, but however she behaves will call for skillful description. The protagonist carries a significant share of the workload in the whole process of storytelling, and your readers' first impression of her is crucial.

That skillful description can't stop with the first scene; neither is it restricted to major characters. Most of your characters—perhaps even down to the boy who delivers a telegram and is never seen again—will need to be sufficiently described so that your reader can get a good picture of them. I've never *physically* seen John D. MacDonald's protagonist Travis McGee, other than the various actors who have played him in movies, but based solely on MacDonald's descriptions of him in his many novels—the way he walks and stands; his gangly, suntanned structure; his haircut and choice of clothing— I believe I could pick him out of a police lineup.

Your goal should be for your descriptions to work that well for your readers, too.

BREATHING LIFE INTO YOUR CHARACTERS

Here are three examples of character description from three fine writers. You will notice that they'll get longer as we progress. But you'll hopefully notice something else, too: Each takes a unique approach to the task.

We'll begin with a few sentences from "A Tree. A Rock. A Cloud." by Carson McCullers:

> The boy went toward him. He was an undersized boy of about twelve, with one shoulder drawn higher than the other because of the weight of the paper sack. His face was shallow, freckled, and his eyes were round child eyes.

McCullers gives only physical description and leaves this boy's attitude, motivation, and worldview until later in the story.

Now look at these sentences from the beginning of William E. Barrett's *Lilies of the Field*:

> His name was Homer Smith. He was twenty-four. He stood six foot two and his skin was a deep, warm black. He had large, strong features and widely spaced eyes. A sculptor would have interpreted the features in terms of character, but Homer Smith's mother had once said of him that he was two parts amiable and one part plain devil.

Here, the author uses short, to-the-point sentences to give us a few physical traits, then dovetails the image of this man in with something his mother said about him. In a mere sixty-one words, we not only know what Homer looks like; we have our first good peek into who he *is*.

Now, let's have a little something from Flannery O'Connor, but none of her philosophy about writing this time, rather a taste of her fiction itself. Here are the first few sentences from her story "Good Country People":

> Besides the neutral expression that she wore when she was alone, Mrs. Freeman had two others, forward and reverse, that she used for all of her human dealings. Her forward expression was steady and driving like the advance of a heavy truck. Her eyes never swerved to left or right but turned as the story turned as if they followed a yellow line down the center of it. She seldom used the other expression because it was not often necessary for her to retract a statement . . .

O'Connor employs an extended analogy to describe Mrs. Freeman's various expressions, floating us along on a William Faulknerish current of details. At the end of it, we know as much about this woman's obstinacy as her appearance. In your writing, you'll want to do the same thing: convey as much about personality as looks. Don't limit your descriptions to their most utilitarian function: giving the essential facts regarding what somebody looks or sounds like. Work attitude and philosophy and vulnerability and tons of other things in also. Kill a multitude of birds with one smooth stone.

The extent to which you'll describe your characters will depend on what you will have them doing at any given time in your tale, but whatever the situation, and whatever the level of description, you will do well to remember this: Your reader needs to see the people in your fiction as clearly as you do. So two things are essential at the outset: a complete and detailed image of your cast of characters in your mind and an adept conveyance of them to your reader.

Let's look at several ways for you to bring that second part about.

PHYSICAL DESCRIPTION OF CHARACTERS

Providing an image of what your characters look like can come in very short doses—like saying that someone had butter-colored hair—to much longer ones, like this one by William Faulkner (who couldn't write small doses of *anything*) in "A Rose for Emily":

> They rose when she entered—a small, fat woman in black, with a thin gold chain descending to her waist and vanishing into her belt, leaning on an ebony cane with a tarnished gold head. Her skeleton was small and spare; perhaps that was why what would have been merely plumpness in another was obesity in her. She looked bloated, like a body long submerged in motionless water, and of that pallid hue. Her eyes, lost in the fatty ridges of her face, looked like two small pieces of coal pressed into a lump of dough as they moved from one face to another while the visitors stated their errand.

The essence of the physical description here is that this lady is short, overweight, dressed in black, carrying a cane, and her eyes are quite small in her plump face. Remember what I said earlier about the difference between literary and popular fiction; well, saying that Faulkner wrote literary fiction is like saying the *Titanic* was a big ship. He carefully works in detail after detail, like a painter using small strokes with a fine-tipped brush. In a story aimed at readers of popular fiction, you would need to stay a bit closer to what exactly you need the reader to know about this woman. If you need them to know *all* of this—the plumpness versus obesity, the image of a body long submerged in water, the simile with the pieces of coal—then all of it should go in. Just remember that readers of popular fiction aren't as tolerant of long descriptions as readers of literary fiction.

Keep in mind what I said a few pages ago about letting your descriptions carry more of the load than just describing. Here's a good example from David Westheimer, from his novel *Von Ryan's Express*:

> The colonel was tall and conspicuously erect. His dark blond hair was short and bristling, with a scatter of gray at the temples. His face was deeply tanned except for two ovals around the unblinking gray eyes where his skin had been shielded by sunglasses. His eyes were finely wrinkled at the corners and squinted a little from looking into the sun for enemy fighters. His was a tough face, grim almost, with no vestige of softness of any kind. It was, from a distance, a young face, but viewed closely was older than its thirty-six years.

In addition to some detailed description regarding what this man looks like— tall; erect; the color, length, and texture of his hair; the bit about his eyes— we also learn how old he is and get some foreshadowing as to his philosophy: that he's a tough customer rather than a soft one. And that toughness will come into play quite prominently in the story.

One way to go about this multiplicity of purpose in your own story or novel is to list everything that you can think of regarding a particular character in your writer's journal. Get it all down—height, weight, coloring, beliefs, faults, strengths, the way he sits in a chair—anything and everything you can come up with. Don't just put down things that you're pretty sure will end up in your story; your knowledge of this guy will have to be broader than that in order for him to work in your fiction. If he ends up being left in charge of a child in one of your scenes, it's essential for you to know how dependable he is, whether it is important for your reader to know it or not. Good writers know the motivations of each and every character they write: what drives them and what stops them cold. And the only way for you to know a character that well is to immerse yourself in his or her persona. So make the list; you'll be surprised how complex your creations end up being.

Anne Lamott provides a good example, in her novel *Crooked Little Heart*, of something we talked about in chapter four. Sometimes it is quite effective to simply *tell* what somebody looks like or acts like quickly, and get on with it:

> Elizabeth studied James, his wild fluffy hair, his beautiful green eyes, and he looked at her and smiled. She loved being with him; it was that simple. She felt happy when he was around.

The author could have dragged this out, giving us more details about James' appearance, elaborating on how much he meant to Elizabeth and just *how* he made her happy. But she chose to make these things a *given* in the story, since they are obviously a given in Elizabeth's life.

In your own fiction, don't be guided by how much description you can come up with—let's face it: you're a writer, and you can come up with *tons* of it—but by how much something or someone in your story *needs* to be described. Many times, brevity will win out over elaboration, as it clearly does in the Lamott example.

Kent Haruf in his novel *Plainsong* needs to describe two old bachelor brothers who live together and are receiving company in their farmhouse:

> Harold had removed the greasy pieces of machinery from one of the extra chairs and had dragged it up to the table. He sat down solidly. When they were inside the house the McPherson brothers' faces turned shiny and red as beets and the tops of their heads steamed in the cool room. They looked like something out of an old painting, of peasants, laborers resting after work.

The image itself—of the pair of old men who are so unfamiliar with having guests that they must displace farm machinery in the kitchen to make room for them, and so out of their natural element when indoors that they physically change—surpasses simple description; it tells much of the story. Then the author drives the image even further home with the old painting simile.

Load your own description up with tidbits like these—actions and references that help build your overall story. If your character is a teenaged girl on the way to the prom with a boy, but she continuously looks down into her purse at the screen of her cell phone, then your reader will assume that her interest is elsewhere. And a small action will point your readers in the direction that you want them to go.

CHARACTERS BASED ON REAL PEOPLE

Let's spend a little time now on how to describe characters based on real people: those that are based on historical figures or famous people and those that are based on more common folk that you actually know or have known. What the two have in common is that they are each patterned after actual people who drew breath and walked around and lived (or live) their lives outside of just your imagination.

We'll start with people that you know. You can vent here, you understand.

Putting a real person that you can't stand in your fiction, with all their warts and foibles in tact, can be downright therapeutic. But tread cautiously. That old "any similarity to any persons living or dead is purely coincidental" might not prove to be as magically cleansing as most folks think. And if the so-and-so you've woven into your tale is too easily recognizable and still falls into the "living" category, he might cause you some grief. That's not to say that you can't just sort of *slip* him in, or parts of him—the worst parts I suspect.

The other danger of putting in people that you know is to give in to the desire to honor them by making them recognizable in your fiction. This is almost always a mistake, since your characters should be exactly who you need them to be. More precisely, they must be who your *story* needs them to be. Allowing your decisions regarding characters to be dictated by a grocery list of friends that want to be included will dilute this essential process and weaken your writing. People who don't write fiction don't always understand the precision of the craft. Think back on how many times someone has said to you—regarding something cute their child did or something funny someone said—you'll have to put Aunt Mary in one of your stories. What they don't understand is that good writers don't just put things in; they put things in that *fit*. Give your Aunt Mary a free copy of your book, or even dedicate it to her, but leave her out of its pages.

Now, on to real people who are a bit more famous and recognizable than your Aunt Mary. Let's start with the sublime and then move on to someone significantly less than that.

All we know about what Saint Paul looked like comes from two millennia of tradition; there's no good description of him in the Bible and precious little recorded about him by the few historians writing at the time. The two characteristics that wandered down the ages are that he had red hair and that he was not particularly attractive. Taylor Caldwell wrote an entire novel, *Great Lion of God*, about him, and her Paul was redheaded and ugly. Walter F. Murphy in *Upon This Rock* gives a description of Saint Paul before he was a saint—even in fact before he was Paul. He was Saul of Tarsus, before he had that jolting encounter on the road to Damascus. Here's how Murphy paints him in his novel:

> . . . Saul was homely. His face looked like its parts had been thrown together at random. None of his features was ugly, but they did not fit together. His ears were as jug-handled as those of a Celtic legionnaire and protruded at right angles from his head. His hair was a bright, brassy mop of tightly curled red, his complexion light olive instead of fair. His beard was thin and scraggly, more that of a

teenager than of a man almost thirty. It, too, was red, but several shades paler than his hair. If his Roman nose was too long for his face, his mouth was too wide. His teeth were irregular and there was a space between the upper two in front that sometimes forced a half-whistle to punctuate his sentences.

Rather than labeling him as ugly, Murphy goes into some detail regarding *why* he might be considered unattractive. He mentions the Roman nose, wide mouth, gapped teeth, and sparse beard in order to give readers a living, breathing human being—not the image of the ugly redhead they might have brought with them to the reading of the novel.

If you pluck a character out of history and plop him or her down in your fiction, you'll have to make sure you bring the era also. For instance, where Murphy says that Paul's ears were jug-handled, it wouldn't have worked at all to describe them as Bing Crosby ears, since Bing Crosby, though we think of him as a large-eared crooner from the recent past, was, where Paul was concerned, a resident of the distant future. So, while using an allusion regarding his ears will work for you in a story set anytime later than the 1930s, it won't work at all here in the first century.

Murphy and Caldwell could have made their Pauls handsome fellows with blond hair. With the scant historical material to work from nobody could have faulted them for that. But since many of their readers had a preconceived notion of what Paul *might* have looked like, they both chose to conform to the traditional image, each modifying it with their descriptions.

Writing more recent historical or famous people into your story or novel doesn't give you that choice. Let's say you have President Kennedy as one of your characters; then you'd better make him look and sound like President Kennedy, since everybody knows exactly what he looked and sounded like.

When Herman Wouk wrote *The Winds of War* he described many world leaders at the time of World War II, so he had much more data to draw from than Caldwell and Murphy did when they wrote about Saint Paul. There are libraries of biographies and many thousands of photographs of the movers and shakers from the mid-twentieth century, so Wouk had specific parameters in which to work when describing this fellow:

> Hitler was no taller than Henry himself; a small man with a prison haircut, leaning forward and bowing as he shook hands, his head to one side, hair falling on his forehead. This was Henry's flash impression, as he caught his first full-length look at the Fuhrer beside the burley much-medallioned Bulgarian, but in another moment it changed. Hitler had a remarkable smile. His down-curved mouth was

rigid and tense, his eyes sternly self-confident, but when he smiled this fanatic look vanished; the whole face brightened up, showing a strong hint of humor, and a curious, almost boyish, shyness. Sometimes he held a guest's hand and conversed. When he was particularly amused he laughed and made an odd sudden move with his right knee: he lifted it and jerked it a little inward.

Whether describing Saint Paul or Adolph Hitler (and a wider range of human beings would be difficult to come up with) or anyone in between, remember to abide by the clutter rule. Use only those traits and features and actions that serve to move your story along, and avoid teaching a history lesson about the person or their importance.

There's one more category of character that is based on a real person that we need to discuss: the one that you will write about on occasion that is based on *you*. Much is made in some writing books and in creative writing workshops of the importance of keeping yourself out of your fiction. And I agree, up to a point.

Ernest Hemingway will work nicely here as our textbook example. His protagonists were nearly always him, through and through. Hemingway must have been the sort of fellow that an old woman from my youth used to say wants to be the bridegroom at every wedding and the corpse at every funeral, in other words: the center of attention in every situation. And we're all like that, to varying degrees.

We usually write what we know. And what we know best is ourselves. My only advice here is the same I gave regarding using other real people: Use only descriptions that are called for in a particular story or novel. Even so, much of you will sneak in; you should expect it and accept it. After all, you will relate your tale in your voice, so other parts of you will follow along. If you bounce a tennis ball exactly six times before you serve it, then a character in your story might do that also. It's a nice little detail that shows this person is given to superstition or ritual or habit, and the guy in Sheboygan needn't know that you are too.

LETTING CHARACTERS DESCRIBE THEMSELVES

You've heard the old saw "if you want something done right, do it yourself." This can apply to your characters, too. You might want to consider having one or more of them take on the job of describing themselves for the reader. There are several ways to do it.

In *The Deep Blue Good-By* by John D. MacDonald, his narrator Travis McGee tells us about himself:

> I tried to look disarming. I am pretty good at that. I have one of those useful faces. Tanned American. Bright eyes and white teeth shining amid a brown reliable bony visage. The proper folk-hero crinkle at the corners of the eyes, and the bashful appealing smile, when needed.

Notice that MacDonald has his protagonist tell us as much about who he *is* as what he looks like. You might think that this little self-portrait can only be done in first-person narration, but it works just as nicely in third person, as in the following examples. Sometimes, letting your characters dabble in a bit of wishful thinking will be the best way to describe them. That way, the reader is actually getting the opposite of how they really appear. In her novel *Mrs. Dalloway*, Virginia Woolf has her title character consider how she would look if *she* had anything to do with it:

> She would have been, in the first place, dark like Lady Bexborough, with a skin of crumpled leather and beautiful eyes. She would have been, like Lady Bexborough, slow and stately; rather large; interested in politics like a man; with a country house; very dignified; very sincere. Instead of which she had a narrow pea-stick figure; a ridiculous little face, beaked like a bird's.

From that litany of what she wished she was—and then what she actually was—comes a clear picture of this woman.

In that example, a character considers herself and doesn't particularly like what she sees, in this one—from *The Seventh Secret*, a novel by Irving Wallace—another character takes a look at her likeness and is more impressed:

> Evelyn Hoffmann paused briefly to study her reflection in the window of the Café Wolf. What she saw did not displease her. At seventy-three, one could not expect to appear as one had at twenty-three. In the early days she had been a beauty, everyone had agreed. She had been taller than medium height, with ash blonde hair, slender, sophisticated, reserved, with pride in her long, shapely legs.

A passage like this could do a couple of things for you in your fiction. First, it could get the point across that this lady is still attractive, even at seventy-three, and, second, it would serve as a fine lead-in to a backstory where she was twenty-three.

Having characters take on the chore of describing themselves, either in first person or third, is often a better technique than letting another character or an omniscient narrator do it. It is more personal and allows you to work in details and imperfections that only the character might recognize. But use caution: If you don't make this a very natural part of the story—more than just a device used to describe somebody—then it will come off as contrived.

USING DIALOGUE TO DESCRIBE CHARACTERS

Your characters' dialogue should do more than simply report what they are saying to each other. The words and phrases they speak, and the way they deliver them, can be some of the strongest description in your fiction. Listen to these two sentences by Willa Cather from her novel *Death Comes for the Archbishop*:

"Clear off them cheers for the strangers. They won't eat ye, if they air priests."

You've been given not one smidgen of physical description of the speaker of these lines, yet I'll bet you already know a few things about him or her. First, the character is of the earthy variety, hence the use of exaggerated dialect like *cheers* for chairs, *ye* for you, and *air* for are. Second, he or she is addressing a person or persons who might have had little association with priests. Third, the character is hospitable. Fourth, he or she is in some position of esteem or importance, since in just this short declaration they give an instruction and then a reassurance. We know a heck of a lot about this character after merely fifteen words of dialogue.

Your character's words will carry that much weight, also. So choose them wisely, and don't hesitate to infuse them with clue after clue as to the nature and the appearance of the speaker. For example, let's say you have a customer in a general store say this: "My God, Millie, I've done knocked thangs off the shelf agin; why can't you leave enough room for a man to negotiate?" From that the reader will assume that the speaker is either (a) not used to being in stores, perhaps not used to being indoors at all, or (b) is a tad wide in the beam. And there are other traits as well: He likes to blame others, is impatient, perhaps just naturally clumsy, and he knows Millie very well.

When employing colloquial dialect like both Willa Cather's chair-clearing character and the bumbling-shopper use, don't go off the deep end, and write dialogue that readers can't follow. Any puzzles you construct should come in the form of mysteries or unresolved conflicts for readers to ponder, not in dialogue that they'll have difficulty deciphering. *Dodedo* shouldn't be used for door to door; *a nominal egg* shouldn't mean an arm and a leg. But *dawugg* might work as the way your Brooklyn character says dog. *Dawugg* is more easily and quickly translated than *dodedo* or *a nominal egg*, so it won't slow your reader down. To put this briefly: When reading your dialogue becomes a chore, you've gone overboard with dialect.

Be careful, too, when using words in dialogue that have different meanings in different parts of the country or the world. The classic blunder here would be having a little British lady sit down in a teashop in London and order biscuits, only to be served the yeasty lumps of bread that she would receive in America. In England, a biscuit is always what Americans call a cookie, a turtle hull is a boot, and a French-fried potato is a chip. In America, some words either take on or lose certain meanings when they cross the Mason-Dixon Line. For instance, the word *yet* takes on additional meanings in the North than it has in the South. In both places it means *so far*, as in "I haven't eaten yet." But in the South it doesn't mean *still*, as in "Is your mother living yet?" To which in the classic radio joke Charley McCarthy replied to Edgar Bergen, "No, not yet." That line drew huge laughs because of the disparity of the meanings of the word. In your story, having a character use *yet* in one of the two ways will help describe where she is from.

In his novel *Advise and Consent*, Allen Drury paints a wonderful portrait of an old southern senator named Ceep Cooley, who might or might not have been patterned after Everett Dirksen, a legend in the United States Senate for many years. Much of our perception of Cooley comes from what he says (dialogue), how he pronounces the words (dialect), and the *way* he says them (inflection). Listen to this exchange between the old senator and a nominee for Secretary of the State who will be appearing before Ceep's Senate committee:

> "I want to ask you about your virus, Mr. Director" he said, leaning over the nominee and placing a knotted brown hand on his shoulder. "I hope it's cleared up, I surely do."
>
> "All gone, thank you, Senator," Bob Leffingwell said smiling up at him and looking a little more relaxed. "It went over the weekend and I'm feeling good as new now."
>
> "That's good," Senator Cooley said softly. "That's good, Mr. Director. Because I suspect—I just suspect now"—and a slow grin crossed his face and he looked at the listening reporters with a sly twinkle in his eye—"I just suspect that before these hearings are over you may just need your strength. Yes, sir, I just suspect you may."

In chapter three, I talked about being loud and being quiet in your fiction.

In this scene, the old senator is speaking very softly—the author tells us this. But, more importantly, his mannerisms and pauses and general composure are just as quiet and soft. And that quiet softness adds an extra punch to that implied threat at the end: that Mr. Leffingwell should expect one hellacious run through the wringer during the upcoming hearings.

Remember to use that quiet or loud approach when letting your character's dialogue describe them. Look in your manuscripts for places to let what a character says and how they say it replace more conventional description. Rather than telling your reader that Mrs. Abernathy is a woman who screams at children, show it:

> "Get out of my azaleas!" Mrs. Abernathy bellowed from the porch. The children looked in her direction and gingerly retreated.

One way to emphasize a character's inflection in dialogue is to italicize all or part of a word, as in "I could smash you like a *bug!*"

Listen to this brief line from John O'Hara's novel *Ourselves to Know*: "Well, if I know Mr. *Mill*houser, . . ." The emphasis on just the first syllable of the name is proof that the speaker *does* know Mr. Millhouser. And that he is unique in some way.

SHOWING A CHARACTER'S MOTIVATION

You'll need to know exactly what motivates your character before you can convey him or his situation to a reader. Maybe you've created a guy who is set on embezzling some money from his job. He's pretty sure he'll get away with it—almost all would-be criminals think that—and he's willing to take the risk. Now, your description of this guy will depend at least partly on *why* he wants the cash. If he intends to blow it all on loose women and hard liquor and gambling in Atlantic City, then your description will be altogether different than if he needs the money to pay for an operation for his ailing wife.

Consider how Donald Westlake—writing as Richard Stark—shows the motivation of his central character, Parker, a professional thief who is being solicited to take part in an upcoming heist in *Comeback*:

> Liss said, "You still there?"
>
> "Yes."
>
> "We could get together someplace, talk it over."
>
> "Maybe."

"You want to know who else is aboard." And again Liss waited for Parker to say something, but again Parker had nothing to say, so finally Liss said "Ed Mackey."

That was different. Ed Mackey was somebody Parker did know and had worked with. Ed Mackey was solid. Parker said, "Who else?"

"It only takes three."

Even better. The fewer the people, the fewer the complications, and the more the profit. Parker said, "Where and when?"

Parker is obviously not interested in the project at the beginning, and just as obviously not too impressed with Liss. Then, when he decides to consider the job, it is because he learns of the participation of someone he *is* impressed with. More precisely, the author shows us one of Parker's motivations here, some essential thing that he *had* to know before committing: that he is to work with someone that he can trust and have confidence in.

There are other ways of showing a character's motivation than just dialogue. Backstories and flashbacks are very useful, perhaps where some injustice was dealt out to your character and revenge becomes his impetus or some kindness shown to him in his youth turns him into a philanthropist. Once you've determined what the motivation will be, make sure you find ways throughout the story or novel to remind readers of it, through the character's actions, thoughts, words, and descriptions.

Knowing what your characters need, want, and are capable of doing—in other words, what drives them—will determine how well you define them. Once again, I encourage you to make that data sheet (like the one on page 113) for each and every character, and make sure you include their motivations.

SHOWING A CHARACTER'S MOOD

By mood, I really mean their overall state of mind in a given scene. And this is a wide range of possibilities indeed, covering everything from happiness and contentment to anger and depression. In real life, everybody's constantly in one predominant mood or another, so the people who populate your fiction should be also.

Look at how V.C. Andrews shows a character's fear in *Into the Garden*:

All I could do was listen and wait. The floorboards creaked. I thought I heard what sounded like a skirt rubbing against a leg as someone crossed from the

Making a Character Profile Sheet

If you expect your reader to know *some* things about your character, then you'd better know *many* things about him or her.

Profile sheets like this one will help you define who you'll be using in your story. Just look at it as your character filling out an application to be in your fiction. When you're done, put it in your writer's journal for quick and easy reference.

PROFILE

Full name _____

Nickname _____

Married/children _____

Age _____

Occupation _____

Color hair/eyes _____

Build/weight/height _____

Religious beliefs _____

Fears _____

Strongest belief _____

Biggest secret _____

Biggest regret _____

Political persuasion _____

Favorite color _____

Favorite type of movie _____

Favorite food _____

Strongest personal relationship _____

Weakest personal relationship _____

Unique mannerisms _____

Dependability _____

Peculiarities _____

Who would he/she have voted for in the last presidential election?

_____

door toward my bed. Shadows darkened. I took a deep breath, closed my eyes and then with all my might sat up.

"Who's there?" I cried.

The author uses several of the standard "things that go bump in the night" devices that we all have sensed more than once and not just in reading. The use of them here—the creaking floorboards, the darkening shadows, deep breathing and closed eyes—paints a more vivid picture than simply telling the reader that this character is afraid.

Always look for ways to show rather than tell in your description of a character's mood, as David Guterson does when describing his lonely protagonist in *East of the Mountains*:

> He found a fire ring full of charred fence posts, a rusted coffee can holding dry, leached stones, and a plastic bucket turned upside down, tattered and torn along its flanks where shotgun pellets had passed through it. Two beer bottles were set against a strand of rusting, low barbed wire, and then no further sign of people. Ben felt right in his loneliness. It was just as he had wanted it.

Notice all the remnants that the character sees, leftovers from people who are no longer there—things that are used up and discarded, no longer of any use to anyone. These things reinforce the solitude that this man wants at this point in the story, and this bit of description does a much better job of showing it to the reader than just reporting that he wants to be by himself.

In the Andrews example, the character's mood is implied; in the next one it is identified toward the end as loneliness. There's no rule of thumb for me to give you to help you decide which approach to take other than this one: Avoid starting out with a declaration like *He was lonely*. It's much more effective to show this to the reader than tell it.

That's not to say it is easier. It would be infinitely easier for a writer to simply tell the reader what kind of mood a character is in. But if you haven't noticed by now that the easier path is hardly ever the best one for a writer, then the odds are that you won't end up being a very good one.

SHOWING A CHARACTER'S FLAWS

Odysseus was full of himself, brimming with the excessive pride of self that the Greeks called *hubris*; Achilles had that vulnerable heel; Don Quixote was a dreamer (and arguably a nut); Hamlet could not for the life of him make a decision; and your Uncle Chester can't hold his liquor. Everybody has a flaw.

And your characters better have at least one, too. Perfection is a trait that just doesn't pop up in real people, neither should it in the ones you create.

In *The Great Santini*, Pat Conroy includes this scene where some children are watching their military father prepare to begin a family outing:

> He arranged the things on the dashboard very carefully. On his far left, he stacked three road maps. Beside the maps was a box of Tampa Nuggets cigars, blunt. On top of the cigars was a pair of aviator's sunglasses. Then, putting his hand into the pocket of his flight jacket, he pulled out a .22 pistol from it and laid the gun gingerly beside the cigar box.

The precise description of this man's actions shows us primarily two things: (a) he is quite the perfectionist when arranging things, and (b) there is something definitely wrong with him. Fathers don't as a rule place a pistol on the dashboard when taking their family on an excursion. Despotism and obstinacy prove to be the flaws of Santini—who turns out to be not so great after all—and Conroy, rather than telling us this up front, slowly establishes the image with descriptions of little scenes like this one. Think back to this example when *you* write. The careful building up of details, like choosing just the right cobblestones and then laying them precisely in a walkway, is far more effective than reporting the situation all at once.

Let's take a look at one of the classic flawed parents in American literature. This time, however, the child worships the character and wants more than anything for him to be as estimable in other people's opinions as he is in hers. This is from Betty Smith's *A Tree Grows in Brooklyn*:

> Yes, everyone loved Johnny Nolan. He was a sweet singer of sweet songs. Since the beginning of time, everyone, especially the Irish, had loved and cared for the singer in their midst. His brother waiters really loved him. The men he worked for loved him. His wife and children loved him. He was still gay and young and handsome. His wife had not turned bitter against him and his children did not know that they were supposed to be ashamed of him.

Notice that the author begins with a little catalog of people who loved Johnny and ends with a reference to the fact that all of that adoration might be unwarranted, that there was something about him that should cause his family to be ashamed of him. In your story or novel, look for ways to make irony work for you in your description of characters. People not really being as happy as they seem to be—or as rich, or as clever, or as good—make for fine irony. And one of the best ways to pull this off is to build up one image and then deflate or alter it with a hint at another one, as Smith does in that paragraph.

Not all flaws in people—or in fictional characters—are emotional or behavioral; sometimes they are physical. Ahab's missing leg and Captain Hook's missing hand provide motivations for their obsessions, and Flannery O'Connor's one-legged philosopher, Hulga—in "Good Country People"—is bitter and incomplete, just as her body is incomplete.

Look at how Robert Phillips, in his story "Night Flowers," uses a physical flaw to determine a character's career choice:

> Because he had no nose, Thetford Collins took the job as night stationmaster at the Public Landing train station. It was the only job he could find where people didn't look at you.

The flaw gives the reader a vivid description of Thetford, not just the absent nose—though that is graphic enough—but, more than that, his reaction to the condition: taking a job where he will not be gawked at. Look for places in your fiction where physical flaws might provide motivation for a character—or cause them to be unmotivated. Deformities and imperfections are useful ways for you to let characters overcome things, to become more complete in spite of something fate has thrown in their way, like Helen Keller. They can also be a crutch for your character, keeping him from overcoming anything, like Thetford.

STEREOTYPICAL CHARACTERS

So, have you heard this one?

The Texan and his wife are driving through New England to see the fall foliage, and they stop to visit with a New Hampshire man who is raking his lawn. The Texan swaggers out of his Cadillac and hitches his thumbs in his wide belt. "How many acres yah'll got here?" he wants to know. The New Hampshire man tells him he has one and a half. The Texan breaks into a wide grin, slaps his Cadillac, and says that, back home on his place, he can get in this here car and start driving and, two hours later, he won't be off his own property. The New Englander listens, nods, and finally says "Ayah, I used to have a car like that."

If that joke works for you, it's because you brought some stereotypical baggage in when you read it. You assumed the New Englander would be stoic and practical, and you knew the Texan would be pompous and blustery. In the joke, both characters are stereotypes. In your fiction, they probably shouldn't be.

In reality, not all New Englanders behave as their stereotypical image suggests, and not all Texans bloviate loudly about the biggest and the best (I am a Texan, and refrain from bloviating on most occasions). There are exceptions to every rule, especially when it comes to stereotypes. So beware making most of your characters exactly what your reader is expecting.

That's not to say, however, that you won't draw on that reader's preconceived notions from time to time. You should, and you'd be foolish not to. Let those notions help to make your fiction work, just like your stereotypes of New Englanders and Texans might have made that joke work.

Here's how F. Scott Fitzgerald taps into his readers' expectation of how an old-money, East Coast society matron might see things in his story "The Rich Boy":

> Just before Christmas Mrs. Hunter retired to a select Episcopal heaven, and Aaron became the responsible head of the family.

Fitzgerald could have said Mrs. Hunter died. But he had more intentions for that sentence than to report her demise; he wanted to convey a stereotype of a very wealthy society dame who wouldn't condescend to do anything as common as dying. *Retiring to an elect Episcopal heaven* is an altogether grander accomplishment.

Using stereotypical, expected images of your characters will work in some places in your writing (as it did in that one from Fitzgerald), but it won't in many others; it will depend entirely on the uniqueness of the particular story. Loading up your fiction with stereotypes will provide your reader with nothing more than a cast of those cardboard, one-dimensional people that we've talked about. Much better to give them folks who surprise them, characters who break out of their stereotypes.

SUMMARY: THE OCCUPANTS OF YOUR FICTION

The characters that people your fiction must come through clearly in order for your story or novel to work. Your reader should see something of themselves in some of them and, via your writer's voice, even something of you. The key to how that reader perceives your characters is how well you breathe life into them. In this chapter, we've looked at a few ways to do it effectively.

Pay close attention to the physical description of all of your characters. Believe me, one of the most stinging and damning criticisms that you can get is that someone didn't "see" your characters. So, *make* the reader see them; give the reader plenty of things *to* see. Go beyond the obvious traits like weight and hair color and clothing and work in small details like the way they hold a cup of coffee or wave for a taxi. Be careful when patterning your description on real people, making sure that you walk the fine line between straying too far from reality and making the character a mere stereotype of himself. Consider letting some of your characters describe themselves, and let much of the work of your description be done in their dialogue.

The brush you use to paint these people for your reader should be a fine one, capable of infusing small details, but the canvas should be broad enough to work in more than just what they look like. Your descriptions should also include people's motivations, moods, and flaws.

All of these approaches will overlap in your writing, and you should make sure that they do. Many times the best way to show a character's mood is in her dialogue. That lady that we visited earlier who started her day lamenting that it's not even worth getting out of bed is a far cry from another one who wakes up, reaches for the phone, and starts blabbering sweet things to her boyfriend. One is sad; the other is happy. And we know that without having been told that it is so. Just like we know in some stories that a man is in a particular mood because of something that motivates him or that another is influenced by his flaws or his stereotypical heritage.

The people who do and say the things and words that you put in your fiction are, in large part, what makes your story work for your reader. So treat them well. And describe them well.

EXERCISE 1

Stand in front of your bathroom mirror—or sit yourself down with one of the handheld variety—and take a good, hard, long look at yourself. Now write down what you see in such a way that somebody that has never laid eyes on you might *see* you through your description. Don't limit yourself to simply physical description: Work in hints of character, flaws, a spiritual awareness, or that evil gleam in your eye that an elementary teacher saw long ago.

Using one of your manuscripts choose one character, major or minor, and look for ways to use your description of him for more than just to report what he looks and sounds like. Consider ways that you can work other elements—foreshadowing, prejudice, fear, a deep, dark secret—into your overall delivery of this fellow to your reader.

EXERCISE 3

Now dig through one of those manuscripts one more time, this time looking for any characters that might benefit from some stereotypical description (attributes and characteristics that the reader expects) but, more so, at how you might "destereotype" some of them. Maybe, in your story set in 1958 in Mississippi, let that rural white southern sheriff say a kind word to a black sharecropper rather than snub him. A bit of irony will have taken place, your reader will be surprised, and at least one of your characters will emerge as something more than a one dimensional cardboard figure.

chapter 7

[TIME AND PLACE]

In chapter four I pointed out that it is essential when writing fiction to tell a story rather than write a report. The reason is simple: Stories are more enjoyable than reports and easier to digest. You want proof of that? Dust off your Old Testament and start reading, not for any spiritual enlightenment but just for comprehension. You'll probably like Genesis, what with Adam and Eve misbehaving and Noah getting his odd instructions regarding a particular boat and Abraham's test and many other things. Then read on through Exodus, with God continually asking Moses "What's *with* these people? I promise them all these neat things, give them food that falls out of the sky, and all they do is *whine*." That's good stuff, best-seller material if ever I saw it.

Now take a stab at Leviticus, which is a long catalog of specific dietary and ritualistic rules. Leviticus has undoubtedly brought legions of people intent on reading straight through the Bible from start to finish to a screeching halt.

In Genesis and Exodus there is drama; there are murders, betrayals, and interesting characters with various motivations in various dilemmas. In short, there are stories. In Leviticus there is just that seemingly unending list of decrees.

And there is one more difference—perhaps the single most important one—between the Old Testament's first two books and its third. All of those stories are grounded in specific times and places. They each have a definite setting; Abraham looks out across the vast unknown territory that he has been told to traverse, Noah watches the waters cover up the world and gets bumped around by all those animals in the close quarters of the ark, and Moses actually *sees* the promised land, rather than just hears about it. Readers see it too, since they are right there with him. There's none of that in Leviticus, since the reader is never given any particular place to *be*.

Nothing so solidly anchors a work of fiction in readers' minds as knowing when and where something is taking place. Settings provide bases of operations for everything that happens in your story or novel, and, as importantly, they—along with the characters that will do things in there—provide you with a means to actually tell a *story*, rather than simply report information.

In this chapter, we'll look at a few ways for you to put your readers in the times and places where those stories can emerge.

THE CREDIBILITY OF YOUR SETTING

One night my wife was watching television while I tried to read student manuscripts. Bits and pieces of whatever she was watching began to mingle with the words I was reading, and soon I began to realize that I was paying as much attention to the movie as I was to what I was supposed to be doing.

The plot involved a middle-aged woman who had fallen into a romance with her young renter, who had taken to cavorting with the woman's teenaged daughter. The whole mess ended tragically for the mother and daughter—a hatchet was involved—with the amorous renter languishing away in an insane asylum. When I commented on the absurdity of the situation, my wife looked at me and said these words: "It's based on a true story." Then she leaned forward and secured the story's credibility with this surefire endorsement: "It really *happened*."

Those words come close to carrying magic, don't they? We seem to be constantly on the lookout for some level of reality—of credibility—in real life that we seem to think fiction denies us. That's why the phrase "stranger than fiction" packs such a punch. That's why when someone says that a particular movie or book is "based on a true story" they are implying that that fact somehow elevates it from events and characters that have been fabricated by a storyteller.

Now here's the deal. For you as a writer, every one of your stories should really happen in the mind and eyes and ears of the reader. They should happen as surely in fiction as they would if actually transpiring in fact.

We're really talking about two things here: (1) establishing your characters and their situations and the details of the setting so completely that it all *could* possibly take place (the overall credibility) and (2) the effective conveyance of those characters and situations and details so that the story *does* take place. One of the very best ways to ensure that both of these things happen is to pay close attention to the description of your setting.

Let's look to Hemingway for our example. In this opening paragraph from his story "In Another Country," he takes us to a time before most of us were born and to a place where most of us have never been. And yet, through his description and the use of small details, the reader is actually there, seeing the things that the narrator is seeing, feeling the biting cold of a long-ago evening:

> In the fall the war was always there, but we did not go to it anymore. It was cold in the fall in Milan and the dark came very early. Then the electric lights came on, and it was pleasant along the streets looking in the windows. There was much game hanging outside the shops, and the snow powdered in the fur of the foxes and the wind blew their tails. The deer hung stiff and heavy and empty, and small birds blew in the wind and the wind turned their feathers. It was a cold fall and the wind came down from the mountains.

For the reader, this event really happens as surely as the events that inspired that movie my wife told me was "based on a true story." More than eighty years separates Hemingway's writing of the words in that paragraph and my writing of these, and yet when I read his, that little scene comes through as clear and crisp as if I were standing on the sidewalk on that cold night, looking at the game outside the shops.

Your fiction should seem that real to your readers. The only way to make it happen is to pay close attention to the details that you want, and *need*, to convey in a scene and then to choose the very best words that you can come up with in order to describe the details. A list—kept close by when you are writing—of all of the images that you feel need to be included will be quite helpful to you; that way you can check off the things that you include, cross out the ones that you've reconsidered, and make little notes—like "do later"—beside others. Also helpful will be other lists, perhaps of adjective possibilities or metaphor or simile candidates.

The end result of all of this thinking and scribbling will be—you can only hope—a work of fiction that will bring your readers in and give them a realistic sense of where things will be taking place.

THE BIG PICTURE AND THE SMALL

One of the first decisions you'll have to make when conveying your time and place will be how to provide your reader with that always-important first impression of your setting. There are numerous ways for you to bring the location to life and then keep providing a strong sense of the setting throughout the entire story or novel, but before you can do any of them, you'll need

Making a Plot Graph

Completing one of these for each and every scene in your short story or novel chapter will help you to locate, and then remember, all of the details that you need to establish your setting. Then place each one side by side to provide you with a linear representation of your overall plan. It also lets you see at a glance if some of your minor characters are popping up too frequently or not often enough. Prominently placed on the wall in the room where you do most of your writing, this graph will let you pinpoint problems and make modifications. It might also provide you with the assurance that progress is actually being made, something that all writers need to feel when working in the trenches of a project.

PLOT GRAPH

Scene Number _____

Time _____

    Month/Year _____

    Clock Time _____

Place _____

Weather Conditions _____

Geography _____

_____

Architecture (Layout of Room or Place)

_____

_____

Food _____

Characters in This Scene _____

(Very) Brief Summary of Action

_____

_____

Things, Actions Needing Description

_____

_____

to decide if you're going to start with a wide frame and tighten your focus or begin with that narrower viewpoint and work within it.

You will probably employ the latter most of the time, but there will be many opportunities for you use the wider vision. Let's take a look at both approaches.

The Macrocosm

The word *macrocosm* actually means the totality of everything, as in a universe, but for our purpose it indicates a large setting as opposed to a specific one. In fiction, a macrocosm can be a more far-reaching series of events than one little action by a character or two, as in a single soldier going about the business of staying alive inside the gigantic thing swirling all around him that is a world war, or two kids who fall in love within the ancient feud in *Romeo and Juliet*. In chapter ten we'll look at how the larger view can help to move your fiction along, but here let's consider it in a much more specific way: at how you can give just a *glimpse* of this totality to your readers then move them into a smaller, more detailed place.

This bird's eye view can be done rapidly—sort of slipped in—with a mere mention of the distant viewpoint, as John Steinbeck does in the last sentence of this offering from *The Moon is Down*:

> Near the mine entrance the guards watched the sky and trained their instruments on the sky and turned their listening-instruments against the sky, for it was a clear night for bombing. On nights like this the feathered steel spindles came whistling down and roared to splinters. The land would be visible from the sky tonight, even though the moon seemed to throw little light.

Or you can go into more detail, taking advantage of this lofty perspective to establish your setting, as I did in *The Windows of Heaven*, when describing Galveston Island:

> From the air she would resemble an awkward creature trying to take flight, her head, wider and heavier than the rest of her, making an effort to lift all of her up and away, the long, slender body lagging behind. The side of her short wings, straining to pull her up, was the pointed jut of land above Offats Bayou, and most of the rest of her was sand and salt grass, the curving beach separated from the flats and marshes by sand dunes, odd shaped structures born of wind and tide. Only toward the head of the creature had much civilization taken hold, as if the town had grown out of the thing's brain, and been blown back over its body by the wind accompanying its ascent.

You might notice that I transform the island into a living thing so that my readers might see it more clearly. On a map, Galveston does indeed look like a bird taking off, so I played that to the hilt. If you decide to use this approach, spend some time looking at either aerial photographs or maps of your large setting, trying to come up with things that they look like (I've always thought the continental United States resembles a hefty side of beef, with Maine as the thick neck, Florida as the stubby front leg, and Baja California as the tail). Once you've come up with a visual image that works, try different ways to work it into your description. A metaphor might be the way to go: *Don't underestimate Italy, the slender boot poised to kick a field goal with Sicily*, or maybe a simile will be your best bet: *Cape Cod stretched itself into the Atlantic like an arm flexing its muscles, its fist clenched tight against whatever the ocean might bring.*

Whether you choose to take the stealthy, brief approach—like Steinbeck's—or the longer, more elaborate one—like mine—will depend on what you want a reference to do for your reader. If you just need a different perspective, then brevity will work just fine, but if you want to help establish what will be an important place, where important things will happen, then you'll need to dwell on it somewhat longer and in more detail.

Another way to convey the big picture is to let your reader's mind's eye move *across* the setting, rather than down into it, like the slow panning of the camera across a landscape in a widescreen movie. Look at how Stephen Harrigan does this in his novel *The Gates of the Alamo*:

> The light crept down the hills, then swam across the shallow river valley until it reached the field where the Alamo stood, and then moved on to the river and the village beyond. In a cypress tree along the banks, a hawk sat ruffling its feathers, shaking off the cold that had seeped into its bones during the night and beginning to rouse its mind from the sleep that held it fast.

This use of visual description is considerably more effective than simply saying the sun rose. Harrigan also makes nice use of personification, not by comparing the entire scene to a living thing, as I did in the preceding example about Galveston, but by having just one thing, the light, creep and swim. Notice, too, that he moves that light *gradually*, first over the Alamo and then into the village and past it, as if illuminating the set where important things are about to commence. Then, when he's got his wide stage lit, he focuses on the smallest of things: a single, sleepy hawk in a tree. By the time he gets around to some action—and plenty of it in the form of one of the most famous battles in history—readers are well aware of the setting. They have front row seats.

The use of dialogue offers yet another opportunity to establish a tiny setting within the enormity of a larger one. A classic example is in *Our Town* by Thornton Wilder, when one character tells another one about some recent mail:

> "I never told you about that letter Jane Crofit got from her minister when she was sick. He wrote Jane a letter and on the envelope the address was like this: It said: Jane Crofit; the Crofit Farm; Grover's Corners; Sutton County; New Hampshire; United States of America . . . Continent of North America; Western Hemisphere; The Earth; the Solar System; the Universe; the Mind of God—that's what it said on the envelope."

You will more than likely not make your macrocosm as all-inclusive as Wilder's, but search for opportunities to occasionally give your readers the big picture—the panorama or bird's eye view—before you focus in on a much smaller place and situation. If your setting is a brownstone near Central Park in Manhattan, it might be a good idea to drop in slowly, showing the entire island at first and then coming down to where your story will take place, like the opening scene in the movie *West Side Story*. This overall view won't be something that you'll want to use more than once in a short story, and probably not any more than that in a novel, but it does serve to remind your readers that your specific setting is only one piece in a much larger puzzle.

Description of or reference to a macrocosm will work nicely for you occasionally, but its opposite, the *micro*cosm, is where you will be setting most of your fiction.

The Microcosm

We're talking here about a *little world*—a world in small. The home you grew up in might have been exactly that for you, populated by people who sometimes went out into the bigger world but always came back to that more important one. It might have offered safety and stability; it almost certainly provided nourishment and shelter and, hopefully, love and support. It was probably—at least in your youthful, naïve perspective—a self-sufficient, independent place. To borrow a phrase from Robert Frost (which I've already stolen outright as a title for a novel) it was "a place apart."

To your way of thinking, that home—and perhaps your entire hometown—was incredibly clearer and more distinct than the wider world beyond it. And that clarity and distinction is what you should aim for in your fiction. If a particular room in your story or novel is going to be important—or if important things are going to happen there—then it should not just be a *generic* room, essentially no different than countless other rooms. It should be *the* room that you envision in which something in your story will be played out.

In this bit from *The Ghost Writer* by Philip Roth, a young narrator is shown into a room by a famous writer.

> The living room he took me into was neat, cozy, and plain: a large circular hooked rug, some slipcovered easy chairs, a worn sofa, a long wall of books, a piano, a phonograph, an oak library table systematically stacked with journals and magazines . . . Beyond the cushioned window seats and the colorless cotton curtains tied primly back I could see the bare limbs of big dark maple trees and fields of driven snow. Purity. Serenity. Simplicity. Seclusion. All one's concentration and flamboyance and originality reserved for the grueling, exalted, transcendent calling. I looked around and I thought, This is how I will live.

That room makes quite the impression on the narrator, so it should make equally as much of one on the reader. Look back at the fine details Roth puts in to make this just the right room: the comfortable, worn furniture, that table stacked with books and journals, the nice scenery through the window, even the author's succinct, one-word assessments. Then look at that declaration at the end, leaving no doubt that this is a room the narrator won't soon forget.

It's not unlike the vivid, detailed description of that room in *The Shipping News* we looked at in chapter one. And you will need to use details just like that in your fiction in order to bring rooms and streets and parks and many, many other places to life for your readers. Let's say you've got a character being interviewed for a job; she's sitting in someone's office and answering the questions as he asks them. This sort of scene would seem to lend itself to a dialogue-driven treatment, but don't overlook making the setting work for you also. What sort of room is it? Is it a corner office with a breathtaking view of the city, which would indicate the person conducting the interview is a big cheese? Are there photographs of his family on the wall? Is it a dark place, lots of oak paneling and leather chairs, or a bright one, with huge windows and rows of track lighting? What is there about this room that might help the reader see more clearly the personality of the man who inhabits it or the nature of the position that this woman is seeking? Maybe there are documents scattered around on the desk that are obviously confidential, alerting her to a possibility of impropriety or unprofessional laxity.

Or maybe the setting you are describing is someone's backyard. If the shrubs and trees are all neatly trimmed, a pair of Adirondack chairs in precise alignment, the lawn perfectly manicured and raked, the birdfeeders topped off, and a vase of fresh flowers on the patio table, then your readers will assume that a particular type of person lives there. If the grass is overgrown, the flowerbeds full of weeds, and cheap plastic folding chairs sit upended on the unswept patio, then they will assume someone quite different.

In short, make the settings of your fiction more than just places to be. Make them repositories of numerous details that help to tell your story and define your characters. A very good way to do this is to look for microcosms—little worlds—in your settings, scene by scene and in the work as a whole. When you do this, you'll come closer to being able to convey the settings—and the treasure trove of details they contain—to your reader.

A PAIR OF ESSENTIALS

When using those details, don't overlook two areas that are vital to a full representation of a particular time and place: weather and geography. If your readers don't get some idea of what the climate and the landscape are like, then there will be some awfully big holes in their overall perception of the time and place. These are two constants in everyone's daily lives, so it would be a mistake to ignore them when describing your settings.

Weather

I'm a big believer in plot graphs (as seen on page 123), linear representations of where things are taking place in a story and where things are generally heading. For each scene of a story or a chapter in a novel, I make sure I put down things that will help me focus on details that will be essential in my writing. One of these is weather. Even if the scene takes place inside a room that has no windows, *I* still need to know what the climate and conditions are outside, especially since scenes usually come wedged in between other scenes, which *might* take place outdoors. And because characters are more than likely affected by the weather. If you're at a place in your war novel where a group of commanders are at a staff meeting deep inside a bunker, you won't be expected to describe what the weather is doing outside (since there are no windows). But you *do* need to convey these men's crankiness due to the fact that it's been raining for a week and showing no signs of stopping in spite of the fact that a major landing is on for tonight.

Bright, sun-washed skies, driving rain, howling winds, a Winnie the Pooh blustery day—all of nature's various moods and conditions are some of the best tools in your kit. So don't forget to use them.

Look at how Belva Plain, in her novel *Her Father's House*, came up with a better way of telling the reader that the weather outside is frightful:

> Still frazzled, he boarded the train. Red-faced passengers, people with wet coats and windblown hair came in stamping their feet and rubbing their cold hands . . .

That's a classic example of showing rather than telling. We've all seen cold, wet, red-faced people step inside and stomp their feet and rub their hands. So we know *exactly* what the weather is like without having it reported to us. Now think about how much stronger the image is in readers' minds than if they had been told that it was a cold, wet day. As I said in chapter four, it's always a good idea to go on a hunting expedition in your manuscripts, looking for places where showing will work much better than telling.

And, as I also said in chapter four, there will be places where telling might work just fine, as it does in this sentence from *Harvard Yard* by William Martin:

> It was one of those March evenings when the lingering light promised spring, but the air was as cold as February, and January still whistled in.

This is still better than simply telling that it's cold out. The author calls upon the reader's preconceived notions of weather conditions of three months in this example. So, rather than spend too much time describing that lingering light and cold, whistling air, he chooses to convey the image in one fell swoop. The plot, at this point in his novel, is not dependent on what the weather is up to, but this brief description makes the setting more realistic. It's a small detail that adds to the overall image that a good writer is constantly striving for.

When writing about the weather, or anything else, it's not always a bad idea to bluntly state the obvious. Remember, showing is usually better than telling, but that's not *always* the case. The first sentence in the first chapter of the first book I ever wrote is *It is snowing*. You can't get much more straightforward than that. It just so happened that I wanted my readers to know this from the get-go. So I chose for it to be the initial image.

When planning your story or novel, know—for every scene—exactly what the weather is up to. And make sure you let the reader know it, too.

Geography

Most of us are impacted—positively or negatively or probably bits of both—by the physical landscapes that we live in. Let's face it: A person who lives in the big sky, wide-open vista of Wyoming is apt to have a different worldview than someone who lives in a congested, noisy city. And that worldview will undoubtedly spill over into his or her life in many ways.

Here's an example. It might be true, as John Donne maintained, that no man is an island. But more than a few live or have lived on one, and island folk are usually quick to tell you how hearty and independent they are. And—guess what?—more often than not they are. Maybe they've convinced themselves of it, or perhaps being an island dweller actually *does* set people apart from mainland inhabitants. I don't know. But I do know this: When I wrote my novel about Galveston Island, I met many, many of its citizens. Those who had actually been born there always told me quickly they were a BOI (born on the island), a distinction they wear as proudly as if it were a Medal of Honor.

I would have been foolish, when writing that novel, to have not described that pride and grit and independence in those Galveston people. Because those qualities determined entirely by geography were essential components of who they were and are.

In your own fiction, look for places to instill those qualities and quirks and mannerisms that derive from the land itself. But be careful not to end up with a cliché. The stereotypical western loner, out there on the sweeping western range, looking for no more companionship than his trusty horse, will be all too predictable if he wanders into your story. Using elements of that independence and standoffishness in a character might work just fine, but to transplant the Marlboro Man into your fiction whole cloth will be a mistake. Remember, stereotypical characters are usually much too unsurprising and one-dimensional. The same applies to settings; Texas is not all cactus and prairies any more than England is all heather and hedgerows.

Your more common use of geography will be the actual description of it. In most cases the lay of the land won't be any more pivotal to your plot than the weather is, but, like your occasional references to the weather, the reader needs, and wants, to know what the landscape looks like. Here are Sherlock Holmes and Doctor Watson in a railway car on their way to the country in "The Adventure of the Speckled Band" by A. Conan Doyle:

It was a perfect day, with a bright sun and a few fleecy clouds in the heavens. The trees and wayside hedges were just throwing out their first green shoots, and the air was full of the pleasant smell of the moist earth. To me at least there was a strange contrast between the sweet promise of the spring and this sinister quest upon which we were engaged.

Notice the carefully laid on springtime images both meteorological and geographical at the start: *perfect day, bright sun, fleecy clouds, the first green shoots, the pleasant smell of the moist earth.* Then all of these niceties give way to something not so nice, to this *sinister quest* that will be the business of the remainder of the tale.

Doyle calls upon both the weather and the landscape to help him introduce that quest. In your fiction, do the same thing: Use whatever is going on around your characters and their actions to give the reader a clearer view. If you've got something happening on a seashore, make sure you describe what kind of beach it is. A beach in Maine with rocky cliffs and tall evergreens is likely to be altogether different than one on the gulf coast, where the land is as flat as the sea. The very colors of the sand and water are different in those two places, so you'll need to get it right.

Which brings us to this word of caution: Do your research. Make sure when you mention mountains or hills on the horizon that you are placing them where mountains and hills would actually *be.* Having a character stumble over kudzu in Colorado would be as silly as having someone pick edelweiss in Mississippi. My novel set in northern Ohio has a photograph on the cover with a crepe myrtle tree in a front yard. The problem here, as more than one northern Ohioan informed me, is that there are no crepe myrtle trees in that part of the world.

CREATING BELIEVABLE SETTINGS IN IMPOSSIBLE PLACES

In Mark Helprin's novel *Winter's Tale,* the setting is New York City early in the twentieth century, but with a few modifications. For instance, there is a constant fog bank so thick that it scrapes and sometimes dents the tops of trains that rumble through it. And the novel starts one early morning with a bored horse that strolls across the Brooklyn Bridge and eventually learns to fly.

Both things sound impossible, don't they? And of course they are. But, owing to the fine storytelling from this talented writer, they aren't *unbelievable,* anymore so than the existence of evil Nazi-like rabbits in Richard Adams's *Watership Down* or the dogged persistence of an unassuming hobbit in saving Middle Earth in *The Lord of the Rings* trilogy.

Whether or not your setting works for a reader is not dependent on whether or not it is physically *possible*, but on how well you establish its credibility within the context of the story. I'm fairly certain there isn't *really* a land somewhere over the rainbow, with wicked witches and grumpy apple trees and Munchkins, but that doesn't keep *The Wizard of Oz* from working on every level at which a good story must work. The Lion doesn't evolve as a believable character because he's a lion, or even because he's cowardly, but because he finally locates the compassion and courage that he didn't think he had, and because we've sometimes surprised ourselves also and can relate to him. The expedition on the Yellow Brick Road doesn't work because of all the odd adventures and strange places along the way, but because we've all made difficult journeys.

If you choose to place your story or novel in an impossible setting, you'll need to remember that the setting is only a stage for the more important business that you'll be about: the interaction of your characters and the situations in which you place them. If you have a colony of people living on a planet in a galaxy far, far away—having been transported there by a technology that hasn't yet been developed—you'll need your story to depend on how these characters behave in *that given setting*. In other words, you'll need to place them in situations that we earthbound readers in the here and now can identify with. Let's face it: stealing a canister of hyrocaspicular mertatron on the third moon of Salantgris isn't all that different from robbing a bank in Grand Rapids. They're both stealing, and they both involve the inevitable planning and nervousness and suspense that are part and parcel of all theft. Most certainly, you will have chosen your setting for a reason; it will have some significance in the story and sometimes the setting itself will *be* a character.

When writing about impossible—maybe we'd better say *improbable*—places, it's essential that you create a system of rules for that world and that you stick to them. Your rules might not be anything more complex than a group of space travelers not being able to breathe the atmosphere of a given planet without wearing helmets or they might include various levels of things, as J.K. Rowling employs in her Harry Potter series, where the physical laws of nature are altered considerably. When you build such a system of rules, you'll have to apply them consistently in your work, for an oversight here will lose readers quickly.

Remember, let your characters and their motivations and actions drive your story, not the setting. If you do that, then go ahead and make the time and place as impossible as you want to. Your solid story will render it entirely possible within the context that you have established.

BEWARE THE COMFORT ZONE

When I pick up one of the Travis McGee novels by John D. MacDonald and plop myself down in my hammock to reread it, I get a sense of coming home. Here again is Travis tinkering around on his houseboat, *The Busted Flush*, in a St. Petersburg marina. And here is his friend and sidekick Meyer, the old economist whose home floats in the next slip. The Florida sun shines down, the early 1960s creep slowly along, and all is well. I'm so contented with the setting and the characters that I haven't yet been able to forgive MacDonald for dying and depriving me of more novels.

That comfort zone—that relaxed, good feeling you might get when you delve into a new book or story—is a good thing. You should only hope that your readers feel that secure and comfortable when reading your fiction; it means you satisfy them as a writer and that they will continue to buy your books. But here's a warning regarding the comfort zone: As a writer, you should avoid falling into it yourself.

John D. MacDonald never got so cozy with his setting and his characters that he had page after page of that Florida sunshine and tinkering on the boat and chatting with Meyer over scotch on the rocks. MacDonald understood that one of the unbreakable tenets of good fiction is that it has to *move*, and at a pretty steady clip. This is especially true when writing for a popular fiction audience, as opposed to one with more literary tastes. He infused his stories constantly with all of the elements that make me feel so at home with McGee and his sun-kissed, laid-back lifestyle, but he kept the plots churning along, often times putting his characters and that lifestyle in harm's way.

Let's say you've got a character who grew up in the city and buys herself a nice little house in the country. Here's a fine opportunity for you as a writer to have her fix the place up, plant some petunias, paint the mailbox, meet the neighbors, join the church, and do countless other things. Here's the opportunity, also, for you to have her do *only*—or mostly—these things, rather than pushing a story forward that will hold your readers' attention. All of those things that she does should be a subplot, each woven carefully into the bigger plot that will center on the box of old love letters she discovers in the basement or the body in the flower bed or the strange man who lives next door who just might know something about the checkered—or downright criminal—past that she moved to the boondocks to escape.

Remember, Holmes and Watson don't always sit cozy by the fire in their Baker Street rooms on foggy London nights, they get up and *do* things. And

Miss Marple, Agatha Christie's sleuth, doesn't just putter around the garden of her cottage in St. Mary Mead, she spends much, much more of the story's time snooping around to see who poisoned the vicar.

There's nothing wrong with your reader feeling a comfort zone in your fiction, at least occasionally. But make sure you make them feel it in little doses, not in long descriptions. As importantly, you should avoid getting so caught up in it that it impedes your more important goal: to relate a compelling, active series of events.

FRAMEWORK SETTINGS

Frameworking—the inclusion of several things into a larger context or frame—is one of the world's oldest literary devices. Odysseus's adventures were all played out in the bigger story of the return to Ithaca after the Trojan War, and *The Canterbury Tales*, perhaps the most famous framework piece, is comprised of stories told by pilgrims on their way to visit the shrine of Thomas Becket. So all of these individual stories of Cyclopes and killer whirlpools and talking roosters and the Wife of Bath are little pieces of something bigger, in these cases two journeys: from Troy to Ithaca and from London to Canterbury and back again.

The physical settings of fiction can also be frameworked, not by actions or events this time, but by the places themselves. For instance, James Michener's novel *The Source* covers several thousand years by focusing on one small place throughout all of that time. And the framework that he chooses to employ is an archeological dig in which several artifacts are discovered at different depths. Each jar and spearhead and buckle that is excavated has its own story to tell as it turns out, and those stories become the many chapters of the novel.

Even if you don't undertake such vast time travels in your writing, a bit of frameworking in your own setting might make your story or novel more interesting. Maybe you've got two old siblings reunited at the house they grew up in, and the crumbling house becomes, in a flashback or a back story, a newly built, handsome structure. This way, the disintegration of the house itself serves to highlight similar changes in the old men. Or maybe you've got a couple on their honeymoon in France, ending up at the very same little hotel where one of their grandparents had their own honeymoon many decades before. Perhaps you'll have one of your characters come across a dilapidated old building that becomes the setting of the backstory that will be the major plotline, as Fannie Flagg does in her novel *Fried Green Tomatoes at the Whistle Stop Café*.

Using a framework can be a very effective and creative way to tell a story. If you choose to do it, make sure that your major emphasis is on that *story* and not the framework. Remember, the Canterbury *tales* are the important things, not the fact that their tellers are on a common journey.

SUMMARY: BEING THERE

There is a wonderful place in *The Martian Chronicles* by Ray Bradbury where two characters have a chance meeting on a Martian plain on a nice night. One is from Mars and one is from Earth and at first they can't communicate. Then the Martian makes a technical adjustment and begins speaking English, and in not too many minutes they each begin to notice that the other one is not really *there*. In fact, what each of them sees off in the distance—a group of ruins for one and a vibrant, active town for the other—isn't really there either. We finally see what is going on: that the two characters are at the same place, but the *times* at which they are there are actually separated by tens of thousands of years. After a while, these two decide that, rather than try to figure out how this oddity came about or what they might do to fix it, they should each accept the settings they are in and enjoy them.

I've come to believe that that is exactly what good fiction does; it allows us to be immersed in a particular time and place for awhile. Your job as a writer is to deliver those settings.

We'll look in the next chapter at ways to establish settings in particular types of fiction. Here we've considered several ways to do it in general. The times and places in our fiction must be sufficiently credible to make your readers believe they *can* exist (even in impossible places), and they must be sufficiently delivered to make readers believe they *do* exist in the context of your plot. Look for ways to incorporate the larger view (by offering a bird's eye view or a framework) and such things as the weather and the landscape. Good settings are comprised of many details, and good fiction is comprised of nicely crafted settings.

EXERCISE 1

Using one of your manuscripts, find places where you can go into more detail regarding weather conditions and geography. You'll be surprised how much more clearly your setting will emerge when your reader is aware of these things.

Take down your world atlas and start flipping through its pages. Look specifically at the shapes of states, nations, and continents. Now, determine how you might go about describing a few of those shapes for your reader. Every place can look like *something*, and your comparison might be a good way to establish your setting. Pick a couple of places, and write a paragraph or two in which you bring those places more clearly into your readers' minds.

Using that manuscript again, or another one, search for places where you can let your characters' dialogue help establish your setting. You might use inflection or dialect that is unique to a particular place, or your might have your character refer to a city or region.

chapter 8

[DESCRIPTION AND SETTING IN SPECIALIZED FICTION]

Now that we've spent some time considering a few ways to establish your settings and better use of description, let's focus on how to put them to work within several specific types of fiction that are sometimes considered to be outside the general, or mainstream, offerings.

Many talented authors write in more than one of these genres. Just look at several titles of novels by the late Dan Parkinson: *The Guns of No Man's Land*, *Gunpowder Wind*, *Blood Arrow* (westerns), *The Fox and the Flag* (a buccaneer swashbuckler), the Dragonlance Dwarven Nations series (fantasy), *Timecop: Viper's Spawn*, and the Gates of Time series (science fiction).

He was able to successfully publish in these (and even other) genres because he never forgot something that we've talked about more than once already: Good fiction is not finally dependent on the time and place of the story, but on the story itself.

Let's consider an often used device—the journey motif—that always involves some character or several characters attempting to *get* somewhere. It's a literary vehicle as old as literature itself, and it works as effectively in modern novels like *Cold Mountain* as it does in ancient epics like the *Odyssey*. Sometimes the journey is a geographical one—like Huck and Jim floating down the Mississippi in *Huckleberry Finn*—and sometimes it's a completely internal voyage, like Helen Keller groping to find her way out of her blind, deaf world in *The Miracle Worker*. Whatever the particular circumstances, the journey always elicits a change in the central character and usually in others as well. It is this change, and the character's reactions to the journey and its consequences, that allow the journey motif to work effectively in *any* genre.

Here's how. The settings are worlds apart in *Cold Mountain*, the *Odyssey*, *Huckleberry Finn*, and *The Miracle Worker*, as different in fact as in

The Lord of the Rings and *The Wizard of Oz*. But what these works all have in common are not their times and places, but the journey that has to be made.

And what ties Dan Parkinson's many novels together is not the fact that some of them take place in the distant future on planets countless light years away, others on high seas fraught with pirates over two centuries ago, and still others on the plains of the American West in the late 1800s. What makes Parkinson's work accessible and enjoyable is that none of his novels are *about* those places or times. They are about the characters and the dilemmas and struggles and obstacles they face and sometimes overcome. In other words, they're about the *story*.

Believe me, there really isn't much new under the sun, at least when it comes to basic story lines. What *will* be new is the unique spin you put on it in the context of the genre you choose, the setting you create, and the description and fine wordsmithing you employ.

You might end up overlapping or you might find a genre that you enjoy writing and stay within it for several books. Some authors of certain genres publish dozens of novels, or sometimes hundreds of stories, over the course of their careers and never choose to try anything different. That's not a crime. Frankly, I'm delighted that a number of my favorite writers have stayed within what they consider to be *their* genres, since they are such exceptional practitioners of that distinctive type.

Whatever you decide to do—to write within one genre or move around among several—remember two things: (1) the story that you are going to tell will more than likely work within several of the types of fiction and (2) because of that, you'll need to read some good examples of each and keep an open mind when making your decision. Those three characters that you've decided to push into a love triangle in your fiction can go about that dubious enterprise in the suburbs of Spokane or in Dodge City in 1874 or on the eighth planet of Zennotutha or in London during the Nazi blitz. What you have to decide is which setting will let you best highlight the actions of those characters and their situations.

When you get to the place, in a few pages, where I discuss several of the genres each in their turn, don't skip over those that you think are of no interest to you. Consider each one. You just might surprise yourself. Maybe there's a darn fine fantasy story in that imagination of yours, one that you never intended to write.

DOING YOUR HOMEWORK

If you have received many rejection slips from publishers (let's face it, we all have if we've sent off very many queries or samples), you've no doubt come across some version of this phrase: "We suggest that you read some of the books (or stories) that we have published."

That's good advice, indeed.

Publishers are looking for specific types of stories and novels—and require that they be written in specific ways—because the people who buy their offerings expect certain things. Someone who purchases a Western novel expects to *get* one, with all of the requisite gunplay and slapping of leather against horsehide and dust clouds billowing up out of canyons and corrals. And that reader will be mighty put out if something called *The Maverick of Broken Axle Canyon*, with an illustration of a lone cowboy on horseback galloping under a crimson sky, turns out to be a romance involving a tax attorney and a housewife seeking meaning in her life.

Readers generally know what they want. So when you decide to write a particular type of fiction, you need to know what they want, too. Make sure that one of the very first things that you do is read several novels or stories that are representative of that genre. And don't let the fact that you *have* read some of them keep you from this essential step in the writing process. Okay, so you're about to tackle writing a spy thriller and you read William F. Buckley's *Saving the Queen* not too many years ago. Read it again, or one of his other Blackford Oakes novels or some other espionage yarn. But this time read it from the perspective of a *writer*, not just a reader. Look closely at how he crafts his plot. Pay attention to the unique wordsmithing that another author might not use in that particular way in a book in another genre. Take the time to acquaint yourself with how successful writers have written in the genre that you intend to be successful at also. It will be time very well spent.

Let's look now at some special attention that you need to pay to settings and description in a few specialized genres. Remember, scout's honor, you're going to read them all.

HISTORICAL FICTION

Historical fiction is a hybrid of both of those things: history and fiction. Being so it carries with it some requirements that you need to be aware of. The most important of these is that the history part—those things in your story or novel that actually *happened*—need to be essentially correct and verifiable.

By essentially, I mean that even though you can tinker slightly with facts and figures and timeframes, you'd better be careful; artistic license only goes so far. Having General Grant knocking back bourbon in a New York bar in a month and year when he was actually in Mississippi conducting the siege of Vicksburg just won't play. You'll be discovered, I assure you. If not by an editor (the best-case scenario, since it can be fixed), or by a critic (the worst-case scenario, hands down), then by some member of the Daughters of the Confederacy or a Civil War reenactment society or just some reader who is sharp as a tack. Inventing dialogue for historical figures is something that all writers of historical fiction do, but putting those figures in places where they could not have possibly been or giving descriptions of those settings or people that are obviously wrong will deal your credibility more than merely a glancing blow.

Just as you can't play too loose and easy with historical facts, neither can you give too much away about what you and your reader know very well will happen later in the story.

The historical novelist is afforded the luxury of hindsight. But that doesn't give her the right to know of future events in the context of her setting and plot. The officers and their wives at the Saturday night Christmas dance at the Pearl Harbor Officers' Club on December 6, 1941, can't know, in your story, that all hell will break loose in the morning. So your descriptions shouldn't be filled with little clues or premonitions. In a scene set on that evening, we'll need plenty of ice clinking in plenty of cocktail glasses, and navy dress uniforms particularly white against skin tanned dark by the tropical sun. We'll need a dance band playing Benny Goodman tunes and everybody smoking Lucky Strikes and Chesterfields. But what we can't have—unless the story involves a clairvoyant or we see things from a different perspective than that of these revelers—is any forewarning of the Japanese planes that are already flying toward them.

Remember, in most historical novels or stories, both the writer and the reader already *know* that the ship will hit the iceberg, the stock market will crash, or the zeppelin will explode when it finally gets to New Jersey. But in order for the stories to work at all, the characters can't know these things. So your job is to make your descriptions of them and of the setting completely realistic for *that moment*, and not serve as precursors for what will happen later. Other parts of the story—the fictional parts that you skillfully weave in among the historical facts—involve things that neither the characters *nor* the readers can predict. And these will be the core of your tale.

When writing in this genre, pay special attention to the tone of your narrative voice, which is the most constant and sometimes the strongest description that you provide. If you write that novel that starts with the Pearl Harbor dance, and your plot winds its way through the several years of war that followed, then you should continuously make sure that your tone doesn't assume the absolute certainty of an allied victory. As anyone who remembers those years can tell you, there was no such guarantee. I've read more than a few American and British novels and stories set during that war that were written and published before its conclusion. Though the voices and tones were usually confident and patriotic, there was something else there, too, almost hidden between the lines. There was a tone of uncertainty.

In order for your depiction of the time and place to ring true, that uncertainty needs to come through just as clearly in your fiction as it does in those books written when it was happening. So when you have two characters talking about the outcome of the war, don't let them be too cocky about it, unless you make it all bluff and bluster to hike up the other's spirits. And when describing a setting that will change when the war is won, be careful not to mention that, since your characters don't know that it will be the case.

Now that we've gotten those two admonitions (regarding the need for accuracy and the limitation on characters' knowledge of the future) out of the way, let's move on to the business of actual description in historical fiction and to your description of settings in particular.

One way to describe a particular location is to provide details about the place itself. Look at how Irving Stone brings Florence of the Renaissance era to life in this paragraph from *The Agony and the Ecstasy*:

> They went with unmatched strides along the narrow streets, past the Street of the Old Irons with its stone palaces and exterior flights of carved stone stairs leading to jutting penthouses. They made their way along the Via del Corso and saw on their right through the narrow slit of the Via dei Tedaldini a segment of the red-tiled Duomo, and after another block, on their left, the Palazzo della Signoria with its arches, windows and crownings of its tan stone tower penetrating the faint sunrise blue of the Florentine sky.

It is certainly evident that the author did his research, with all the streets and churches where they should be. He works in details even down to the color of the masonry. And this infusion of particulars is a good way to convey the era and the locale to your reader. If your story is set in 1906 San Francisco, you might have your young lovers stroll down one of those steep hills, giving the names of side streets and businesses as they pass them. Some research will be necessary, since those same businesses probably aren't there any longer and some of the street names themselves might have changed in the past century. You'd best not put the Golden Gate Bridge out there in the bay, since it wasn't there in 1906. And your happy couple can't have even a hint of the devastating earthquake that will turn their little world on end, literally and figuratively, the next day.

Another way to establish your setting is to describe small actions or events that are indicative of that time and place, as Colleen McCullough does in the following paragraph from her novel *Caesar*. Instead of describing some of the landmarks of ancient Rome, which she does, by the way, throughout the book, and to great effect, here she focuses on an event, on one man standing up to make a speech. But notice how she works in the point-in-time just as effectively as Irving Stone does in his little walking tour of Florence.

> The jury leaned forward on its folding stools when Cicero walked forward to begin, his scroll in his hand; it was there merely for effect, he never referred to it. When Cicero gave an oration it seemed as if he were composing it as he went along, seamlessly, vividly, magically. Who could ever forget his speech against Gais Verres, his defenses of Caelius, of Cluentius, of Roscius of Ameria?

To answer the narrator's question in that last sentence: *I* could forget them, if I ever even heard of them. But it's not at all important that I know the texts of those speeches. From the context of the paragraph, I can determine that they were real doozies—fine orations, most certainly. Many, many little scenes like this one, along with elaborate descriptions of places and people, finally come together in *Caesar* to give us a crystal clear perception of Rome in the century before Christ.

Now how could you use this approach in your San Francisco saga? You might have one of your young lovers pick up the paper and notice that Enrico Caruso is singing in *Carmen* at the opera house that night (he *was* on the night before the earthquake; I looked it up) or make some reference to President Teddy Roosevelt (he *was* the president in 1906; I didn't have to look that one up).

Both of these approaches—physical description of places and focusing on singular events or circumstances—will work well in historical fiction, and in all of the genres.

Remember that overlapping that we talked about a few pages ago? You'll find more of it in this genre than anywhere else. There are historical romances, historical suspense stories, and time travel yarns that most often involve historical settings. There are also historical murder mysteries like those by Ellis Peters whose sleuth is Brother Cadfael, a twelfth-century English monk. And every Western is essentially a work of historical fiction. All of these will require a clearly defined setting and an abundance of good description if they are to capture the time and place.

MYSTERY

Setting and description take on some additional responsibilities when it comes to the writing of a mystery. Here they have to help establish the mood or tone of suspense as well as provide foreshadowing (clues).

Look at how Janwillem van de Wetering uses his setting to establish the mood in his novel *The Maine Massacre*:

> They could see the rowboat left out on the island's shore. The commissaries waited while de Gier went into the shed and came back with a pistol that had a short gaping tube instead of a barrel. The silence of the bay was so vast that the boat's putter seemed like a line of small dark specks on an immense sheet of white paper. A large black bird came gliding from the island and its croak startled the two men, leaning on the jetty's railing.

These two men are investigating a place where a murder was committed, and the author lets the surroundings in which they find themselves paint the backdrop of the scene. The reader is given a number of bleak images all at once: the abandoned rowboat; that ominous gun with the gaping tube instead of a barrel; the vast, silent bay; and even a croaking black bird sweeping in like something out of one of Poe's tales.

This mood, established at the scene of the murder, will be reestablished over and over again throughout the investigation and the final solution of it. In your fiction, do the same thing. Let *things*—like small rowboats in big bays and even croaking birds—highlight the overall tone that you want to set.

There are basically two types of mysteries: those that are particularly realistic in their portrayals of criminal acts and police procedures and those that are more concerned with the nature and lifestyle of a sleuth (who is often not an official investigator at all, like Sherlock Holmes and Miss Marple) and his or her process of detection. In the first sort, your descriptions will tend to be more brutal and to the point than in the second, with much emphasis on the actual inciting event (almost always a murder) and things like forensic reports and the political pecking order in police departments. In the second, which are sometimes called cozies—alluding I suppose to how we're supposed to feel when reading them—you'll probably have an important scene early on where someone finds a dead body, but you won't spend much if any time describing how it got to be that way. At least not until the very end, when the clever sleuth explains what he has figured out involving the particulars of the murder and, most importantly, the identity of the murderer.

Your emphasis in *both* types should be much more on the person or persons trying to sort out the crime than on the crime itself. Perhaps the best model for this is practically any movie directed by Alfred Hitchcock. Very rarely in a Hitchcock film do we see the actual deed being done, the most obvious exception being that shower scene in *Psycho*. What we almost always see are characters' reactions to a crime that they were not an actual witness to, like the James Stewart character in *Rear Window*, whose dubious hobby is looking into other people's windows only to detect a horrible crime that he has difficulty convincing anyone actually occurred. He doesn't see it happen, and neither do we. What we see is him putting the pieces together, slowly and carefully.

And that is what the reader of your mystery should see.

SCIENCE FICTION AND FANTASY

While all of the other genres are usually set in places that either currently exist or did at some specific time, these two usually require complete fabrication on the writer's part. But this is not always the case; a fantastic setting could very well be a real place with a few differences.

In the opening pages of *Foundation*, the first novel in Isaac Asimov's trilogy of that name, a character has arrived at the planet of Trantor, the capital of an immense galactic empire. He makes his way up to the zenith of the tallest building he can find and surveys a sweeping panorama:

> He could not see the ground. It was lost in the ever-increasing complexities of man-made structures. He could see no horizon other than that of metal against sky, stretching out to almost uniform grayness, and he knew it was so over all the land-surface of the planet. There was scarcely any motion to be seen—a few pleasure-craft lazed against the sky—but all the busy traffic of billions of men were going on, he knew, beneath the metal skin of the world.

This relatively short paragraph contains immense detail about a *place*. We see at once—through the eyes of this young man who is taking it in for the first time—the extent of this planet that is completely covered with man-made structures, all its billions of inhabitants hidden beneath its metal "skin."

In your fiction, let your description of futuristic, fantastic places be as fanciful as you want them to be, but remember this: They must be, first and foremost, a stage upon which your characters do something that your earthbound reader can relate to. Consider that Asimov paragraph; what reader hasn't looked out or down or up at something spectacular and felt a surge of adrenaline? Maybe it was the Grand Canyon or the Eiffel Tower or, in my case, looking up at the enormity of the ceiling of the brand new Astrodome splayed out above me when I was a young teenager. So when I read about the young man in *Foundation* looking out at Trantor, I knew exactly what he was feeling. Not because I had been *there*, but because I had been there.

As I said in the last chapter, you must make sure you maintain a consistency in your description when it comes to the rules you've created or those that are already in place, like the actual makeup of the Martian atmosphere. You may have to use more description than usual when creating a futuristic, fantastic place, and you'll have to use earthly terms to do it.

One thing more, the possibility (in all likelihood, probability) of getting proven wrong is something that you shouldn't even consider when writing science fiction, or any fiction that is set in the future. Nobody expects you to be an oracle, just a storyteller. George Orwell missed the mark in his novel *1984*, so did Clive Cussler in *Raise the Titanic*. So what? Neither of them set out to write prophecies; they intended to write fiction. And that should always be your one and only goal.

WESTERNS

Readers of this type are usually quite loyal to the genre, and they have certain requirements. First and foremost, they expect lots of action—gunfights and fistfights and stampedes—and, secondly, they expect these things to be happening, for the most part, *outside*. You'll be allowed descriptions of the interiors of saloons and sheriff's offices and maybe a blacksmith shop or a cabin out on the prairie. But the lion's share of your description should be of the prairie itself. Use the weather conditions and those wide-open Western landscapes to full advantage. Remember, that old Western song goes "home, home on the *range*." It's the range that the reader of your Western is primarily interested in. So give it to them.

You might do that by describing grasslands spread out under a bright sky, the wind rolling along its golden surface like waves on an ocean. Or maybe you'll depict deep, narrow canyons with high, rocky walls, a trickle of a river winding along the bottom. Or you might focus on one of the towns that dotted the landscape of the American West over a century ago. Maybe it will be a mining camp, a boom town high in the Rockies, its streets nothing more than mud after heavy rains, the smoke from its many fires lifting up through pines and aspens on a foggy, cold morning. Or maybe it will be one of the wide-open towns on the prairies that were railheads for cattle drives. Perhaps it will be the cramped interior of a jolting stagecoach, the countryside sliding by outside its windows.

Or maybe you'll invoke the rough, wide-open spirit of the West in your description of a character, making it even stronger by using frontier dialect in your narration. Elmer Kelton does this in his novel *Joe Pepper* when his narrator, an old cowpoke, remembers a girl he once knew:

> I didn't tell you yet about Arlee's sister. Millie was her name. Arlee wasn't much to look at, tall and thin and bent over a little, and had a short scar over one cheek where a Yankee bullet kind of winked at him as it went by. But Millie, she must have took after her mother's side of the family . . . She wasn't much bigger than a minute, and had light-colored hair that reminded me a little of corn silk. And eyes? The bluest eyes that ever melted a miser's heart.

Now, this voice—complete with winking bullets and "must have took" and "wasn't much bigger than a minute"—probably wouldn't carry your story very successfully, or very far, in other genres. But here, where the characters are extensions of the landscape itself, it fits like a hand in a glove, a buckskin one.

Whatever settings you choose for your Western, wilderness or towns, make sure you provide them in detail. The West—at least our perception of the West—is big, so you should make it big in your reader's mind. It was no coincidence that so many Western movies were filmed in splashy-colored, wide-screen formats. Directors like John Ford and Howard Hawks knew exactly what their audience wanted. And so should you. You don't have Cinema-Scope and VistaVision to work with, but you do have all the tools in your kit, your imagination and the ability to wordsmith. So give the guy in Sheboygan the West in all its magnificent glory.

ROMANCE

The major emphasis of romance stories and novels must be *romance*. But for that love story to work, emphasis must be placed elsewhere as well. Readers of this particular type of fiction are especially interested in elaborate descriptions of clothing and décor, of jewelry and limousines, and elegant mansions and penthouse apartments. In other words, they expect descriptions they aren't likely to get much of in other genres. Many romances are played out in these opulent arenas among these shiny baubles, but not all are. Whatever the circumstances or the surroundings, all of those sweet nothings being whispered and schemes and intrigues and infatuations that drive this sort of story will come to nothing if you don't describe them well.

In *Affair,* a historical romance novel set in Victorian London, the author, Amanda Quick, helps to establish the time of the story by mentioning the advent of street lights, the place by adding a patch of London fog, and the mysterious situation by making a character wonder about the "risky activities" of another.

> The weak gas lights that had recently been installed in this part of town could not penetrate far into the fog. So long as he and Charlotte stayed out of the short range of the lamplight, they could be reasonably safe from detection. Nevertheless, Baxter thought it best to make one more stab at discouraging his new employer from her risky activities.

Elsewhere in the novel, we're given this description of a character's gown, which was . . .

> . . . fashioned of yellow muslin, high-waisted and trimmed with long sleeves and a white ruff. A pair of yellow kid slippers peeked out from beneath the severely restrained flounce that decorated the hem.

Almost certainly, we would never see this much description of how someone is dressed in any of the other genres. But such attention to fashion is one of the hallmarks of romantic fiction. And it serves a function other than giving the reader something pretty to read about; it adds significantly to the overall description of the era in historical romances and the level of society in stories set in modern times.

So does the considerable attention that is paid, in this genre, to the physical description of characters, with an emphasis on pleasing traits and qualities in order to make them more desirable.

This is a good time to reiterate what I said a few pages ago about conforming to genre specifications and giving the reader what they want. In the case of readers of romances, they want tons of description about interiors, decorations, clothing, and characters' physical traits. So you'd do well to provide it, in spades.

HORROR, SUSPENSE, THRILLERS

Here you won't need to pay as much attention to what people are wearing and their handsome houses and furniture as to what they are up to, or quite often what they are afraid of. Consider this single sentence from Stephen King's *Salem's Lot*:

> Matt stood on his stoop for almost a full minute after the sound of the car had died away, his hands poked into his jacket pockets, his eyes turned toward the house on the hill.

That house on the hill will, most certainly, prove to be of some importance in the story. And you can bet, before we know what its importance is, we'll have other characters looking up at it or thinking about it, because Stephen King—considered by many to be the master of this genre—uses foreshadowing exceptionally well throughout his stories and novels.

And so should you. If one of your characters has told another one to never, under any circumstances, go up to the attic, then you'd better mention that attic pretty often, or have that character wonder what the heck is up there. Your readers will most likely not *know* what's there until late in your story, perhaps not until the very end. But it should be on their minds. And you the writer are the only one who can put it there. Make references to it, have other things remind the character of it. Maybe have a few strange sounds drift down from up there in the middle of the night.

If that mysterious attic is a major part of your story, then its constant presence in that story might be the most important piece of your setting, even though your major character and your readers won't actually *see* it for a while yet.

Making something frightening when your only tools are words on paper is a tough assignment. But it is exactly what you're signing up to do when you write this sort of fiction. Sometimes the best way to go about it will be with the "less is more" approach, with strong foreshadowing or showing a character's reaction to a scary thing. Other times graphic description of the thing itself will be the most effective way to do it. Think of exactly what you want your readers to see and how you want them to feel and let that guide you in your decision.

SUMMARY: THE SEVERAL SECTIONS OF THE BOOKSHOP

In this chapter we've looked at specific ways to establish and describe settings and to use description in general in several of the different genres of fiction. There are many other types—like humor, satire, action, and war stories, to name just a few. And the techniques we've talked about here will work in those as well. The various writing tools are not restricted to specific genres, not to be used in others. The use of suspense is not limited to a genre that we've chosen to label *mystery*; it will also be called for in Westerns and ro-mances. The infusion of historical facts will be needed in all of the genres from time to time.

Remember, it's a darned good idea for you, as a writer, to spend some of your reading time in more than just a few of the sections of your favorite bookstore or library. You should recall from the first chapter that I'm con-vinced that good writing evolves from a trinity of approaches: (1) making good use of the underlying craft of composition, (2) a variety of models (examples) to learn from, and (3) careful and deliberate wordsmithing. And those models needn't, and shouldn't, come only from one or two specific types of fiction that you happen to enjoy reading. Excellent authors are repre-sented throughout the genres, and you can learn a thing or two (or many) from any of them. So broaden your horizon.

Personally, I shunned science fiction for too many years, suspecting that it was just too *out there*, much unlike the historical novels and whodunits that I preferred. Then a friend insisted that I read *Childhood's End*, by Arthur C. Clarke, and I was fairly blown away by the strong images that stayed with me long after I finished it. Then came Bradbury's *The Martian Chronicles*, which not only impressed and entertained me, but has had as much influence on my own writing as any other single work. Then I branched off into West-erns and fantasies and romances and any number of things that I would have never thought I would read. I'm a better writer because of my metamorphosis. And to say that I have enjoyed partaking at this much wider table would be an understatement of epic magnitude. I have been a glutton there, and con-tinue to be one. Give yourself over to gluttony, too.

A Short (and *Very* Incomplete) Reading List for Those Who Want to Broaden Their Reading Horizons Among the Genres

Note: this is a list of personal favorites and shouldn't be considered as anything other than that. I encourage you to read the blurbs on many more books than these before making your selections.

HISTORICAL FICTION
James A. Michener	*Chesapeake*
Margaret George	*The Autobiography of Henry VIII*
Irving Stone	*The Agony and the Ecstasy*

MYSTERY
Patricia Moyes	*Down Among the Dead Men*
Ellis Peters	*The Rose Rent*
Agatha Christie	*A Murder is Announced*

SCIENCE FICTION
Arthur C. Clarke	*Childhood's End*
Ray Bradbury	*The Martian Chronicles*
Isaac Asimov	The *Foundation* Trilogy

ROMANCE
Joy Fielding	*Whispers and Lies*
Amanda Quick	*Affair* (historical romance)
Sandra Brown	*The Witness*

WESTERNS
Louis L'Amour	*Hondo*
Zane Grey	*Riders of the Purple Sage*
Larry McMurtry	*Lonesome Dove*

HORROR
Stephen King	*Salem's Lot*
Peter Straub	*Ghost Story*
Anne Rice	*Interview With the Vampire*

EXERCISE 1

Look at some story ideas that you've jotted down in your journal or notebook or at some of your manuscripts. Now, consider how those stories would work in another genre. How would your plot play as a Western? Or as science fiction? Fantasy? Romance? Would it work as a murder mystery? You might determine that it works best in the type of fiction you've chosen, or, on the other hand, you might decide that it will work *better* in another. Quite possibly, you'll have to change your setting—and, of course, your description of it—to make it fit into this new genre.

EXERCISE 2

Think of several historical events that interest you and make a list of ways that you might use one or two of them in a work of historical fiction. For instance, the riots at the 1968 Democratic convention in Chicago might make a fine backdrop for a love story between a liberal and a conservative. True love always wins out, right? Well, this scenario will put that to the test.

EXERCISE 3

Go to the library and locate at least three novels (if you've got lots of reading time to spare) or three short stories (if you don't), each of which is representative of a type of fiction that you have never read. If you're a big fan of mysteries and spy thrillers, then find, say, a Western, a science fiction, and a swashbuckler. Now, when reading them, look for ways the authors went about using craft and wordsmithing and specifically at their settings and descriptions. Make good notes. Learn. Then put your new knowledge to work in your fiction.

chapter 9

[USING DESCRIPTION AND SETTING TO DRIVE THE STORY]

I once sat in a parked car on a broiling summer afternoon in Jackson, Mississippi for no other reason than to gaze at a house that was not very much unlike the ones on either side of it. It was an old house situated nicely among old trees across the street from an old college. The reason I was looking at it—along with two or three other people who had stopped to do the same thing—was the old lady who was, we assumed, inside. For this was the home of Eudora Welty.

I was in Mississippi to teach at a writer's conference and the unlucky fellow who had been designated to drive me around sat there with me, both of us watching the house and its pretty lawn as if something was actually going to *happen*. Nothing did, and I didn't expect anything to. But I figured I shouldn't pass up the opportunity to pay some homage, however slight, to one of the giants of my line of work.

Welty, who died not too long after my vigil, shares the upper echelon of luminous southern literati with the likes of Flannery O'Connor and William Faulkner and a few others, all of whom were, obviously, absolute masters of the art and craft of writing fiction. And one of the specific skills that elevated them to that rarified air was their use of setting and description to make their stories and novels *work*, to drive everything forward. Welty was particularly good at that, and it occurred to me, as I watched her house on that summer afternoon, so pleasant amid its sprawling trees, that it would make a perfect setting for a southern yarn, with a Blanche Dubois or a Colonel Snopes standing on the wide porch, mint julep in hand, everything described in an assured, leisurely voice full of the softness and fragrance of magnolia blossoms tempered with a pragmatic tinge of grit and gristle. And a good writer would use that setting for more than just a place for things to happen, she'd make it emphasize other aspects of the story.

So, how can you use a place and time—and description in general—to do such a large part of the work that you have to do in your writing? Look at how Welty did it in her description of an aged black woman talking to herself while walking to town to get medicine for her sick grandson in "A Worn Path," which is arguably her masterpiece:

> "Walk pretty," she said. "This the easy place. This the easy going."
> She followed the track, swaying through the quiet bare fields, through the little strings of trees silver in their dead leaves, past cabins silver from weather, with the doors and windows boarded shut, all like old women under a spell sitting there. "I walking through their sleep," she said, nodding her head vigorously.

The place itself is as much a tangible reality as the old woman. Its stark reality is highlighted by adjectives—*easy, quiet, bare, dead*—and by the use of an unexpected color—silver leaves and silver cabins, both that peculiar color because they've been there too long. Notice that Welty uses the word *silver* twice, when she could have easily used it just once. She wants to make sure that we see it; she wants us to not miss the similarity between the old, used-up land and buildings and the old, used-up woman. Now look at how she employs personification to drive that imagery home even further; the cabins are "like old women under a spell," and the old woman feels like she is "walking through their sleep." Finally, look at the sparse dialect; she uses the fewest words possible, as if every syllable is an effort, which would actually be the case for an elderly person walking a long distance. All of these elements—the fine wordsmithing, the evocation of the land and the dialect, even the mood of exhaustion—make this character's journey come completely alive for the reader.

When writing your story or novel, look for ways to use your setting and description to do exactly what Welty does here. Whatever your time and place, you can find plenty of details to enlarge and amplify your entire story. Three of the best ways to do this are to let your setting and your description magnify some overall theme, convey the general mood, and enlarge one or more conflicts.

MAGNIFYING A THEME

When dealing with themes in fiction, keep this in mind: Don't constantly pound your reader over the head with whatever social, religious, or political message you might be trying to convey. In fact, I'd advise against trying to convey any such messages at all, or at least to a large extent. Sure, Upton Sinclair might have set out to bring about improvements in the meat-packing industry when he wrote *The Jungle* and Harriet Beecher Stowe might have wanted to abolish slavery with *Uncle Tom's Cabin*, but modern readers aren't looking to be reformed. They want to be entertained. So your fiction shouldn't be a crusade; it should be a story. And if you expect to get it published, and then read, it better be a darn good one.

One way to make it that good is to let the setting and your description emphasize a theme. First off, the term theme, or at least my perception of it, needs some clarification. Many people come away from their English classes thinking that literary themes are a precious few haughty ideals—like *pride*, *truth*, or *equality*—that are chiseled deep into granite. Teachers who advance such a notion do a great disservice to the literature itself and to their students, because very few things in either reality or fiction can be so conveniently fit under such all-inclusive umbrellas. My idea of a theme is anything that the writer is attempting to convey in a particular scene. So, instead of *everlasting love*, your theme in the sixth scene of your story might be *trying to get a date*. Instead of having one lofty theme, your story will have several, probably many.

One of the strongest themes in Greg Tobin's novel *Conclave* is the excessive manipulation and intrigue that sometimes occurs in powerful places, in this case during a papal election in the College of Cardinals. Look at how he uses delicate description and the ominous presence of the surroundings—an assemblage of cardinals, ecclesiastical movers and shakers of the highest order—to get that point across:

> The camerlengo turned to Mulrennan. "You may address the assembly."
>
> Again Vennholme started to protest, but Portillo directed him to his seat with a firm shake of the head. Vennholme stood in place a moment, looking at the faces of his brethren, then complied.
>
> Timothy Mulrennan walked to the head of the room and turned to face the senate of holy elders whom fate, or perhaps Divine Will, had made his judges.

The tension is high in that room, and between those characters and the author's deft description of it—the aborted protest, the study of somber faces, the slow approach to the front—serves not only to show that tension but to magnify that theme. Allen Drury utilizes the same theme in *Advise and Consent*, relocating the setting to confirmation hearings in the United States Senate, and you might use it in a setting not anywhere so imposing or powerful as the Vatican or the Senate chamber. After all, manipulation and intrigue occur in any number of places. Maybe your story is set in a break room in a factory, where one of your characters is about to undercut a union election that will send thousands of workers out on strike. Use the room itself—the slow ticking of a clock, the raspy gurgling of a coffeemaker, the drab, completely utilitarian carpet and walls—to highlight the dreariness and tension. Or introduce a morsel of intrigue at a breakfast table, when a sly teenager who intends to finesse a scheme gets his comeuppance from his father, who is wise to the scam. In that case, maybe a toaster should loudly launch two slices of bread at exactly the moment that the teenager realizes the jig is up. Or maybe you could describe him as catlike, since cats are as stealthy as he thinks *he* is.

Let's turn now to a classic work of nonfiction, to see how a good writer can use description of a physical setting to emphasize a theme, something that is not physical or tangible at all. In C.S. Lewis's *Surprised by Joy*, a chronicle of his early life, he carefully paints a word picture of his surroundings on the afternoon of his purchase of a book that will ultimately nudge him from atheism to Christianity. It is, as you might imagine, an enormously important moment in his life, and he wants his readers to see, hear, and feel the place itself, to get a real sense of the prospect of change, of new possibilities that are not only within him but manifested in the everyday, commonplace bit of the world that surrounds him. Here's how Lewis describes the long ago October afternoon when he reached into a bookstall and lifted out a secondhand copy of George MacDonald's *Phantastes*, a book that would quite literally change his life:

> I and one porter had the long, timbered platform of Leatherhead station to our-
> selves. It was getting just dark enough for the smoke of an engine to glow red
> on the underside with the reflection of the furnace. The hills beyond the Dorking
> Valley were of a blue so intense as to be nearly violet and the sky was green
> with frost. My ears tingled with the cold. The glorious weekend of reading was
> before me.

He, the young man on that platform, is about to undergo a change, even though he is quite unaware of it. Notice that the setting is changing also; darkness is falling, the colors of the distant hills and the sky itself are changing. He uses things that are there—the train station, the last light of the day, the chill, those hills—to call attention to something that is not there, the great alteration that is about to occur inside him. And he ends with a statement about the promise of a good weekend of reading that lies ahead of him, not realizing the fulfillment of greater promise that is in his future, which will be initiated by the small used book that he will begin reading on the train.

Your fiction should contain an abundance of places like that station, where your description of the setting calls your reader's attention to whatever theme you are striving to convey. If one of your characters suffers from low self-esteem or an unflattering self-image, then you might do well to plop her down in an ice cream shop, shoveling down Rocky Road and watching large people wedge themselves into small booths. The fact that the inhabitants of those large bodies aren't doing anything about their problem points your reader to the conclusion that your character isn't either. So, you've utilized a setting and its description to magnify a theme that will make the character's situation clearer for your reader and will drive the story toward some sort of resolution or lack thereof. She'll either do something about her problem or she'll get another scoop of Rocky Road.

CONVEYING MOOD AND TONE

Whatever mood you find yourself in will pretty much determine how your day goes. The same holds true for the characters in your fiction and for the stories themselves.

In the *Iliad*, Achilles spends most of those long years on the wide plains of Troy pouting in his tent, trying to decide if he should fight for Greece or take his men and go home. Since the *Iliad* is about those years leading up to the business of that giant wooden horse and the climatic battle itself, and since Achilles is, perhaps, the major player among the Greeks, his mood pretty much determines the brooding, ominous tone of the entire saga.

When, at long last, he bursts out of his tent—and out of his snit—and flies into action, making short work of Prince Hector and any other Trojans who make the mistake of getting in his way, things perk up considerably. The overall mood changes from one of quiet contemplation, plotting, and endless waiting to one of loud, sword-clanging, bugle-blowing action. The mood of the entire story changes because the mood of one character changes.

This will happen in your fiction, also. Or, at least, it should. The mood of a place or a character should *drive* your story, as Achilles' moods drive the *Iliad*.

Often, the prevailing mood doesn't come from a character at all, but from the setting itself. And your description will have to establish it. *It was a dark and stormy night* is one way to do it. But it's not your only option, nor usually the best. Both setting and description—and description *of* a setting—can be mighty useful here. Consider this sampling from Nicholas Meyer's *The Seven-Per-Cent Solution*, one of his Sherlock Holmes novels:

> It was impenetrable. All about me was a wall of sulphurous smoke, stinging to the eye and noxious to the lungs. London, in a matter of hours, had been transformed into a creepy dream-world where sound replaced light.
>
> From different quarters my ears were assailed by horses' hoofs striking upon the cobbled street and by street vendors' cries as they hawked their wares before invisible buildings. Somewhere in the gloom an organ grinder creaked out a sinister arrangement of "Poor Little Buttercup" . . .

In those two paragraphs, the overall mood is established entirely by the description of the place. Look back at how it is done: the fog (notice that the word itself is never used) is many things at once; it is impenetrable, a wall of sumptuous smoke, stinging, and noxious. Then, when we've seen and felt the setting, we shift sensory gears and *hear* it. We listen to horses' hoofs on cobbled streets, vendor's cries, and finally an unseen organ grinder playing a tune. Notice the strong use of a verb, *creaked*, and an adjective, *sinister*, to secure the gloomy, baleful mood for the reader. Think back to all that we talked about in chapter five regarding the use of sensory description. When establishing a mood or tone, making the reader see, hear, feel, taste, or smell the physical surroundings might be the best way to do it.

So, now that the reader is fully immersed in all this fog and gloom, how does the immersion serve to push the story along? Here's how: No reader, after having been given a description like that one, is going to expect a happy-go-lucky love affair or a syrupy sweet plot involving a boy and his faithful dog. They expect murder most foul, crafty criminals and clever sleuths, and suspense and plenty of it. Once you've established a prevailing mood, you've pretty much set the course of your story. So careful attention to the establishment of that mood is some of the most important work you'll do in your writing.

There are many ways to do it. Often it is best brought about by describing simple actions, as Dashiell Hammett does in *The Maltese Falcon*:

> Spade mashed the end of his cigarette in his plate and made one draught of the coffee and brandy in his cup. His scowl had gone away. He wiped his lips with his napkin, dropped it crumpled on the table, and spoke casually: "You *are* a liar."
>
> She got up and stood at the end of the table, looking down at him with dark abashed eyes in the pinkening face. "I am a liar," she said. "I have always been a liar."

We don't have to be told that these are two tough cookies. Because we have been *shown* that they are. And that tough, edgy tone is evident in more than just the characters. Look back at the specific wordsmithing that brings this image to life for the reader: the slow mashing of the cigarette butt and the one gulp of coffee and brandy, then the quick use of the napkin and dropping it crumpled on the table. And all of these important—yet very common and simple—little actions *before* the important words that are spoken about being a liar. Then, a tiny action of the female character's own—standing up and then looking down (with those "dark, unabashed eyes"). Finally, notice that Hammett gives us no instructions as to how she delivers those lines. He used italics to indicate how the man's words should be heard, but nothing here. This is a good example of that; we can hear this gal deliver those few words in several ways. But each of them is chock-full of an attitude. Each of them leaves no doubt that she is what Hammett might call a cool and collected dame, which fits perfectly into the mood that he wants the reader to perceive.

Now, you might be thinking that I've made entirely too much of those two short paragraphs; after all, my dissection and explanation of them is longer than the paragraphs themselves. That alone should prove my point: that every word and phrase that you decide to use should work toward the effect that you are trying to achieve, and every syllable beyond that is clutter. This extra work on your part is essential to keeping that desired effect front and center in your reader's mind.

In your story or novel, if you want to convey a festive, carefree mood, then you might choose a festive, carefree setting, like a carnival or a sunny day in the park. Or you might rely on the description of a character's actions or mannerisms. Maybe a normally subdued fellow is suddenly overcome by giddiness and flicks water from his glass on a lunch companion.

Remember, never resort to the easy, obvious approach of simply telling readers that "the mood that day was festive and carefree." *Show* them, by either the surroundings or some action, or a combination of both.

When Shakespeare put King Lear up on that cliff howling at the storm, he couldn't very well have him screaming out how much he *loved* his daughters. The mood of the character and the mood of the day had to coincide in order to be effective; the tempest within Lear—his sense of betrayal by his children and his anger because of it—had to be equal to the lightning, thunder, and wind that surrounded him. In the same way, allow mood to drive *your* story.

ENLARGING CONFLICT

When it comes to writing fiction, there are very few absolutes. Here is one: If there is no evidence of any degree of conflict, then you don't have a story. And a good way to ensure that you do is to use your description and setting to enlarge conflicts.

In *Ethan Frome*, Edith Wharton gives us the following exchange between the title character and Mattie, the young woman who works for Zeena, Ethan's wife, who has gone on an errand to another town. Ethan and Mattie have begun to realize the mutual attraction they feel and—given the social and religious boundaries that would have been rigidly in place in a small New England village in the first years of the twentieth century—a fine, festering conflict grows up around that little farmhouse. Ethan has just mentioned that he hoped Zeena made it to her destination before bad weather set in:

> The name set a chill between them, and they stood a moment looking sideways at each other before Mattie said with a shy laugh, "I guess it's time for supper."
>
> They drew their seats up to the table, and the cat, unbidden, jumped between them into Zeena's empty chair. "Oh, Puss," said Mattie, and they laughed again.
>
> Ethan, a moment earlier, had felt himself on the brink of eloquence; but the mention of Zeena had paralysed him. Mattie seemed to feel the contagion of his embarrassment, and sat with downcast lids, sipping her tea, while he feigned an insatiable appetite for dough-nuts and sweet pickles. At last, after casting about for an effective opening, he took a long gulp of tea, cleared his throat, and said: "Looks as if there'd be more snow."
>
> She feigned great interest. "Is that so? Do you suppose it'll interfere with Zeena's getting back?" She flushed red as the question escaped her, and hastily set down the cup she was lifting.

Look at how dexterously this awkward predicament is played out. A much lesser writer would have reported that these two were nervous around each other and gone onto something else. But that doesn't even come close to what Wharton wants to convey. Here is something between flirting and trepidation; both speakers tiptoeing around a gorilla of a dilemma, both knowing what they want, and knowing they can't have it. Now there's a conflict worthy of the designation.

Wharton tells us about the chill that exists between them, then proceeds to prove it, with all that *feigned* interest in unimportant things, like the cat and the meager supper. Then, notice, things perk up when the possibility of

Using Home for Something More Than a Place to be

When choosing a setting, don't limit yourself to what you know. Many of my students feel that they can only write about places they've been, that they can only adequately describe places they have personally seen, touched, tasted, smelled, and heard. There are, I agree, obvious advantages to writing about a place with which you are familiar. But remember all those science fiction and historical authors who had no firsthand experience at all regarding their settings. Remember, too, that Shakespeare, whose greatest works were set in Denmark and Italy, never left the British Isles. They pulled it off, and so can you.

On the other hand, many fine authors have chosen to locate their fiction in places where they grew up and have chosen to live. Faulkner created Jefferson, Mississippi, and pretty much stayed there for all of his fiction, as did John O'Hara with Gibbsville, Pennsylvania. Anne Tyler never strays very far from Baltimore in her novels. And though Mark Twain wandered as far away as Arthurian Britain, any high school student even half awake knows that his best work is played out on the Mississippi River.

While it's certainly true that these writers stayed in their own backyards, so to speak, the much more important thing is that they used those times and places to be considerably more than stages for the action; they put them to work driving the entire story or novel along.

more snow is mentioned, for that means that Zeena won't be coming home tonight and that presents undreamed-of possibilities. Instead of telling us this, Wharton *shows* it in that perfect last sentence. Mattie's actions and mannerisms enlarge the overriding conflict as surely as those two in *The Maltese Falcon* amplify the mood of that scene.

When using your setting and your descriptions to enlarge a conflict, think of things or actions that will help bring this about. Let's say you have a woman who hasn't spoken to her son in over a quarter of a century, and now a situation has arisen where she will have to. The perfect way to call the reader's attention to the conflict might be to set the reunion in the house where she raised her son, among things that he hasn't seen in all that time, maybe working in bits of backstory that tie in a sofa, a picture on the wall, the fireplace. Or you might want to highlight the conflict by describing their mannerisms when they have to acknowledge each other at the door.

Either approach, or both, will be tremendously more effective than telling your reader that these two are laying eyes on each other for the first time since the Carter administration.

SUMMARY: DESCRIPTION, SETTING, AND THE WRITER'S VOICE

In this chapter, we've looked at three ways to use setting and description to help drive your entire story. By emphasizing themes, moods, and conflicts, you can better deliver a work of fiction that your reader can connect with.

Description is a matter of wordsmithing, of selecting precisely the right words to create certain images. So you need to make every description count; make every adjective or phrase serve to bring things into clearer focus in your reader's mind. The setting is another thing entirely and depends on more than just the careful selection of words. The setting is securely anchored in geography and time. It is a fact; either your story takes place in Seattle in the 1860s or it doesn't. So one of a writer's most important jobs is to choose a place that will be more than *just* a place and a time that is more than *just* a time. It should be a time and a place that serves other, bigger functions in the story, like theme, mood, and conflict.

EXERCISE 1

Remember all that nervous tea sipping that Ethan Frome and Mattie did? That's because Edith Wharton wanted the reader to feel and see the tension brought about by that particular conflict. Look through one of your manuscripts and find places where specific details might add to the reader's perception of a conflict, theme, or mood.

EXERCISE 2

Come up with at least one *thing* that might represent each of these common broad themes: (an example, aggravation: a prescription bottle that won't open.)

- infatuation
- anger
- deception
- joy
- hope
- indecision
- manipulation
- superficiality
- credibility
- lack of credibility
- capriciousness
- vulnerability

EXERCISE 3

In that manuscript you already have out, find places where you used setting or description to accomplish one or another of the three things—magnify a theme, convey a mood or tone, enlarge conflict—we've discussed in this chapter. Then look to see if that same setting or description doesn't work for one or both of the other two, also. For instance, look back at those paragraphs from *Ethan Frome*. We saw how the description enlarged a conflict, but doesn't it also convey a mood (nervousness, awkwardness) and amplify a theme (sidestepping an issue)? And if it doesn't, maybe it wouldn't take too much tinkering to make it serve more than one function. After all, the clearer the image you present to your reader, the better.

chapter 10

[WORKING THE MAGIC]

When attempting to teach the fundamental components of a story—interesting characters, a well-established setting, one or more conflicts, and some degree of resolution—I often use *The Wizard of Oz* as a model. One reason I use that particular film is that most people have seen it, and, even if they haven't, it has woven its way so completely into the fabric of contemporary culture that they usually have a general idea of the plot. But my primary purpose in using it is that it does everything that a story should.

Because I mention it so frequently—and sometimes even resort to playing a cassette recording of its rousing overture when my charges need recharging—more than a few students over the years recommended that I read a novel called *Wicked: The Life and Times of the Wicked Witch of the West* by Gregory Maguire. To put it mildly, I didn't leap at the prospect. I've read some novels based on existing characters created by other writers and, with the exception of John Gardner's *Grendel* and a few of the Sherlock Holmes resurrections, I haven't been that impressed.

But *Wicked* is indeed a horse of a different color. It is, in fact, one of the best-crafted and most enjoyable novels that I've read in a while. Here's why: The author, Gregory Maguire, infuses his story with excellent description page by page, actually line by line. As importantly, he sustains suspense and drama throughout, in a time and place that was already sufficiently fantastic, in my mind, and is enormously more so here. Add to that a cast of characters that I really came to *care* about, including the witch, who I certainly never cared about before, beyond trying to hide my quivering, six-year-old body under the seat in the old downtown movie theater in Palestine, Texas, the first time I made her acquaintance. Maguire gives her and the other characters doubts and inclinations and motivations that are not all that much unlike mine and creates a setting—complete with Munchkins and yellow brick roads—that is entirely believable in its context. In short, he works considerable magic.

There are many ways to bring this magic about, and in this chapter we'll focus on a few of them. But first, let's take a look at the opening paragraph of *Wicked* and see what Maguire used to set his story in motion:

> A mile above Oz, the Witch balanced on the wind's forward edge, as if she were a green fleck of the land itself, flung up and sent wheeling away by the turbulent air. White and purple thunderheads mounded around her. Below, the Yellow Brick Road looped back on itself, like a relaxed noose. Though winter storms and the crowbars of agitators had torn up the road, still it led, relentlessly, to the Emerald City.

Notice the perspective we are given in the first sentence. We aren't actually in the setting but far *above* it, looking down at something specific: the curving road. Remember the macrocosm that we talked about in chapter seven? That bird's, or in this case witch's, eye view gives us a glimpse at where the story is going to take place before we swoop down into it, *it* being both Oz and the story itself. We immediately have a witch, which is in most cases unbelievable, in some turbulent weather and dark thunderheads, which are commonplace occurrences. Then we have the yellow brick road, which we already know something about; but it is in bad repair due to winter storms—that makes sense—and crowbar wielding agitators, foreshadowing of a conflict that we hadn't expected. It's no coincidence that the simile regarding that road involves a noose, which is hardly ever a harbinger of anything cheerful. The end result of all of it, at least for this reader, is that it is a mix of things I expected and things I didn't. And that's a perfect formula for making me want to read on.

First impressions are—as your parents and your high school speech teacher used to tell you—quite important. And this paragraph certainly makes a dandy one. But one thing that sets excellent authors apart from simply good ones is how they maintain the level of wordsmithing used at the first all the way through till the end, as this writer does.

So how should you go about it?

The complete answer to that would fill up a shelf full of books. But let's have a look, paying special attention to setting and description, at five things—alteration of reality, selection of the title, crafting of the first sentence, placing a specific setting within a much larger one, and blending your story and your voice—that will help you accomplish this artful manipulation that is at once difficult to pull off and absolutely essential to the success of your fiction.

MODIFYING REALITY

Often, in order to end up with fiction that comes off as realistic, the author has to do a good bit of tinkering with what is *really* real.

To find proof of this, you might not have to look any further than your kitchen on a typical weekday morning. Let's say you're about to write a scene that involves a husband and wife having their last cups of coffee before they each leave for work. So you figure you'll record your and your significant other's dialogue one early morning, word for word, so as to infuse your novel with authenticity. When you play the tape back, here's what you might have to work with:

> "Almost out of coffee."
>> "Get the dark roast this time. This is too weak."
>> "Don't put in so much water. You put in too much water."
>> (Shuffling of papers)
>> (Pause)
>> "Get the dark roast."
>> "We need milk. Two percent."
>> "Can't go today. Gotta meeting."
>> "I'll go."
>> (Shuffling of papers)
>> (Pause)
>> "This stuff is worthless. Get the dark roast."

Now, our subject in this chapter is working magic in your writing. Well, I've got news for you; if you use *that* little conversation verbatim the only magic that will ensue will be your reader making your book disappear.

I stated in chapter two to be on the lookout for details everywhere. And I haven't changed my mind now that we are in chapter ten. But *finding* all of those particulars doesn't mean you have to use all of them, and it also doesn't mean that you, as a writer, shouldn't manipulate them in order to make them fit into your story. Sure, you shouldn't change the date or the location of the *Titanic*'s demise, but you can—and you'd *better*—modify that business about the coffee that we just read.

In your scene that takes place in the kitchen, you'll want little details to show the reader where things are taking place. You can have these two finishing off the coffee, and maybe even have one of them suggesting that they try a darker roast. But to have this pop up for absolutely no purpose is clutter. In real life, things like this pop up all day long, but in fiction everything should be there for a reason. For instance, maybe one of the characters in your novel wants to make some big changes in his life, and this little thing—wanting a different kind of coffee—will call the reader's attention to those bigger alterations. Remember, seemingly insignificant details are often the best ways to amplify a theme, mood, or conflict.

In the first act of *Death of a Salesman*, Willie Loman comes home late from a business trip. He's tired, argumentative, and worried about the fact that he's pretty much washed up as a traveling salesman. To cheer him up, his wife suggests that he eat a little something; she tells him she bought some new kind of cheese. "It's whipped," she tells him. Willie goes on with his tirade about his current dilemma and then stops, thinks, and asks "How can they whip cheese?" It's a great line. Not because Arthur Miller might have heard it somewhere and decided to use it in his play, but because it enlarges what Willie is feeling. The world is changing too quickly around him, leaving him behind, and something as inconsequential as whipped cheese calls attention to it.

Look back at the transcript of that morning conversation. Words are left out; sentences are incomplete; there's no connective theme. It's a mess.

So how could you use it? Answer: You *change* it. You lift out exactly what you need—that bit about wanting stronger coffee to spotlight your character's desire for bigger changes—and you rework the dialogue:

> Ted glanced at the headlines, then flipped over to the sports section to see if the Dodgers won. He sipped his coffee.
>
> "This stuff is horrible," he said. He put the mug down on the counter. Pushed it away from him. "It's like colored water."
>
> Alice looked up from the metropolitan section. She looked at him over the tops of her half-frames.
>
> "It's the brand we've used for years," she said. "I make it the same way every day." She put the paper down; took off the glasses. Thought. "You've never complained before."

Now we've got something that comes a heck of a lot closer to working in a story or novel. The dialogue is smoother and makes more sense. The little conflict is obviously there for a reason, and the wife just might be picking up on the reason there at the end.

When writing fiction, you'll have to modify reality constantly in order to work your magic. That oddly decorated pawn shop you pass on the way to work every day will work much better in your story in a different location. The mutt in your neighbor's back yard becomes a Great Dane. The cute newscaster on Channel 11 becomes in your novel the weather girl with whom your protagonist is infatuated.

The many, many tidbits of reality that you gather will ultimately need to be adjusted, enlarged, narrowed, or modified in some other way to finally fit nicely into the story that you want to tell.

YOUR TITLE

The single most important first impression your fiction will make on your potential reader—other than the cover of your novel or the illustration of your story, neither of which you are likely to have any control over—is your title. So you'd better spend some time coming up with a perfect one.

Sometimes titles will emerge from your own manuscript, bubbling up out of your wordsmithing like *The Catcher in the Rye* must have for J.D. Salinger. Other authors have used the title to magnify a significant theme, as Robert Harling did when calling his play about a group of scrappy southern women *Steel Magnolias*. I am among the legions of writers who have stolen their titles outright from the Bible, *The Windows of Heaven* (Genesis 7:11), and from poets, *Into That Good Night* (Dylan Thomas), *A Place Apart* (Robert Frost). I haven't pilfered from Shakespeare, who has provided more titles than any other single author, but I'm not done yet.

When it comes to setting and description, your title can work wonders for both. Many titles evoke the primary setting in the reader's mind before they have read one word of the text. Just a few examples are *Chesapeake*, *London*, *Across the Great Divide*, *The Bridge of San Luis Rey*, *Dubliners*, and *Winesburg, Ohio*. Other titles aren't so bold, but only hint at the *type* of place or the geographical location, like *The Big Sky*, *Snow Falling on Cedars*, *The Cider House Rules*, *Islands in the Stream*, *Tobacco Road*, and *Where the Red Fern Grows*. And many authors use the title to help define a character, conflict, or situation; some examples are *The Ugly American*, *Rich Man, Poor Man*, *A Time to Stand*, *Bound for Glory*, *Girl With a Pearl Earring*, *Our Man in Havana*, *In Dubious Battle*, and *The Once and Future King*.

Choosing a title might be one of the last things you do in the writing process. In fact, I'm inclined to suggest that it *should* be; as your plot and characters constantly change in your thinking, the perfect title might emerge. When writing a novel that begins with a little boy waiting for the first cold front of the season on his grandfather's farm and ends with that little boy having become an old man, I had a short list of several titles that I had lifted from several sources. Finally, I settled on *Touching Winter*, which hadn't been on my original list at all, and which I didn't have to steal from anyone, because of the double meaning of the boy waiting for the season to change and the old man in the winter of his life.

Face it, your title is an extremely important bit of business. It is the moniker by which everyone will refer to this thing that you sweated and strained over for so long; it is the flag that will fly over your book or story for as long as people read it and refer to it. So choose wisely.

Here's one last thing regarding titles. More than a few have firmly rooted themselves in the public mind, so leave those alone. Whatever the legal or ethical implications, if any, you'll look mighty foolish sending your novel set in Dallas and Fort Worth in to a publisher with *A Tale of Two Cities* on the cover sheet.

FIRST SENTENCES

I once heard about an acquisitions editor in New York who takes three manuscripts to work with him every morning on the subway, because there are three subway stops between his apartment and his office building. He gives each of the manuscripts exactly the time it takes the subway to make its way from one stop to the next, and if the author hasn't grabbed his attention by then, that project is down the drain, at least as far as that editor and that publishing house is concerned. This may or may not be a true story; I can't vouch for it. But, fact or fiction, it's a good reminder for writers who want to be published to provide their reader with the very best first sentence, and paragraph, and page they can concoct.

The primary function of that initial sentence is to make the reader want to read the second one, so it has to be a real grabber. "Once upon a time" won't cut it, and "There lived, once, in the city of Paris a . . ." isn't likely to, either. It needs to be engaging, maybe a little quirky, and it wouldn't hurt if it had a smidgen of mystery or foreshadowing.

When brand new fiction writers in my classes and workshops bring in their first stories to the critique table, we have to sometimes wade through a great pile of clutter before we get to what might serve as an effective first sentence. Often it is buried in the second paragraph, or the second or third page, hiding there like a gold nugget waiting to be dug out. That's because human beings usually have an innate propensity to take a long time getting to the point. Either that or they've been so thoroughly trained to write thesis statements that their first sentence might be something like "The murder of Erica Bennington was committed by Wallace Weeks, her spurned lover." Which, provided this story was supposed to have been a whodunit, would hardly be the best way to begin.

Just keep this in mind: This first arrangement of words is your reader's initial taste of both your story and your voice. So work substantial magic here. And it sometimes offers an excellent opportunity to get a toehold into your setting and description.

Let's look at several first sentences and consider *why* they work. We'll forego the very famous ones—like "It was the best of times, it was the worst of times . . ." and "Call me Ishmael"—and concentrate on some that are equally as effective but are probably less well known. Here's how J.R.R. Tolkien begins the first chapter of *The Fellowship of the Ring*, the first volume of the *Lord of the Rings* trilogy:

> When Mr. Bilbo Baggins of Bag End announced that he would shortly be celebrating his eleventy-first birthday with a party of special magnificence, there was much talk and excitement in Hobbiton.

First, there is the pleasing alliteration of the name, followed closely by that unexpected number—*eleventy-first*—and finally the promise of something exciting that is going to happen: a party. Then there is the first use of two of Tolkien's magical place names—Bag End and Hobbiton—which begins to establish the setting. Much is accomplished here, in not very many words. It's a fine little attention-getter of a sentence that pulls the reader quietly into a riveting, oftentimes horrifying saga that will wind its way through the next thousand plus pages.

In her novel *Summer*, Edith Wharton starts with this:

> A girl came out of lawyer Royall's house, at the end of the one street of North Dormer, and stood on the doorstep.

At first glance, it seems simple enough, almost as if it had been dashed off quickly in order to get a start. But I suspect Edith Wharton never dashed off a line in her life. Closer examination shows the thought and craft that went into this beginning. We have, in this first little taste of the novel, a girl for whom we are not given a name or an age; Wharton knew that sometimes the best description is no description. The owner of the house is identified as a lawyer, which throws open several possibilities; the girl might be his daughter, or then again she might be a client. Then we're given the name of the town or city, North Dormer, which might make some readers wonder if there is a South Dormer, followed quickly by proof that it is most certainly a town, and a small one, since there is only one street. These twenty-three words provide a good bit of information, and one important question: Who is this girl and what is she up to?

Now here's Jeffrey Archer's opener for his novel *First Among Equals*:

> If Charles Gurney Seymour had been born nine minutes earlier he would have become an earl, inherited a castle in Scotland, 22,000 acres in Somerset, and a thriving merchant bank in the city of London.

This one foreshadows a character's actual situation—whatever it might turn out to be—with what it *would* have been, had fate been a bit more prompt. Archer chooses to start with irony, and one that most if not all of his readers have had some experience with: the old *woulda, shoulda, coulda* slings and arrows that destiny sometimes hurls. Beginning with something that the reader can identify with is a very good way to launch a story or novel. In your own writing, look for situations that might make the reader connect with the story, and you might have found a fine place to begin.

Another good way is to start with a relationship, more than likely one that involves a conflict. Frederick Busch begins his novella *A Handbook for Spies* with this:

> Willie thought of his parents' life together as an inverted pyramid, a vast funnel, a tornado that stood still.

There's any number of ways this author can go from here. But you can safely bet the narrator's parents—and their odd relationship—will be a large part of it. So he anchors it in the reader's perception at the outset. Sometimes it's best to provide readers with a strong image like this one right up front, one that will stick with them throughout the story.

Whatever your leadoff sentence ends up being, it had better be interesting and promising enough to keep your readers on board. And the best way to do that is to give them just enough to make them wonder what's up, and to make them want to stick around to find out.

YOUR SPECIFIC SETTING WITHIN
A LARGER ONE

In my creative writing classes and workshops I call this "the thing and the bigger thing."

The "thing" is the specific storyline or, more often, an individual scene. And the "bigger thing" is something that impacts more people than the few characters in the scene. For example, here are Huckleberry Finn and Jim, the runaway slave, drifting along on their raft on the wide Mississippi, the countless stars spread out above them in the night sky. That scene is the "thing," but it is just one small component of several bigger "things," like the Fugitive Slave Act and the prejudicial societal norms of that era.

In regards to setting, this disparity between the two things—the small setting and the much larger one (which includes not only places but other things, like philosophy and customs, as well)—provides an excellent opportunity for you to firmly establish the time and place where your story takes place.

Go back to chapter one and look over those paragraphs from *Underworld*. The specific setting is a baseball game at the Polo Grounds in Brooklyn in 1951. But notice that the setting is significantly more than that. It is other places in greater New York where people are listening to the game on the radio, it is four famous people who we recognize, it is the love affair of a city and a nation with baseball, and it is the advent of the age of nuclear weapons, to name just a few.

Now, how can you use this enlarged, wider macrocosm to enrich your own setting and description?

Let's revisit that husband and wife that we left with their weak coffee. We'll say that the coffee is being drunk in a kitchen in an old neighborhood of Oxnard, California, with tree-lined streets and lots of picket fences. That neighborhood—along with the husband who wants to make some changes in his life that don't include Oxnard or, perhaps, that wife who is staring at him—is the "thing" of your story or at least of this one scene. The "bigger thing" might be the entire state of California, or of the western seaboard, that is undergoing energy cutbacks that affect our characters and their situations. Or maybe the divorce laws in California are stricter than they are in other places—I don't know that. Look it up; it's your story, and that impacts this fellow's decisions. Or maybe something going on on the other side of the planet affects these two and the changes the man wants to make; maybe their son is in the front lines of a war.

Here's the point. When writing fiction, look beyond the obvious setting and situation that you establish. One reason to do it is to keep yourself out of trouble with your editor. If you have a lawyer in your novel flirting with a pretty woman in the front row of the jury box during a trial in 1903, you'd better think again. Because there would, almost certainly, have been no women in jury boxes in this county in that year. But a better reason to set your sights higher and wider is to take advantage of the many societal, historical, and geographical implications that you can use to make your story stronger and better.

LEAVING YOUR READER WITH A TASTE OF YOUR STORY *AND* YOUR VOICE

Some of the strongest magic you'll have to work will be after the fact. You'll need to leave your reader with a lingering flavor of both your story and the voice in which you told it.

So how do you do that?

Here's the one and only answer: *constantly*. This fusion of these two effects on the reader isn't something that you can go back in and fix after you're done. You've either built a fine story line by line or you haven't. And you've either conveyed it in a dependable, consistent, unique voice or you haven't. If you haven't done these things, you have a real problem on your hands. If you *have* done them, then you might just be home free.

A good way to check to see if you are balancing story and voice is to print out chapters or scenes as you finish their first drafts and read them back over carefully. I have two suggestions here that might or might not work as well for you as they do for me. First, make sure you actually print the text out on paper and read it with pencil in hand. I maintain that we bring a slightly different mindset to reading something on a page than we do to seeing it on a screen. Unless you end up publishing your work as an e-book, your reader will see it on paper, so it's a good idea to read it back to yourself in the same medium to see if your story and your voice are emerging. Second, put the printed pages away for a day or so before reading them. Go on and start working on the next part, and come back to this section later. That way, the words won't still be ringing in your head as you look at them again. That fresh viewpoint, even if it is only a day removed from the first one, will make a great difference. And you'll see things, good and bad, that you are likely to overlook when reading what you have just written.

Waving the Magic Wand

Here's a checklist to help you make sure you did the best job possible on that manuscript that you're ready to start sending out to prospective publishers:

- Is the title representative of your story and will it elicit a reader's interest?
- Is your opening sentence a "grabber"?
- Is your narrative voice consistent and user-friendly?
- Are the characters and the setting credible?
- Is there a recognizable overall mood or tone?
- Is there some evidence of settings and situations that are *larger* than your specific settings and situations?
- Are there enough resolutions to tie up all loose ends that need to be tied up?
- Have you wordsmithed thoroughly? Have you chosen the best word and phrase in *every* case?
- Have you varied the length and structure of your sentences and paragraphs?
- Have you shown more than you've told?
- Have you provided sufficient description?
- Have you provided too *much* description?

Will the finished product be something you'll be proud of?

There's no one model that I can share with you here, because these things have to work throughout entire stories and novels, not in just a paragraph or two. But think of a piece of fiction that you particularly enjoyed and that stayed with you, then look back over it and determine *why* it worked so well for you. There will be many, many little things that the author did to warrant your overall satisfaction. But I'll bet the main reason you were impressed and entertained was this combination of story and voice.

SUMMARY: THE LITTLE MAN BEHIND THE CURTAIN

In this chapter, we looked at several places where you can work some of the magic required to tell a story effectively. Modifying realistic things and actions so that they will fit smoothly into your fiction is essential, as is choosing a good title and first sentence. You might use a specific setting within the larger context of a more inclusive one, and you will definitely need to balance the story you are telling and the unique voice in which you are telling it.

Since we opened this chapter with references to *The Wizard of Oz*, it seems only right that we close it with one.

Do you remember when Toto runs forward and pulls the curtain away to reveal that the horrific, fire-breathing Wizard is nothing more than a not very impressive little man pulling at levers? Well, I hate to burst your bubble, but that's you back there. And it is me.

The writer is that little man behind the curtain, working constant magic and manipulating and tinkering and wordsmithing to such an extent that, if he or she is any good at it at all, readers won't see any of the seams or the inner workings. What readers should see is a smooth telling of a good story that appears to have been no trouble at all to dash off.

We know better, don't we? We who sit down in quiet, lonely places and put ourselves through the rigors of writing know that, however proud and contented we might feel when the work is done, the writing itself is often a staggeringly painful and aggravating enterprise.

But that can be our little secret.

EXERCISE 1

Go on a shopping trip for a title for that manuscript you've been writing. Look in all of these places and come up with one from each:

- the Bible (*East of Eden* has been taken; choose another)
- Shakespeare (ditto for *The Winter of our Discontent*; darn that Steinbeck)
- Some of your favorite poems (you can't have *For Whom the Bell Tolls*)
- Nursery rhymes (sorry, *All The King's Men* is spoken for)
- A single word that encapsulates an overall theme or mood (forget *Misery*)
- A common creed or phrase unique to a character's profession (nix on *Protect and Defend*)
- Your characters' dialogue or a situation in your own story (this be fertile ground; go for it)

Now choose the best one, close your eyes, and imagine it in bold print above your name on the cover of a bestseller.

Using the same manuscript, circle any sentences in the first several pages—or maybe even further along—that might work as the very first sentence of the story or the chapter. You might just come up with one or two that will be better than the one that currently occupies that place of honor.

Jot down five adjectives that you believe describe your creative voice, the unique style that you employ to tell a story. Just a few possibilities are *friendly*, *laidback*, *serious*, *humorous*, *ominous*, *dynamic*, *ironic*, *formal*, and *informal*. Then, when you're confident that you've chosen the five best words, look for examples of each in your writing. You will probably confirm your self-appraisal, but, who knows, you might discover that your voice is actually different than you thought.

chapter 11

[TOO LITTLE, TOO MUCH]

We've spent ten chapters now looking at ways to make your descriptions better and your settings stronger and more realistic. So now let's take some time to consider some things that you should *not* do.

I thought about calling this one *Minimalism versus Excess*. But, in addition to its sounding entirely too technical, it implies that all we're about to discuss is short sentences like some of Hemingway's as opposed to page-long ramblers like many of Faulkner's. That perception would be misleading, since there is nothing at all wrong with using very short or very long sentences, as long as you use them correctly and well. And this chapter will be about things in your writing that *are* wrong and need to be made right.

By *too little, too much* I mean the wide pendulum swings of not giving the readers nearly enough to bring them into the story or understand it and giving them considerably more than they need, or want, to know. Your job as a writer is to stay in the middle ground, and sometimes that proves to be a delicate bit of maneuvering.

DEALING WITH CLUTTER

In Stephen King's *On Writing*, he tells about a sort of epiphany he experienced in high school when he got back a page of copy from the old newspaper editor who had just hired him. Much—perhaps half—of the text was crossed through, and what was left was exactly what he (King) had intended to say in the first place. The editor then imparted this gem of wisdom:

> "When you write a story, you're telling yourself the story," he said. "When you rewrite, your main job is taking out all the things that are *not* the story."

If that precept could be somehow injected into everyone who intends to write, then we'd have better writing, writing teachers would have fewer headaches, and editors would either have considerably less to do or be out of a job altogether.

Let's look now at some elements of writing that are rich loam for "all the things that are *not* the story," and at some ways to avoid letting that clutter creep into your fiction, especially into your settings and description.

Dialogue Tags

These little fellows—. . . *said Mary*, . . . *he answered*, . . . *she replied*—are often necessary, but not nearly as often as many writers seem to think. They carry enormous clutter potential.

I have two rules regarding dialogue tags that I try to pound into my students: (1) if there is any way not to use them, *don't*, and (2) keep adverbs out of them.

Regarding the first one: If you have two characters in a scene—even in a scene that is dialogue driven—you shouldn't need more than a grand total of *two* dialogue tags. It's necessary to distinguish who's talking at the start of a conversation, but then the reader should be able to keep up. It gets trickier if more than two speakers are involved, and more tags will be required. Even with several characters babbling, if you've done a good job of describing them, giving them unique personalities and voices, then readers will know who is speaking by what they are saying, and they won't need tags very often.

Now, about those adverbs. Not much that a writer can do will put me off faster than constantly using them in tag lines to describe something or someone. Listen:

> "My goodness," Eloise said, hopefully, "that *is* good news. Don't you think?"
> "Not really," John responded, sadly. "It all might come to nothing."

This conversation is quickly coming to nothing, as far as I'm concerned. If the writer wants Eloise to be hopeful and John to be sad, then she should have them do hopeful and sad things. Or describe them as hopeful and sad. Better yet, let their words stand for themselves; Eloise's dialogue *is* hopeful and John's response to it *is* sad. The reader can discern both moods without being told what they are.

When writing, you should be as watchful for things to leave *out* as you are for things to put in. Things that don't have to be there—like useless tags—do nothing more than slow readers down and divert their attention away from the story you're telling.

Clichés

As we discussed in earlier chapters, where clichés are concerned, fewer isn't good enough; you should aim for *none*. To say in your fiction that a landscape is *pretty as a picture* or a character is *as quiet as a church mouse* or *running around like a chicken with its head cut off* is just bad writing, top to bottom.

Using clichés in dialogue sometimes works. A character who spews them out might add a little needed comic relief in your story, but having more than one do it is a bad idea. And for *you* to use them outside of dialogue will lose you many a reader.

If the image conveyed by a cliché is one that will be useful for your description, then come up with other ways to say the same thing. There are plenty of alternate—and better—ways to say or show that someone is inebriated than resorting to saying they are *tight as a tick* or *three sheets to the wind*.

Creative writing should be *creative*, and there is nothing creative about using clichés. They're nothing more than crutches that keep you from having to conjure up your own descriptions. So, unless you're going for the *film noir* voice of Mickey Spillane—"She leaned against the file cabinet, her face like a mile of bad road"—you'll need to avoid clichés.

Repetition

We talked about cadence in chapter three; now let's spend a minute or so on how to avoid its evil nemesis: repetition.

It works its way into our writing quite naturally, since most people tend to repeat themselves in conversation, and if something is weighing heavily on our mind, we rerun things over and over in our thinking. In writing, repetition stands out (if I hadn't just delivered that little diatribe regarding clichés I'd say *like a sore thumb*).

Perhaps the most common culprit is the adverb, which seems to be drawing considerable fire in this chapter. Please understand that some of my best friends are adverbs; I use them all the time in my writing. But the problem is that they are *so* useful. They are just too handy and sometimes keep us from giving a better description. Most often, since they are very *telling* modifiers, they keep us from *showing* a trait in a character or place or situation. For instance, if you say that a character quickly ate her dinner, that might be all you want to say about it and it will certainly suffice. But if the fact that she is shoveling it down at breakneck speed is important to your plot, then you should show her doing just that, in as much or as little detail as you feel is needed for the scene.

One adverb in particular—*very*—is quite possibly the most common single-word violator of the clutter rule. We are in love with this word in our language and tend to use it when other words or phrases, or the absence of them, would work much better. If we want a house in our novel to be larger than most houses, we say that it is *very* large. For a writer purporting to write well, that is *very* bad. There are so many ways to show the enormity of a house other than resorting to using a description that is too generic to carry much useful imagery. Needless to say (I hope), the way to make that house even bigger is *not* to add yet another *very*, making it a *very, very* big house. Following that formula, you could tack on six or seven more *verys* and have yourself a house of gargantuan proportions, and a bit of description that is abysmal.

The most common repetition that lifts its ugly head in manuscripts—it's regularly ferreted out in critique sessions (peer workshops)—is when a writer uses a word or phrase that has just been used. For instance, if you say that a character ordered the smoked salmon for lunch and, in the same paragraph, that he smoked a cigarette while waiting for his check, that's using the same word too often too closely together. Granted, the first *smoked* is an adjective and the second is a verb, but the reader hears the same thing both times, and that repetition keeps your story from flowing as smoothly as it could if you changed the second *smoked* to *had*.

Even words that sound alike, or almost alike, can be repetitious. Donald Westlake once said that if he had known that his character Parker would work himself into an entire series of crime novels, he might have chosen another name for him. Because over the years, Westlake has had to grabble many times with how better to say *Parker parked* his car.

In addition to being always on the lookout for common words and phrases that you've repeated, be just as diligent when looking for the uncommon ones—like *scatterbrained*—which will work only once in a great while, probably only once in an entire novel. *Smoked* popping up here and there is fine, but *scatterbrained* is too unique to be effective more than once. And be careful to not let phrases reemerge in your dialogue. "Oh, my God!" has been uttered, screamed, or barely whispered in more novels and stories and movies than perhaps any other. When your character says it, if it fits in your story, then join the parade, and it will probably work just fine. But if that character says it again, or others use it, then your reader will stop seeing those words and start seeing a cliché.

Didacticism

More than a few professional writers are also teachers, and sometimes it's hard to keep teaching out of our fiction. If it does creep in and becomes too apparent (that is, if the object becomes instruction rather than storytelling) then it's given a name: didacticism. Which is, you should note, not a commendable trait in fiction; it's certainly not a word that you want mentioned in your reviews.

Let's say your historical romance is churning along nicely and you need your reader to know that right about here is when Thomas Becket is slain in Canterbury Cathedral. Now, first of all, unless it's important for your readers to know this in regards to your story, then it's not your job to tell them. Let her go to T.S. Eliot's *Murder in the Cathedral* or a history of England for that. But if that event *is* essential to what's going on in your fiction, then you'll need to find another way of imparting it than stopping the flow of the story and giving a lecture about it. Maybe one of your characters can learn about it from another one—in dialogue or perhaps in a letter. Or you can make references to it in your narrative. Another option is to set one of your scenes right there in the cathedral on that blustery December night and have the martyrdom become part of your plot. Ken Follett does this very thing, with this very event, in *Pillars of the Earth*.

Remember, readers of historical fiction expect to be given bits and pieces of history. But they don't want, and probably won't tolerate, history *lessons*.

Another thing readers aren't likely to abide is being preached to, which is a form of didacticism. Unless you're aiming for a particularly specific audience, like readers of Christian fiction, then you'd do well to leave out anything that might come across as a sermon.

Ethical teachings or implications are like symbols when it comes to writing. If they need to be there, or if the reader wants them, they will emerge naturally from the story. It's not your job to point them out. Summing up your story or novel with either some character or the narrator cataloging the virtues of a person or the rightness of an action or situation is much too over the top; you might as well conclude with "and the moral of this story is . . ."

The moral of *this* story is don't tell the moral of the story. If there really is one, *show* it—in the story itself.

Verbosity

Verbose, along with *didactic*, is another of those words that you'd rather not find in a review of your fiction. A few of the many synonyms for verbose are *wordy*, *longwinded*, and *rambling*; none of which are good references for an author.

Whether your writing is clear or verbose depends on your individual writer's voice. And yours should lean toward the former. We're not talking about using a lot of words here, which is the common misconception of what verbose means. Larry McMurtry's Pulitzer Prize-winning *Lonesome Dove* is a huge novel that consists of one heck of a lot of words, but the story is told in a crystal clear voice. So it is not verbose. Another writer might write a short, short story in which he is much more intrigued with the beauty of his own language than with the story he is telling, and that brief offering would indeed be verbose.

Becoming enamored with grandiose descriptions and language is a pitfall that modern writers should avoid. Many first time poets and writers of fiction think back to those things by the romantic poets and Charles Dickens that they read in high school and they try to squeeze their poems and stories into antiquated structures and phrasings. Then they'll flop around in them long enough to finally realize (I hope) that their fiction just looks silly dressed up like that.

Two centuries ago, a writer might have said that a character "may have taken the exaggerated view" but, today, you'd better just say that he is lying. Unless you're writing historical fiction in the narrative voice of that era, your readers will not likely tolerate having to swim through your wordiness. Your readers want a story nicely told in language and description that is, at least sometimes, beautiful and moving. But what they mostly want is clarity.

Another type of verbosity that should be avoided at all costs is the use of the passive voice. I don't know who is responsible for perpetuating the myth that intelligent sounding things get delivered in this odd vehicle, but they should be punished harshly for it. Nobody in their right mind is going to wander up to the gathering at the office water cooler on Monday morning and seriously say "a fine football game was watched by me yesterday afternoon." Neither should you use passive voice in the telling of your story or in your dialogue.

So, leave out *alas*, *lo*, *suited the action to the word*, *a fine time was had at the ball*, and rambling sentences that are obviously meant to impress the reader with your vocabulary. The reader knows that if you are a writer you are in possession of a thesaurus, so using big words is not going to be nearly as impressive as you might think.

Wandering Offtrack

I believe that it is essential for you to know, in every scene of a story or chapter, what it is you should be up to. When writing scene three of chapter six, you should have no doubt that *this* is what you want to happen, *this* is who you want it to happen to, and *this* is the result. In terms of setting and description, this means that you are always aware—at every stage of your story and your writing of it—of the specific time and place and of what needs to be carefully described and how you intend to do it.

Then, when you've determined that you've strayed off your course, which you almost certainly will, you can avoid wandering off in the wrong direction. But bear this in mind: It might not *be* the wrong direction. It's quite possible that the straying will turn out to be a *good* thing. I've had interesting characters and places pop up that I hadn't planned on at all. If this isn't the case, then you'll have some clutter to deal with. It might be well-written, clever clutter— "a rose by any other name," etc.—but it still has to go.

I suggest that you become something of a packrat when it comes to things that you discard. There's an interesting story regarding Rogers and Hammerstein, the collaborative authors of some of the finest works in the American musical theater. I can't vouch for its accuracy, since I heard it from another writer at a conference, and writers, given the nature of our profession, sometimes fabricate at will. True or not, this one is instructive. When writing *South Pacific*, either Rodgers or Hammerstein wrote a peppy little song called "Getting to Know You" for a young Navy lieutenant to sing to his Polynesian lover. The other member of the writing team thought it was a ridiculous thing for a naval officer to be singing so they scrapped the song and wrote another one. But they saved the first one, which ended up working perfectly in a later musical *The King and I*.

So don't be too quick to throw things away. That long description of a child waiting for a school bus in the rain might not fit at all in the story you removed it from, but it may be just what you need in another one.

Useless Information

The light blue phone in your story or novel shouldn't be light blue unless it *matters* what color it is.

Description simply for the sake of description is clutter. Any details that you provide should be ones that will help your reader better see a character, place, or situation. That ornate china cabinet that you inherited from your grandmother might be an absolute joy to describe, and you might do it extremely well, but unless it serves to move the story along, it has no place there.

Remember, elaborate description of a person, place, or thing—especially in work intended for readers of popular fiction as opposed to literary—can stop a story dead in its tracks. And good stories and novels never stop; they keep *moving.*

Flannery O'Connor maintained that even though details are essential to the writing of fiction, piling them up, one on top of another, is counterproductive to what you should be about: telling a story.

When writing your story or novel, always consider what the reader *needs* to know. What you'll almost always end up with, if you give them more than is needed to make the story work, is loose ends at the conclusion. Remember, when you describe something or someone, you are intentionally calling readers' attention to that thing or person. So they have the right to assume that the thing or person is of some importance and that they will reemerge in the story. We'll let the great dramatist Anton Chekhov have the last word on this subject of making sure that everything in your fiction is there for a purpose. He said that if there is a gun on the wall in act one, by act three it should fire.

WHEN THE BEST DESCRIPTION IS NO DESCRIPTION

Sometimes the best way to tell or show something is not to tell or show it at all. It's always a good idea to make the reader do some of the work in your fiction, and this is particularly true when it comes to description.

Here's one of the best examples I can think of. There is a fine short story by Saki, the pseudonym of H.H. Munro, titled "The Interlopers" in which two old enemies find themselves trapped under a fallen tree deep in the forest on a cold winter night. While waiting for one of their groups of men to show up to rescue them, they manage to resolve their differences and to bring a generations-old feud between their two families to an end. When they finally hear some commotion on the ridge above them, one of the men asks the other, who has a better view of the ridge, which group of men it is:

> "Who are they?" asked Georg quickly, straining his eyes to see what the other would gladly not have seen.
> "Wolves."

Chilling, isn't it? And the main reason that it *is* so chilling is something that the author *doesn't* do. He doesn't describe the horrors that we know are

A Checklist for Clutter

If you have to put a checkmark beside any of these when reading through
your manuscript, then you've got some clutter to either modify or dispose of.
- repetition of words or phrases
- useless tag lines
- too many adverbs
- too many adjectives
- modifiers that mean the same thing
- useless information
- useless characters
- too much description
- too verbose
- too didactic
- resorted to a cliché

coming. After all, the men are trapped and the wolves are wild and no doubt
hungry; you get the idea. And it's that *idea* that he wants to emphasize, not
the gnarling, bloody business that he could have described in great detail. He
isolates that final, terrifying word with no instructions or suggestions about
even how it is delivered by the speaker. It might be a shout, or a pleading.
But I've always heard it as more of a whisper. I've always imagined a very
soft, emotionless, statement of an unfortunate yet unalterable fact. And the
impact of that last, single word has stayed with me for many a year since I
first read it.

Look for places where you can leave much, or all, of something to the
reader's imagination. Obviously, when you're writing a mystery or suspense
tale, there's plenty that you'll need to leave out, since much of that overall
suspense will depend on how you write your descriptions. But carefully chosen omissions will serve you well in any genre.

This intentional lack of description can work for settings also, but to a
lesser degree. My first two books had been particularly dependant on their
settings—one was about the town I grew up in and the other was about an
island that was hit by a horrendous storm—so I wanted my third offering,
A Place Apart, to be a story that could take place practically anywhere. So I

set it in Ohio, a place for which I didn't have a fixed idea. But I found early on that I still had to describe many things about that time and place in order for the novel to function at all.

Having your story play itself out in a time and place that is completely generic—with absolutely no description of interiors or landscapes or what the weather is doing and no clue regarding past, present, or future—will take away much of what makes good fiction work. But there will be places where it's just not important for the reader to know if the story is in Vermont or California or the Ukraine. Backstories often fall into this category. If a character's grandfather once taught her an essential life lesson, then it might not matter *where* he taught it. But be careful. Remember, readers like to know where and when things are taking place.

SUMMARY: KEEPING THE WHEAT, TOSSING THE CHAFF

Several times in this book I've referred to what I call the clutter rule, the principal that anything that you include that doesn't serve to move your story along has to go. It's exactly the same thing, of course, as when Stephen King's old boss told him to take out everything that was *not* the story. However you conceptualize it, this really should be one of the golden rules when it comes to the writing of your fiction. Nothing short of just plain bad writing will slow your reader down or stop him altogether faster than having to wade through an overabundance of clutter. That and not giving him enough information or detail to bring him on board in the first place.

I told you at the start of this chapter that it is sometimes difficult to stay between these two extremes. But you'd best do that reckoning constantly when writing. Drifting too far in one direction or the other will weaken, or destroy, what you want to be a fine bit of storytelling.

EXERCISE 1

Pull out one of your manuscripts and start looking for places where you have used description. Now, consider for each place how your story or novel might benefit by having less description there, or none at all. Let the impact on your reader be your guide. You might omit some fine writing, but your story will be the better for it.

Relying on your writer's craft and your fine wordsmithing, write a short phrase that will work *better* than each of these that contain clichés. Remember, the object here is to remove the cliché and retain the image or description that it created.

- Don't let her pull the wool over your eyes.
- He's as drunk as a skunk.
- His eyes are like a deer's caught in a headlight.
- Suddenly, the girl felt as light as a feather.
- Toby, as mad as a hornet, slammed down his fist.
- When it comes to handiwork, he doesn't know his head from a hole in the ground.
- Elliott knew that, when it came to this boss, he was behind the eight ball.
- What goes around comes around.
- You can't teach an old dog new tricks.
- *Que sera, sera.*

Open a novel or a story by a good writer—be forewarned: this exercise won't work if you choose a bad writer—and start looking in the text for places that he or she obviously chose another word to keep from repeating one that they had recently used. You'll be surprised at how lucrative your search will be, and seeing how they did it will influence how *you* will do it.

chapter 12

[DESCRIPTION AND SETTING IN THE WRITING PROCESS]

Once you've made the decision to write a short story or a novel, or anything else of a creative nature, you place yourself in the company of countless storytellers that reaches back through several millennia to the first oracle who stood up, cleared his throat, and told the first tale. Most of them followed pretty much the same process from the genesis of an idea to the delivery of the final product, and so will you.

In this last chapter, let's briefly consider how setting and description, specifically, should fit into the *process* of writing fiction.

THE IDEA

The sources of story ideas differ from writer to writer. Many authors draw heavily on personal experience and childhood memories; others let their imaginations run wild and dream everything up out of thin air. Something as seemingly unimpressive as an old man walking beside a busy highway might be enough of a spark in one writer's mind to end up as a 500-page novel, but a downright harrowing personal experience might not be sufficient for another one to translate into what he or she feels would be a worthwhile project.

In short, wherever you come up with your idea is your business, and I'll leave you to it. But our two major concerns—setting and description—should factor into your selection.

I often encourage my students to locate their piece in a setting that interests them, in a time and place that they would like to know more about. Anyone intending to write something that happens in Chicago in the 1920s will need to do some considerable research. And the eventual description of all those flappers and mobsters and G-men and speakeasies and Model Ts will undoubtedly affect the entire story.

Should the choice of a primary setting and the anticipation of some impressive description be the ultimate determiner of the story itself? Probably not. But it can—and in all likelihood *should*—have a great impact on your decision.

Maybe you've been toying with the possibility of penning a murder-for-hire saga. You know it's going to involve a love triangle and some sailboats (you like sailboats), but that's about as far as you've thought through it. Love triangles and murders-for-hire can occur just about anywhere, but those sailboats require a large body of water. So, the setting is already one of your first concerns.

Now, where you finally *do* locate this steamy bit of business will greatly determine many other things in your fiction. A yacht club deep in the heart of Dixie will be completely different—geographically, philosophically, architecturally, etc.—than one in the northeast. The locals will have a different mindset; the customs and even some of the laws will differ. Then there's the landscape; if you intend your hired murderer to toss someone off a cliff, then you'd best not set your story anywhere on the Texas gulf coast, since you won't find a cliff there capable of inflicting any more damage than a sprained ankle. Those sailboats you're so interested in might themselves even differ from place to place; maybe an altogether heartier sort of wood and design are called for in the icy waters of the far north than is needed in the balmy currents of the tropics.

Where and when your story or novel takes place, and the descriptions you employ to tell it, is an essential element in your fiction. So make it an important component in your initial idea.

PLANNING

Now that you've made your decision—your sordid, three-way love fest/bloody betrayal is going to play out on Lake Ouachita, Arkansas—you've got some real planning to do.

Remember, it is not only important but *essential* for you to know where you're going. I've had students and workshop participants tell me that they don't believe in planning, that they just *write*. They just give their muse free reign and follow where she leads. When I've read their stories, I believe them. Because what you'll almost certainly end up with if absolutely no planning goes into the process will be a rambling collection of clutter. There must be method to your madness, and the *method* is a plan.

When making your plans, setting and description should be constantly on your mind. However you go about it—many writers use detailed outlines; I'm a big believer in plot graphs—you should pencil in loads of details regarding the time, the place, and things and people that will need describing in each scene. If you actually *go* to Lake Ouachita, take along a camera, your writer's journal and/or a fat notebook, and a sharp pencil. But if your budget forbids such an excursion, then get on the Internet or write to the chamber of commerce and find out about the topography, trees, customs, and anything else that you might need in order to take your reader there.

When your reader settles down in their hammock on a nice summer afternoon or in a comfortable chair beside a roaring fire on a blustery winter night, they should, when they begin reading your story or novel, *be* at Lake Ouachita. They should smell the pine trees and see the small, rocky peninsulas that jut out into the water. The Ozarks should lift up there in the distance. And here are some of those sailboats that you've envisioned, their white sails puffed full of afternoon breeze, their sleek hulls skimming across the crystal blue lake. And over there, at the Mountain Harbor Lodge, two parts of that lover's triangle are plotting against the third, and your story is set into motion.

Before any of that can happen, you have to do considerable planning. As you can see, the time and the place, and the description you will use to deliver them to your reader, need to be very important ingredients of that planning.

WRITING

I am a firm believer—some of my students might say to the point of fanaticism—in the idea that this most important and creative stage of the process should be separated completely from the others. A writer who is serious about his or her task should set aside a block of time each and every day for writing. This time should never be for planning, researching, revising, or editing. Perhaps most important, it shouldn't be for *thinking* about writing (writers are, if you haven't already noticed, great procrastinators). This predetermined daily time should be for *writing*. And it should be sacred time.

My block is from four until half past five every morning. And I try awfully hard to write for that hour and a half seven days a week. Now, this isn't meant to imply that I *only* write for an hour and a half. Many days I log many more than that. What I want to you to understand is this: I write for at least that amount of time *every* day. I know; you're probably not an early riser. That's fine; then your block shouldn't be when mine is. Maybe yours should be late at night, when mine *absolutely* shouldn't be. I'm very much a "morning person," and I doubt if I could compose even a coherent grocery list at midnight. I'm a better writer early in the morning, and I've discovered that a strong advantage to my predawn ritual is that nobody ever bothers me. Believe me, if the phone rings that early in the morning, it's either a wrong number or an emergency.

So one of my unbreakable rules is that I am at the keyboard for that hour and a half every day. The other one is that I am writing for all of that time. Many mornings I feel pretty certain that what I'm writing is garbage, and sometimes it turns out that I'm right. But the funny thing about garbage is that there is usually something buried in there that can be salvaged. The worst thing a writer can convince himself of is that he doesn't feel like writing today. I encourage my students to make believe, every time they sit down to write, that they have a deadline to meet for a tough city editor on a daily newspaper. Envision him as a scowling, Lou Grant-type character who doesn't care a fig what you feel like. He just wants your copy on his desk, pronto.

When it comes to setting and description during the actual writing of a story or novel, I've found it very helpful to have photographs, floor plans, or schematics of the specific setting where I can look at them when I write. When constructing that scene about Lake Ouachita—with its blue water and mountains and pine trees—a postcard tacked up over your monitor would be a good idea. And a list of possible adjectives and phrases that you've jotted down in your planning will be essential, as will frequent dips into the thesaurus to scan several options that might work better in your overall wordsmithing. But avoid a spell check and grammar check during your actual writing. Save those for revisions. You don't want anything slowing you down in this, the most crucial phase of your task.

Usually, when writing a chapter of a novel or a section of a story, I won't tackle it in the order that it will eventually play itself out, but will start with the clearest image that I have in my mind and then write "around" it. For instance, if your most vivid image is of those sailboats on Lake Ouachita, then that might be the best place for you to begin. Here again is proof positive that your choice of setting is very important.

REVISION

Now's the time to check over everything and make the first of many changes. I always print out the pages that I've just written and sit down on the couch in my study (not during my sacred block of writing time; remember: that's only for writing) and make plenty of notes on the manuscript with a fine-point mechanical pencil. I draw arrows to indicate when I want to move words, phrases, or whole sentences. I take things out and put things in. I declutter and make things clearer. Sometimes I scribble out entire new paragraphs in the margins, their sentences wandering around the edges of the page like rats in a maze. Sometimes I reward myself with little checkmarks for a bit of nice wordsmithing. Everybody needs a pat on the back occasionally, even if it is self-inflicted.

This stage of the writing process is the most likely candidate for being shortchanged, I suspect. After all, we all know full well how enormously important planning and writing is, and we sometimes look down on revision as something less creative than the first two. But believe me, revision is every bit as essential if you intend to finally come up with a finished product that is both publishable and readable. Revision is your refiner's fire; it is the polishing of your work to the highest possible shine. So build in enough time to make a proper job of it. The revision phase is the time that I pay very close attention to my description and my setting. I weigh every adjective against other possibilities. And I try to *become* the guy in Sheboygan, who has never been to Paris (if I am writing about Paris) or to Lake Ouachita. It is essential that I attempt to see my writing through his perception, to make sure that I have adequately described the time, the place, and the characters.

FEEDBACK

When I am first working my way through an idea for a story or novel, and then when I do the planning, writing, and initial revisions, I make it a point not to seek any outside input or to accept any. Too many cooks in the kitchen early on will indeed spoil the stew. In fact, when people ask me what I'm working on, I usually lie and tell them nothing at the moment. If I tell them I've got an idea for a story or a novel, they will inevitably ask what it's about, and that is exactly what I *don't* want to go into at that stage of the process. This thing—whatever it ends up being—will have to work in *my* voice, from *my* perspective. So I need to be the lone ranger in the first vision, the planning, and the first and maybe second draft.

Then, I throw the doors to that kitchen open wide to other people whose opinion I respect. Patricia Soledade, a fellow teacher and a wonderful friend, is my constant reader, and her input has been invaluable over the years. But

Pat never hears about possible ideas, never sees plot graphs, and never sees first drafts. That's when it would be detrimental to have her, or anybody else's, ideas tripping over mine.

When I take a chapter or a story to Pat, it has been planned, written, and revised. Then she digs into it and brings me back the thoroughly marked-up and Post-It-noted manuscript. I spend a lot of time with that batch of papers, considering each of her recommendations, changing some things and leaving others as they were. And, of course, I ask her for clarification on some things. The ultimate decisions are mine, but my work is stronger because of the skillful input I've received from an excellent and dependable sounding board.

Finally, I make my next round of revisions and send the manuscript off to my agent and my editor. Then, of course, there are things they want changed or enlarged or done away with. Sometimes I yield, sometimes I compromise, and sometimes I dig in my heels. Every once in a while, it can be a frustrating process, but it's always ended up being a productive one.

One last thing, if you aren't fortunate enough to have a Pat Soledade, I suggest you get yourself into a writer's critique group that meets frequently in your community. Go online to locate one, or call a local bookstore or your library to see if they know of any. There will be, I assure you, one or two Pollyannas in that group that won't be of much use to you because they'll gush over every offering and never find anything wrong with anybody's writing, and there will be a Scrooge or two who will find *everything* wrong and never anything right. But there will also be, if you are very lucky, a core group of talented writers who will provide fair, constructive feedback from which your fiction will benefit greatly. And you will do the very same thing for them.

SUMMARY: THE FINISHED PRODUCT

I get asked fairly often to speak to writer's groups like the ones I just described to you. They usually meet in bookstores or in the community rooms in shopping malls and, though their main order of business is to critique each other's fiction, they do sometimes invite published writers in to say a few words and to answer questions.

The vast majority of questions put to me over the years have regarded how to go about finding a publisher or an agent or—this is the most frequently asked question—how to make the most money at this writing gig. Rarely am I asked any questions that I can actually *answer*, like how to better

A Fews Good Rules for Good Writers

- Set aside a specific time for writing. Then *write*. Don't look out the window. Don't listen to the radio. Don't talk on the phone or check your e-mail or hook paperclips together. Don't edit. *Write*.
- Wordsmith. Make sure every word and phrase is the *best* choice.
- Read! Read! Read! Someone once told me that good writers are just avid readers that spilled over.
- Plan! Know where you're going.
- Show more than you tell.
- Leave out more than you put in.
- Use the five senses to describe.
- Make characters and situations and dialogue believable.
- Make your setting more than *just* a setting. Put it to work in your fiction.
- Don't preach.
- Don't imitate. Locate and polish your own voice.
- Don't clutter.
- Take your time.
- Revise! Revise! Revise!
- Plan, write, and revise autonomously; then seek feedback.
- Be open to constructive criticism and willing to make the changes necessary to make your writing better.
- Don't worry about fame, fortune, or a national book tour. Just write well!

develop a character or instill a bit of irony or make the best use of setting and description. Sometimes, these John Grisham wannabes seem disappointed that I was invited at all. And the fact that I'm there, instead of John Grisham, should have been a dead giveaway that I don't know anything about making a lot of money from writing. People who do that generally charge a lot of money to speak to groups that can get somebody like me for free.

All I can tell those groups is what I have tried to tell you in these pages: Wordsmith the very best story or novel that you can, crafting every word, sentence and paragraph precisely, in your unique voice. Work it through as many revisions as it needs. Then get yourself a good resource full of agents' or publishers' names and—armed with a perfect query letter—wander into a marketplace that will likely break your heart many times before it makes it glad. Be persistent. There is on a shelf in my closet a shoebox crammed full of rejection letters that came my way in regard to my first book, which was finally published by Farrar, Straus, & Giroux, one of the most prestigious publishers in New York. That book went on to make the short list of finalists for a national PEN award. But during the writing of it, I didn't let myself focus on anything other than the story I was trying to tell and the best ways to do exactly that.

In a nutshell, don't worry about agents or publishers or marketing your wares when writing. Just concentrate on writing well, on using all the tools in your kit, not just the two—setting and description—that we have been talking about. If you do that, then you'll end up with something that will be worthy of your faith in it and of the persistence you'll use to put it "out there."

You will be a wordsmith. Welcome to the club.

EXERCISE 1

Look over these basic story ideas. Then jot down several possible primary settings (times and places) where the ideas might be fully realized. Think of places where you have been or places you have an interest in and would *like* to visit. And consider reasons to set the story in one place (or time) rather than another:

- two old friends end up on opposite ends of a labor dispute in a canning factory
- the ghost of a slave appears a century and a half after his death
- a tale of espionage in a large hotel
- the old man befriended by a young couple at a resort might, or might not, be a Nazi fugitive
- a spoiled, city teenager who survives a plane crash must endure a wilderness and find her way to civilization
- a woman returns to her old hometown to make amends for a bad thing she did years ago
- a murder is done at a famous landmark, and an innocent tourist is implicated

EXERCISE 2

Make a list of at least five people you know that will be good readers for your second draft manuscript. I suggest you don't put down your significant other, since he is too close to you, and perhaps to your writing. Friendship shouldn't be your only criteria, or even a major one; choose people who do a lot of reading of fiction and ideally someone who has done some creative writing themselves.

EXERCISE 3

Using two markers—one red and one green—dig into a manuscript that you've been working on. Circle strong, clear phrases, sentences, or paragraphs with the green marker, then locate their counterparts, the sections that need work. You might just notice a pattern emerging; the green passages are good for certain reasons, and the red ones are found lacking for other reasons. Get to work pulling the red ones up to snuff, transforming them into green.

appendix

[POINT BY POINT—A QUICK AND EASY REFERENCE TO MATERIAL COVERED]

CHAPTER ONE: THE IMPORTANCE OF DESCRIPTION AND SETTING

- Good writing is never entirely dependent on the setting, but any work of fiction without a clearly depicted time and place will almost certainly fail.
- Your fiction should have a setting rich enough to match the story you intend to tell.
- Fiction is essentially made up of two things: the craft that a writer uses to create a story and the unique voice in which he or she conveys it.
- Improvement in writing can occur when you focus on three things: the underlying craft of fiction (the tools of the trade, so to speak), models (examples of published authors' works), and wordsmithing (the careful selection of each and every word).
- Giving the lay of the land (actually describing topography and geography) is one way to introduce your setting, and it will work especially well if you intend for that land to play a vital role, almost as a character in its own right, in your story. MODEL: John Steinbeck, *East of Eden*.
- The use of intricate details is another option. Here, though, you would do well to consider the audience you are aiming for: literary or popular. Readers of literary fiction will be more receptive to long passages of description while devotees of more mainstream or popular stories and novels want less of that and considerably more action. MODEL: Don DeLillo, *Underworld*.
- Yet another way to introduce the setting is to appeal to the reader's five senses, paying special attention to what things look, taste, smell, sound, and feel like. MODEL: Margaret George, *The Memoirs of Cleopatra*.

- The tone (the prevailing attitude or mood) will determine how your fiction will be perceived and to a large extent what will actually happen in your story or novel. MODEL: Jack Finney, *The Night People.*
- Your close attention to and crafting of description—of your settings, characters, and their actions—must be maintained throughout your entire story or novel, not just at the beginning. MODEL: E. Annie Proulx: *The Shipping News.*
- Within the context of your writing, you have to send an invitation to your readers. Something in the situation you are presenting, in your characters, and in your writer's voice has to be compelling enough to bring them in and keep them on board. MODEL: Robert Frost, "The Pasture."

CHAPTER TWO: LEARNING TO PAY ATTENTION

- Good writers are persistent and meticulous harvesters of detail. MODEL: Morley Callaghan, *That Summer in Paris.*
- When you look at everything with a stronger magnification, you'll end up with more bits and pieces of data than you'll ever use. So you'll have to come up with ways to hold on to them, and then locate them when and if you need them.
- The more time you spend searching for these details, the more interesting and useful details you're likely to come up with.
- One good way to do this is to focus on a time and place in your past. Think of it in present tense—not past—and take plenty of notes, making sure you include sensory details.
- Another approach is to focus on a setting in the present. Select a place where you don't go often or know anyone, so that you won't be influenced by preconceptions.
- A small notebook, kept close at hand most of the time, should be one of your constant tools. Jot down any details, dialogue, descriptions, arrangements, etc. that might be useful to you in your writing.
- Maps, floor plans, or schematics of places real or imagined will help you to better visualize your setting so that you can make it realistic for your reader.
- Movies and television and radio programs are great sources of visual images, intricate details, and the employment and delivery of language that will be useful to you. Other sources are newspaper and magazine columnists as well as daily comic strips that follow an ongoing storyline.

- When looking for details, always be on the alert for any bits of irony. Your readers get plenty of irony in real life, so they expect it to occur in fiction also.
- You need to keep a journal or diary into which story ideas regularly go, as well as bits of overheard dialogue, new dialogue that your characters come up with, details of places or situations, techniques you've picked up from other writers, and anything else that has anything to do with your writing.
- Once you've sharpened your observation skills and taken notes about what you've seen, you need to create the little world in your mind where your story will take place. Because if it doesn't exist there, it won't stand a chance of existing in your reader's mind.

CHAPTER THREE: USING ALL THE TOOLS IN YOUR KIT

- The crafting of fiction is a slow and deliberate undertaking in which you will need to employ, often and well, many of the literary devices and approaches available to you.
- Adjectives and adverbs are the spices that good writers use to flavor their writing. Too little or too much spice can spoil a dish; the same rule applies to modifiers. They should be tested constantly to make sure they're doing exactly what you need them to do. MODELS: Ernest Hemingway, *For Whom the Bell Tolls*; Robert Cremins, *A Sort of Homecoming*.
- Punctuation marks are road signs for your readers, put there to show them where you want them to pause, continue, speed up, and stop altogether. This requires that you *listen* to your fiction.
- Exclamation points should be used sparingly, so as not to diminish their effectiveness. MODEL: Luanne Rice, *The Perfect Summer*.
- Use colons to alert your reader to something that is coming up: a list, a definition, or a clarification. MODEL: Edward Rutherfurd, *London*.
- Semicolons and dashes will prove useful in the important business of giving your sentences a variety of lengths and structures. MODELS: Jeffrey Lent, *In the Fall*; Clare Francis, *Night Sky*.
- Parentheses provide a way for you to tell your reader something *outside* of the story proper. MODEL: Vladimir Nabokov, *King, Queen, Knave*.
- One of the most effective ways to convey a particular image to your readers is to show them what it is similar to.

- Metaphors and similes are excellent ways to imply similarity, and you should use them often. Just make sure you don't get carried away and *over*use them. MODELS: Alex Haley, *Roots*; Aidan Chambers, *Postcards From No Man's Land*; Ken Follett, *The Hammer of Eden*.
- Sometimes you'll need to lay out an exact comparison, not an implied one. That's when an analogy will work better than a metaphor or a simile. MODELS: Lori Aurelia Williams, *When Kambia Elaine Flew in From Neptune*; James Michener, *The Eagle and the Raven*.
- When using an allusion, make sure it is wide enough for your readers to pick up on. MODELS: Kurt Vonnegut, *Cat's Cradle*; Tony Kushner, *Angels in America*; Anne Rice, *The Tale of the Body Thief*.
- Personifications provide excellent ways for you to paint a visual, active image in your reader's mind. MODELS: William Shakespeare, *Romeo and Juliet*; Ann Packer, *The Dive From Clausen's Pier*; J.K. Rowling, *Harry Potter and the Goblet of Fire*.
- Symbolism should occur naturally in your fiction, with no need for you to intentionally *plant* symbols. MODEL: Aaron Elkins, *Fellowship of Fear*.
- When employing onomatopoeia, weave it into the fabric of your sentences, letting the sound words have their effect in small doses. Avoid using them as one-word sentences followed by exclamation points. MODEL: Zane Grey, *Riders of the Purple Sage*.
- Cadence is good; repetition is bad. Cadence provides a flowing, musical aspect and taps home strong images, while repetition is simply saying something you've already said. MODELS: John Grisham, *Bleachers*; William Gay, *Provinces of Night*.
- Flashbacks, backstories, and future stories are good ways to establish setting and provide description by diverting your readers' attention from the present plot to another time and place. MODELS: William Styron, *Sophie's Choice*; M.M. Kaye, *The Far Pavilions*.
- Foreshadowing provides small clues of what's to come, and is quite an effective way to keep your reader interested. MODEL: Alice Sebold, *The Lovely Bones*.
- Readers get tired of sentences of the same pattern and length coming one after the other, and the same is true of paragraphs. So give them a variety. MODELS: Patricia Cornwell, *From Potter's Field*; Shelley Mydans, *Thomas*; D.E. Stevenson, *Miss Buncle's Book*.
- Let moderation and a sense of balance determine which literary techniques and devices you choose for your story or novel.

CHAPTER FOUR: SHOWING, TELLING, AND COMBINING THE TWO

- Use a combination of showing and telling in your writing, but tend to show more than your tell. MODELS: Toni Morrison, *Sula*; Masuji Ibuse, *Black Rain*.
- In your fiction, plug your readers' into images—situations and emotions—that they can relate to. One of the best ways to do this is to immerse them in those images by showing rather than telling. MODELS: Kathleen Cambor, *The Book of Mercy*; Charles Frazier, *Cold Mountain*.
- Sometimes a combination of showing and telling works best. MODELS: John Gardner, *Grendel*; Ray Bradbury, *The Martian Chronicles*.
- Don't tell what you've already shown.
- Deciding when to show and when to tell becomes an instinctive process, but you should always test each passage or image to see if it might not work better in the other way.

CHAPTER FIVE: SENSORY DESCRIPTION

- The success of your story or novel will depend on many things, but the most crucial is your ability to bring your reader into it. And that reader will be most completely in when you deliver the actual sensations of the many things that comprise your fiction.
- The extent to which you should do this will be determined somewhat by the audience you are aiming for. Readers of literary fiction will tolerate lengthy passages of sensory description in order to get a wide canvas on which the story can take place. Readers of popular fiction want the description also, but they want it more quickly. MODELS: William Goyen, *The House of Breath*; Joy Fielding, *Whispers and Lies*.
- The danger of using the sense of sight is to use it too often, to the exclusion of the others.
- When making your reader see something, present it in a way that he or she might not have ever seen it before. MODELS: Cormac McCarthy, *Cities of the Plain*; Walter M. Miller, *A Canticle for Leibowitz*.
- Be careful not to overdo the uncommon, unexpected bits of visual description. They usually work well the first time, but not so again.
- Occasionally you'll need the reader to see only slight differences between things. MODEL: William Martin, *Cape Cod*.

- Smell is the most nostalgic of the senses, so use it to great effect. It can be used to nudge a character's memory, to symbolize something else, to describe something that is difficult or impossible to describe, and to help establish your setting. MODELS: Gore Vidal, *Washington, D.C.*; Marly Youmans, *Catherwood*; Larry Watson, *Montana, 1948*; Patrick Suskind, *Perfume.*
- When using the sense of touch your job is to make the reader recall exactly what it feels like when something occurs in your story or, if they haven't experienced it, what it *would* feel like if they did. MODELS: Dick Francis, *Longshot*; Chuck Palahniuk, *Invisible Monsters.*
- When it's time to inflict a bit of pain and suffering in your fiction, put more emphasis on your character's reaction to it than on the actual description of it.
- Sometimes describing the sense of touch won't show what a character feels, but what you want your *reader* to feel. MODELS: Barbara Kingsolver, *The Poisonwood Bible*; Ron Rozelle, *A Place Apart.*
- The sense of taste can be used to center the reader's attention on a thing, and to help establish a character in the reader's mind. MODELS: Jessica Danes, "Hot Tea," *Houston Chronicle*, January 8, 2003; Gore Vidal, *Washington, D.C.*; Irving Stone, *The Agony and the Ecstasy.*
- Often showing what something *doesn't* taste like is effective. MODEL: Tracy Chevalier, *Girl With a Pearl Earring.*
- Let a character's preference for one taste or another make him or her clearer in your reader's mind.
- Let the sounds that surround you all the time work their way into your stories and novels. MODEL: Louis L'Amour, *Guns of the Timberlands.*
- Sometimes the absence of sound is the best way to convey what something sounds like. MODEL: Robert Frost, "Stopping by Woods."
- Good writers spend much of their time thinking in metaphors; this is especially true when it comes to the sensory detail. MODEL: Robert Penn Warren, *All The King's Men.*
- One way to help describe your characters is to let the reader know what kind of music they listen to, maybe even what their favorite songs are. MODEL: James Baldwin, "Sonny's Blues."
- Use sounds to make your reader curious and build suspense. MODEL: Wallace Stegner, *Crossing to Safety.*

- The sixth sense, intuition, is an excellent way to help describe a character or situation. MODELS: John D. MacDonald, *The Deep Blue Good-By*; Mary Higgins Clark, *Stillwatch*.

CHAPTER SIX: DESCRIPTION OF CHARACTERS

- The characters in your fiction are the actors that will take to the stage in your reader's mind. So breathing life into the characters represents some of the most important work you'll do as a writer.
- Straightforward physical description is the most common approach. MODEL: Carson McCullers, "A Tree, A Rock, A Cloud."
- Mixing physical traits with subtle clues about attitudes and personality is another method. MODEL: William E. Barrett, *Lilies of the Field*.
- The use of an extended analogy is yet another option. MODEL: Flannery O'Connor, "Good Country People."
- Providing an image of what your characters look like can come in very short doses or longer ones. MODELS: William Faulkner, "A Rose for Emily"; David Westheimer, *Von Ryan's Express*.
- Often it is quite effective to simply quickly tell what somebody looks or acts like. Brevity occasionally wins out over elaboration. MODEL: Anne Lamott, *Crooked Little Heart*.
- Load your description up with little telling actions and references that help build your overall story. MODEL: Kent Haruf, *Plainsong*.
- Putting real people in your fiction can be therapeutic, but it can also be risky. So be careful.
- If you choose to use a historical character in your story, do your homework—about both the person and the historical era. MODELS: Walter F. Murphy, *Upon This Rock*; Herman Wouk, *The Winds of War*.
- When using yourself as a model for a character, use only descriptions that are called for in a particular story or novel.
- One way to describe characters is to let them describe themselves. MODEL: John D. MacDonald, *The Deep Blue Good-By*.
- Sometimes, letting the character either dabble in a little wishful thinking or make reference to something they like about themselves provides good description. MODELS: Virginia Woolf, *Mrs. Dalloway*; Irving Wallace, *The Seventh Secret*.
- A character's dialogue can be the strongest description you can give.

MODELS: Willa Cather, *Death Comes for the Archbishop*; Allen Drury, *Advise and Consent*; John O'Hara, *Ourselves to Know*.

- You'll need to know exactly what motivates your characters before you can convey them or their situations to your reader. MODEL: Richard Stark, *Comeback*.
- Showing characters' moods is an effective way to describe them. MODELS: V.C. Andrews, *Into the Garden*; David Guterson, *East of the Mountains*.
- Emotional or behavioral flaws are common in real people, so they'd better be in your characters also. MODELS: Pat Conroy, *The Great Santini*; Betty Smith, *A Tree Grows in Brooklyn*.
- Physical imperfections in characters should provide more than just cosmetic description; perhaps they can be motivating or make a character *not* be motivated. MODEL: Robert Phillips, "Night Flowers."
- Avoid overplaying character stereotypes, but draw on reader's preconceived notions from time to time. MODEL: F. Scott Fitzgerald, "The Rich Boy."

CHAPTER SEVEN: TIME AND PLACE

- Nothing so solidly anchors a work of fiction in reader's minds as knowing when and where something is taking place.
- The credibility of your setting depends entirely on your description of it. MODEL: Ernest Hemingway, "In Another Country."
- One way to bring your reader into the setting is to give them a large view of it—a macrocosm, or bird's eye view. This can be done quickly or in great detail. MODELS: John Steinbeck, *The Moon Is Down*; Ron Rozelle, *The Windows of Heaven*; Stephen Harrigan, *The Gates of the Alamo*; Thornton Wilder, *Our Town*.
- Another—and much more commonly used—approach is to give the reader a microcosm, a world in small. MODEL: Philip Roth, *The Ghost Writer*.
- Remember to let your reader know what the weather is doing at any given time in your story; it's an important, and often overlooked, aspect of your setting. MODELS: Belva Plain, *Her Father's House*; William Martin, *Harvard Yard*.
- Just as important is letting the reader know about the geography—its actual description and its influence on characters' personalities. MODEL: A. Conan Doyle, "The Adventure of the Speckled Band."

- When describing weather and geography for particular places, do your research.
- Whether or not your setting works for your reader is not dependent on whether or not it is physically *possible*, but on how well you establish its credibility within the context of the story you are telling. Let your characters and their motivations and actions drive your fiction, not the setting.
- Beware the comfort zone, where your characters are cozy and comfortable in the setting you've provided for them. Your story has to be constantly moving.
- Frameworking—the inclusion of several things into a larger context or frame—is an ancient and quite effective way to tell a story. If you choose to use it, make sure that your major emphasis is on the specific story you are telling, and not on the wider framework.
- Good fiction allows the reader to be immersed in a particular time and place for a while. Your job is to deliver those settings.

CHAPTER EIGHT: DESCRIPTION AND SETTING IN SPECIALIZED FICTION

- The story you are going to tell will more than likely work within several of the genres of fiction.
- Because of that, it is important that you read some good examples of each genre, and keep an open mind when reaching your decision.
- Historical fiction is a hybrid of both history and fiction, so you'd do well to do the necessary research to get the historical facts right.
- Though the readers of historical fiction usually know how certain things will turn out, the characters must not have any such knowledge.
- One way to describe a particular historical location is to provide details about the place itself. MODEL: Irving Stone, *The Agony and the Ecstasy*.
- Another way is to describe small actions or events that are indicative of the time and place. MODEL: Colleen McCullough, *Caesar*.
- In mysteries, setting and description can help establish the mood of suspense and provide foreshadowing. MODEL: Janwillem van de Wetering, *The Maine Massacre*.
- When writing science fiction and fantasy, your settings can be as fanciful as you want them to be, but they must be—first and foremost—a stage upon which your characters do something that your earthbound reader can relate to. MODEL: Isaac Asimov, *Foundation*.

- Readers of Western fiction expect considerable action, and they expect it to take place outside. Give your reader plenty of vivid description, and invoke the rough, wide-open spirit of the West in your description of characters. MODEL: Elmer Kelton, *Joe Pepper*.
- Readers of romance novels and stories want elaborate descriptions of clothing, décor, and characters. MODEL: Amanda Quick, *Affair*.
- When writing horror, suspense, or thriller fiction, use foreshadowing extensively, and focus on your character's fears and suspicions. MODEL: Stephen King, *Salem's Lot*.

CHAPTER NINE: USING DESCRIPTION AND SETTING TO DRIVE THE STORY

- Your setting should be more than just a place for your story to play itself out. Aspects of it should impact your characters, their actions, and your overall plot. MODEL: Eudora Welty, "A Worn Path."
- Let setting and description magnify a specific theme. MODELS: Greg Tobin, *Conclave*; C.S. Lewis, *Surprised by Joy*.
- Mood and tone can also be conveyed by setting and description.
- One way to accomplish this is to let the mood emanate from the setting itself. MODEL: Nicholas Meyer, *The Seven-Per-Cent Solution*.
- Another possibility is to let your description of your characters' actions determine the mood of the story. MODEL: Dashiell Hammett, *The Maltese Falcon*.
- Showing the prevailing mood, by either the surroundings or some action, is more effective than telling it.
- Use setting and description to enlarge conflicts in your fiction. MODEL: Edith Wharton, *Ethan Frome*.

CHAPTER TEN: WORKING THE MAGIC

- First impressions are just as important in fiction as in daily life, perhaps even more so. So you must begin the careful weaving of craft and voice in the first sentence and paragraph. MODEL: Gregory Maguire, *Wicked: The Life and Times of the Wicked Witch of the West*.
- Often, in order to end up with fiction that comes off as realistic, the author has to modify what is total reality. The many realistic details that you gather will ultimately need to be adjusted, enlarged, narrowed,

or changed in some other way in order to fit in your story or novel. MODEL: Arthur Miller, *Death of a Salesman.*

- Wherever you find your title—the Bible, poetry, song lyrics, dialogue of your own characters—make sure what your choice is a very good one. That title will be the first taste the reader has of you.
- Titles can be particularly helpful in establishing your setting.
- The primary purpose of your first sentence is to make the reader want to read the second one, so it should be a real grabber. It needs to be engaging, maybe a little quirky, and it wouldn't hurt if it had a bit of mystery or foreshadowing. MODELS: J.R.R. Tolkien, *The Fellowship of the Ring*; Edith Wharton, *Summer*; Jeffrey Archer, *First Among Equals*; Frederick Busch, *A Handbook for Spies.*
- The disparity between your specific setting and a much larger one—which includes not only bigger pieces of geography, but prevailing customs and philosophies—provides an excellent opportunity for you to firmly establish the time and place where your story takes place.
- A good way to check if you are balancing story and voice is to print out manuscript pages you've just written, put them aside for a while, perhaps overnight, and then give them a fresh reading.

CHAPTER ELEVEN: TOO LITTLE, TOO MUCH

- Be as watchful for things that you leave out as you are for things you put in. Anything that is not directly serving to move your fiction along is clutter and should be removed.
- If you have two characters in a scene—even in a scene that is dialogue driven—you shouldn't need more than a grand total of two dialogue tags.
- Rather than resort to the use of adverbs in dialogue tags, *show* what you would have conveyed with the adverbs in the characters' words and their actions.
- The only acceptable use of clichés is in a character's dialogue or in a very colloquial narrative voice, and even these should not be overdone. Creative writing should be *creative*, and there is nothing creative about resorting to clichés.
- Avoid using modifiers that simply tell; find ways to *show* a trait in a character, place, or situation.

- Avoid repeating words and phrases, even words that have different meanings but sound somewhat alike.
- Readers of fiction don't want to be taught lessons, they want to be told a story. Neither do they want to be preached to. So avoid being didactic, and don't overemphasize the moral implications of a situation.
- Don't use passive voice.
- When you wander off track, and end up discarding paragraphs or pages of text, don't throw them away. What doesn't fit in one story might work beautifully in another.
- Description simply for the sake of description is clutter. Any details that you provide should be ones that will help your reader better see a character, place, or situation. Always consider what readers *need* to know and avoid giving them useless information.
- Sometimes the best description is no description. Look for places where you can leave much, or all, of something to the reader's imagination. MODEL: Saki, "The Interlopers."

CHAPTER TWELVE: DESCRIPTION AND SETTING IN THE WRITING PROCESS

- Wherever you get your story idea, setting and description should factor into your selection. The place and time where your fiction will take place will impact every aspect of it: characters, plot, mood, conflict, and theme—to name just a few.
- Once you've got the idea, setting and description should be constantly on your mind when making your plans. Look for things that you will want to emphasize in your description and make notes.
- A writer who is serious about his or her task should set aside a block of time each and every day for writing. It shouldn't be used for planning, researching, revising, or editing. Neither should it be used for *thinking* about writing. It must be an inviolable time for wordsmithing.
- During the actual process of writing, it is essential to have any ancillary materials—maps, plot graphs, outlines, floor plans, character trait lists, photographs—close at hand so you won't have to take time to look for them.
- It is not essential that you write everything in chronological order. It might be best to start with the strongest image, or scene, in your mind. Then write *around* it.

- Revision is your refiner's fire; it is the polishing of your work to its brightest shine. So build in enough time to make a proper job of it.
- Attempt to see your setting through the eyes of a reader who has never seen it before.
- In the early stages of the writing process—the formation of the initial idea, the planning, the first draft—you need to work without any input from others.
- Then, it's essential that you get helpful feedback from readers that can point out what's working and not working in your manuscript. One dependable reader that you trust might be all you need, or it might be a good idea for you to locate a writer's group in your community, one that workshops manuscripts on a regular basis.
- Don't worry about agents or publishers or marketing your wares when writing. Just concentrate on writing well.

index

Printed in the United States
by Baker & Taylor Publisher Services.

Printed in the United States
by Baker & Taylor Publisher Services